THEY CAME TO THE HOLY LAN

They Came to the Holy Land

WHAT PILGRIMS, TRAVELLERS, AND ADVENTURERS EXPECTED AND WHAT THEY FOUND

BERND BRUNNER

TRANSLATED BY
LUCY JONES

PRINCETON UNIVERSITY PRESS
PRINCETON AND OXFORD

First published in Germany under the title *Unterwegs ins Morgenland. Was Pilger, Reisende und Abenteurer erwarteten, und was sie fanden*

Published by Princeton University Press
41 William Street, Princeton, New Jersey 08540
99 Banbury Road, Oxford OX2 6JX

press.princeton.edu

GPSR Authorized Representative: Easy Access System Europe
- Mustamäe tee 50, 10621 Tallinn, Estonia, gpsr.requests@easproject.com

ISBN 978-0-691-29173-4
ISBN (epub) 978-0-691-29558-9
ISBN (PDF) 978-0-691-29177-2
Library of Congress Control Number: 2026947744

British Library Cataloging-in-Publication Data is available

Editorial: Ben Tate and Josh Drake
Production Editorial: Karen Carter
Jacket/Cover Design: Katie Osborne
Production: Danielle Capurso
Publicity: Alyssa Sanford and Kathryn Stevens
Copyeditor: Catja Pafort

Jacket/Cover Credit: Louis Haghe after David Roberts, *The City of Jerusalem Viewed from the Mount of Olives*. Coloured lithograph, 1842. Courtesy of the Wellcome Collection.

This book has been composed in Arno

Printed in the United States of America

10 9 8 7 6 5 4 3 2 1

MIX
Paper
FSC
FSC® C183721

"The man who finds his homeland sweet is still a tender beginner; he to whom every soil is as his native one is already strong; but he is perfect to whom the entire world is as a foreign land."

—Hugh of St. Victor, Didascalion
[trans. Jerome Taylor] (1176–77 [1961])

"I cling, however, to a blind belief in my Bible, and think that this was once a fertile plain like the Garden of Eden, until the crimes of men and God's anger made it what it is."

—Isabel Burton on the Dead Sea,
The Inner Life of Syria, Palestine,
and the Holy Land (1875)

"Does the stretching of the ten fingers have more meaning for Protestants, I ask, than the prostration before God among the Orientals, or the sinking to their knees among the Roman Catholics?"

—Titus Tobler, A pleasure
trip to the Orient (1839)

"It is not possible to imagine the rapidity with which news circulates from mouth to mouth in Arabia; it is known already at Damascus, Aleppo, Latakia, Saide, and Jerusalem, that a stranger is arrived in Syria, and is about to travel through those countries. In a country where there is little movement in affairs and minds, the most petty circumstance of an unusual nature becomes all at once the topic of every conversation; it circulates with the rapidity of speech from one tribe to the other; the lively and exalted imagination of the Arabs exaggerates everything, and in fifteen days a renown is gained at a hundred leagues' distance."

—*Alphonse de Lamartine, Travels in the East including a Journey in the Holy Land (1850)*

CONTENTS

List of Illustrations xi

Preface: The Holy Land, a Destination of Longing and Promise xiii

PART I. FROM THE MIDDLE AGES TO THE EARLY MODERN PERIOD 1

God-Inspired Wanderlust—The Lady Pilgrim Egeria 3

Are God and the Holy Spirit Present Everywhere?—How Holy Are Holy Sites? 7

Occidentals Turned Orientals—The Difficult Relationship Between Christian Faiths 14

The Book of a Mysterious Knight—Mandeville and the Consequences 18

The Digressions of Felix Fabri—A Dominican Pilgrimage 21

Pilgrims from Various Countries 30

Amulets, Bone Splinters, and Dubious Likenesses—An Endless Range of Relics 34

Protecting Pilgrims in the Holy Land—Templars and Franciscans 37

Jewish Pilgrims from All Corners of the Earth 41

Pious Muslim Pilgrims 46

Travelling to the Holy Land in the Spirit of Martin Luther 49

Scientists Discover Palestine 56

Among Muslim Fatalists—Constantin-François Volney in the Holy Land 63

PART II: THE NINETEENTH CENTURY 67

Following in the Footsteps of Pilgrims of Earlier Times—Napoleon and de Chateaubriand 69

Skeptical Researchers—Edward Daniel Clarke and Ulrich Jasper Seetzen 77

The Sentimental Journey—A Longing for the Holy Land 83

Half a Library in His Luggage—Alphonse de Lamartine in the Holy Land 90

American Interest in the Holy Land Awakens 94

Arrival in Jaffa and Easter in Jerusalem 107

Where the Human Species Originated—Ida Pfeiffer and Her Adventures 116

Hot Blood Rushing Through My Veins—Maria Schuber, Pilgrim 122

After the Egyptian Occupation of Palestine 127

Forerunner of the Zionists—Moses Montefiore 133

Jews in the Holy Land 140

Encounters in the Harem 150

With the Bible, a Telescope, and a Compass—Archaeology in Palestine 160

In the Babel of Languages—On the Role of Tourist Guides 174

The Land of Milk and Honey 184

Geological and Botanical Curiosities 191

Writers Joining in and a Community of Fanatics 197

The First Package Trip Tourists with Thomas Cook 207

Walking the Fine Line Between Irritation and Fascination—Encounters with Bedouins in the Desert 217

New Settlers in the Holy Land 224

Images of the Holy Land 232

A Painter Turned Emigrant—Gustav Bauernfeind 239

More Americans Arrive in the Holy Land 245

Armenian and Russian Pilgrims 250

An Imperial Caravan 256

Epilogue 262

Acknowledgements 269

Bibliography 271

Index 283

ILLUSTRATIONS

1. The world as a cloverleaf with Jerusalem at its centre as depicted by the German theologian Heinrich Bünting. 20
2. An illustration from Bernhard von Breidenbach's book: "These animals are truthfully depicted as we saw them in the Holy Land." 27
3. Pilgrimage to the Holy Land became a popular topic in publications geared towards a general readership as this issue of *The Penny Magazine* from 1837 illustrates. 87
4. Young [Christian] Girls of Bethlehem, photographed by Felix Bonfils. 92
5. A Christian family from Madaba, Transjordan, in festive attire, visiting Jerusalemn in 1904/5. 103
6. Map of Thomas Cook's Tours in Palestine (1873). 209
7. The steps leading to the Holy Sepulchre (between 1898 and 1914). 214
8. Bedouins in front of their tent, photograph taken by Maison Bonfils. 218

9. The Scottish artist David Roberts travelled to the Holy Land in 1838/39. Here, a group of people who appear to be pilgrims prepare for the last stage to Jerusalem. 233

10. Jerusalem from the Mount of Olives by Frederic Church (1870). 236

11. "The Wailing Wall" (1904) by Gustav Bauernfeind. 242

12. A. E. Breen, author of *A Diary of My Life in the Holy Land* (1906) in Oriental garb. 248

13. One of the earliest maps of Palestine in Hebrew, published in Jerusalem in 1908. 266

PREFACE

The Holy Land, a Destination of Longing and Promise

FOR MANY CENTURIES, the regions at the edge of the Arabian Desert, on the River Jordan, and the shores of the Nile, Euphrates, and Tigris were home to Jews, Christians, and Muslims. Palestine, an inseparable part of historic Syria, was the homeland of Jewish kingdoms before becoming part of the Roman and Byzantine Empires. From early times, it was a transit country and thus a place of encounter and cultural exchange. From the sixth century on, various Muslim rulers and kingdoms followed and from the sixteenth to the beginning of the twentieth century, the region came under the rule of the Ottoman Empire.

The West's view of Palestine, insofar as it can be generalised, has traditionally been shaped by biblical associations. Palestine is considered the land of the Bible, and Jews are the focus of attention. The Holy Land, a slim transit zone between Egypt and Mesopotamia on the eastern edge of the Mediterranean, bordered to the East and South by desert, and to the north by the Lebanese mountains, was a region that held great emotional significance for Christian pilgrims as a destination of longing, utopia and promise. Unlike Rome, which owed its attraction to the martyrs and the papacy, historic Palestine, with its unclearly delineated borders, was synonymous with the events in the Old Testament and what was passed down in the Gospels. Mainly in Galilee, but also other regions beyond modern-day Israel and the Palestinian Autonomous Territories, was where Jesus spent his earthly life.

Although the majority of travellers to the Holy Land came from the Middle East and Russia—Orthodox Christians who could often much more easily travel back and forth to Jerusalem or to monasteries east of the Holy City—those who wrote extensively about the region came mostly from the West. Jews and Muslims were also among those who travelled to Palestine but far fewer reports exist from these explorers in comparison to Christian pilgrims. However, one can assume that no other city in the early modern period attracted as many visitors from different religious backgrounds as Jerusalem. Although there were numerous efforts to describe and even map the Holy Land, the region remained largely a *terra incognita*. But from the late eighteenth century onwards, explorers and adventurers arrived, soon followed by missionaries and tourists, whose paths and intentions sometimes overlapped and sometimes contradicted one another. They certainly cannot all be lumped together. From the mid-nineteenth century onward, Western religious emigrants also came to Palestine. They believed that the Apocalypse was approaching and that Christ would soon be resurrected. Parallel to this, the first settlement attempts took place, stoked by European anti-Semitism. Zionism started to take on increasingly concrete forms.

The region became a literary *topos*, opening up a world to Western readers that seemed familiar in some respects through well-known Bible stories and characters that were all part of the collective memory but was at the same time foreign. The Holy Land became a stage on which people encountered each other, a contact zone where representatives of different religions met. It was a country of dreams, a projection screen for all things biblical, a place of fulfilment or disenchantment. "From our first moment in the Promised Land, we had to become accustomed to looking past the uninspiring present and search everywhere for traces of the great past through eyes of faith," wrote the German Protestant theologian Karl Ohly in his 1898 book, *Recollections of Travels to the Holy Land*. It was indeed a difficult undertaking. Some pilgrims did not find the Holy Land they were looking for; rather, their "prayers on foot" led nowhere.

Travelling to the Holy Land involved a search for past traces of their own religion. However, the Christianity that pilgrims encountered there was different from what most of them expected. The Christian community in Palestine alone consisted of sixteen different denominations. Oriental Christians not only seemed foreign in appearance but also in their interpretation of faith. It is safe to say that the average spiritually inclined traveller was rarely steeped in Greek, Latin, Hebrew or Arabic and had only a fair knowledge of biblical history. What's more, Jews and Muslims who lived there further complicated the picture. While the behaviour of many Christian pilgrims towards Muslims in the Holy Land was problematic, coloured as it was by their orientalist views, the same was true of their behaviour towards Jews in the region, as well as members of other confessions, such as Orthodox Greeks, Armenians, Maronites, and Copts. Those who looked "foreign" to visitors were often lumped together as "Orientals". On the other hand, European and American Christians, whether Catholic or Protestant, were not a homogenous body by any means; rather, they had significant differences of opinion. Interestingly, the relationship between Protestants and Orthodox Christians was less troubled than that between Catholics and Protestants, whose animosity dated back several centuries. Protestants and Orthodox Christians, meanwhile, were united by their resistance to the primacy of the Bishop of Rome.

Despite being a fixture in the *geographia sacra,* Palestine did not become a focus of international attention until the early nineteenth century, as the weaknesses of the Ottoman Empire became increasingly apparent. European powers wanted to secure their position and influence. According to the Eurocentric narrative, Palestine was an underdeveloped Ottoman province—a backyard, even—which now had to be rediscovered and refined.

Reports by pilgrims, nature explorers, missionaries, and fearless adventurers, reveal a colourful and little-known chapter of the West's history with the Holy Land. They act like a window onto historical Palestine before the British mandate, long before the United Nations' partition plan for a Jewish and Arab state and the establishment of the State of Israel. The literature of German travellers who travelled to Palestine complements the work of Edward Said who, in his seminal work on Orientalism, focused on British and French colonial perspectives.

Until the end of the Ottoman Empire, the Holy Land, made up of a Muslim majority population, was a province of Syria and not a self-contained administrative unit. I use this term here primarily because of the places that are—in different ways—sacred to Christianity, Judaism and Islam, the Abrahamic religions.

The term 'Palestine' dates back to the time of the Philistines. It was also the name of a Roman province from the time of Emperor Hadrian. When in 1896, Theodor Herzl referred to Palestine as "our unforgettable historical homeland", it didn't have the politically charged meaning it has today. "Jerusalem" is referred to as such here, even if it is known to Muslims (in the short form) as al-Quds and to the Jewish Israelis as Yerushalayim. It does not imply a political judgment.

The term "Arab" or "Arabs" was not always used unambiguously in the sources, as it could refer not only to Muslims but also to other indigenous people, even if there was no explicit reference to, for example, "Christian Arabs" or even "Arab Jews", which is a very controversial term.

The term "Orient" refers to what is commonly known today as the Middle East. However, the term "Middle East" did not really gain currency until the early twentieth century, therefore "Near East" was used to refer to the territory comprising the lands of the Ottoman Empire and Persia.

All book titles are given in English (even if many of these books have never been translated into English) so as not to interrupt the flow of reading; the titles in the original language (for the most part French and German) can be found in the bibliography.

PART I

From the Middle Ages to the Early Modern Period

God-Inspired Wanderlust—The Lady Pilgrim Egeria

IN 1884, the archaeologist Gian Francesco Gamurrini made an astonishing discovery in the Biblioteca della Fraternita dei Laici in Arezzo, Tuscany: a previously unknown manuscript from the *Codex Arentinus* in the Benedictine monastery of Monte Cassino, dating from the eleventh century and containing a fragment of a pilgrim's account. Gamurrini must have been all the more surprised when he realized from the salutation "loving sisters" that it was a woman who had written those lines, apparently for her spiritual community. The manuscript sat in the archive for seven hundred years.

The preserved notes lead researchers to the conclusion that the pilgrim did not just make a short detour to Jerusalem, but undertook a journey lasting almost four years, which took her to Constantinople, Egypt, the Sinai, the Jordan region, Jerusalem, Cilicia and even beyond the eastern Mediterranean as far as Mesopotamia. Once she arrived in Constantinople, she finally wrote her report in the first-person perspective.

The standard dating for her travels is that the journey took place between 381 and the spring of 384, when she returned to

Constantinople. At this time, a pilgrimage was not only a spiritual quest, it was the only way for women to leave their familiar surroundings and get to know other countries. The report, written in an unusual Latin reads as if the pilgrim, presumably called Egeria, always had the Bible at hand as a "travel guide"—it was newly translated by John Wilkinson (1971). And she even wrote that "the relevant passage from the Bible was always read" as she was visiting the physical landscape. She wanted to locate the biblical stories geographically and was particularly interested in the tombs of martyrs, as well as the places and landscapes hermits had retreated to. She applied the term "holy" to mountains, buildings, and people. In the hermitages, she prayed with the monks, recited psalms and received their blessings. Egeria saw herself as a traveller on behalf of God and wanted to feel close to him. We have to remember that she was a Roman citizen within a Roman and mostly pagan world.

She wrote about Mount Sinai, Mount Horeb, Mount Nebo, and the Tell of Sedima. Her narrative of the Sinai excursion ends with an expression of gratitude to God "that He has deigned to enable me, unworthy and undeserving, to traverse all the places which I did not deserve to see". The report does not contain a description of Jerusalem and the West Bank, as these parts have unfortunately been lost, but there are notes describing the holy week—services and liturgical ceremonies—in Jerusalem's churches and, in connection with this, references to the shape of the tomb building. This was consecrated as part of a church complex under Constantine on September 9, 335, thus about half a century before Egeria arrived—265 years after the destruction of the Second Temple by the Romans under Titus. According to Egeria's notes, there was an outer and an inner room in the tomb, the latter of which she refers to as the "spelunca". She also mentioned a lamp in the inner room and bars. In Jerusalem, she met a woman whom she described as one of her best friends; she is the only one that she mentions by name in her report: "sancta diaconissa Marthana". However, we don't get a real feel for what it was like to be there at the time.

Egeria engaged the people she met in conversations about biblical topics. Foreigners, unless they are clerics and monks traveling with her, were only mentioned in passing: the nomadic Saracens traveling with camels, for example. Otherwise, there is an almost complete indifference to anybody or anything that was non-Christian in her report. However, she must have noticed them, but chose not to write about them. Her focus was simply on other things.

Gian Francesco Gamurrini initially assumed that the pilgrim must have been the Gallic noblewoman Silvia or Silvania, the sister of Rufinus of Aquileia, whose journey to the Holy Land is documented for the year 383. At the beginning of the twentieth century, a letter from Valerius of Bierzo, a Galician monk, dated to the seventh century, led to a new attribution. It mentioned an extremely enterprising nun who had come "right from the other end of the earth". Since she compared the colour of the Red Sea with that of the "Ocean", thus this can be understood as a reference to Galicia in the north-west of the Iberian Peninsula—and set out "with all her strength, undaunted in heart, on the immeasurable journey across the whole world" and was "braver than all the men of the century" (Férotin 1903).

As the original letter is not available, but has only been handed down through other manuscripts from the 10th to 13th centuries, her name appears in different but always melodious variations: as Egeria, Eiheria, Echeria, Heteria, Aetheria and Etheria, although there are several reasons in favour of "Egeria", so that this name is usually used today.

The exact identity of this extraordinary lady pilgrim is still surrounded by questions that will probably never be fully resolved. Presumably she was of a high social status due to the considerable costs of such a journey, and her knowledge of Greek indicates an excellent education. It is also known that the Bishop of Arabia travelled to meet her and accompanied her with a military escort in the eastern Nile Delta, which, at the time, was considered a dangerous zone.

The question of whether she was really an abbess is doubtful: If she was, would it really have been possible for her to take a whole four years off from her responsibilities and duties? Also, there is nothing to be found which could substantiate her wish to return to the West. She wrote: "if I am still alive and able to discover further places, I will either tell you about them face to face, if God grant it, or at any rate will write to you about them if my plans change." Did her correspondents at home ever see Egeria again? We just don't know.

Are God and the Holy Spirit Present Everywhere?—How Holy Are Holy Sites?

THE FIRST FOLLOWERS of Christianity had an unambiguous stance on the question where God can be found: only in the congregation of the faithful did God show his presence, not in a specific place. Jesus arose from the dead and ascended into heaven; but the places where he lived and died were not ascribed any particular importance. "For where two or three gather in my name, there am I with them," as the Gospel of Matthew, Chapter 18, states. The words of Saint Augustine of Hippo, born in Northern Africa in 354, also come to mind: God is omnipresent. In his Confessions, he wrote:

> "And men go abroad to admire the heights of mountains, the mighty waves of the sea, the broad tides of rivers, the compass of the ocean, and the circuits of the stars, yet pass over the mystery of themselves without a thought." Curiosity, which always played a role in pilgrimages, even if hardly talked about, was considered a vice by Augustine.

In a letter written in around 395, Saint Jerome tried to dissuade Saint Paulinus of Nola from undertaking a pilgrimage to Jerusalem:

> "But I do not presume to limit God's omnipotence or to restrict to a narrow strip of earth Him whom the heaven cannot contain. Each believer is judged not by his residence in this place or in that but according to the deserts of his faith. The true worshippers worship the Father neither at Jerusalem nor on mount Gerizim; for 'God is a spirit, and they that worship Him must worship Him in spirit and in truth.' 'Now the spirit bloweth where it listeth," and "the earth is the Lord's and the fulness thereof.' Access to the courts of heaven is as easy from Britain as it is from Jerusalem; for 'the kingdom of God is within you.'"

Considering this passionate plea, it may come as a surprise that Saint Jerome wrote this letter in Bethlehem, of all places, where he lived from 386 and spent the rest of his life. In the spirit of the gospels, then, there was no need for the faithful to travel to holy sites—neither those near their own countries nor those in the far-off Holy Land. Following this line of thought, the Crusades were unnecessary too because it was unimportant to the faithful who was in power in Jerusalem. Despite these objections, the Holy Land retained its appeal, curiosity remained strong: countless groups of pilgrims moved to Jerusalem, despite continual complaints about the city's teeming crowds and the distractions people encountered there.

Egeria was not the first female pilgrim to visit the Holy Land. In ancient times, the leading pilgrim among rich ladies with ascetic tendencies was the Christian imperial patron saint, Helena, who gave the movement a certain respectability. As early as 326/327, she set off for the Holy Land, more than half a century before Egeria. According to legend, she supposedly ordered the excavations that led to the finding of the cross of Christ, including the nails used in his crucifixion, as well as the Holy Sepulchre and the Church of the Nativity. In the late fourth century, Constantine the Great declared some sites sacred that had allegedly come into contact with Christ's body before he ascended into heaven and ordered the building of the Church of the Holy Sepulchre, the basilica above the Church of the Nativity on the Mount of Olives. The original sites mentioned in the gospels had been lost when Hadrian razed ancient Jerusalem to the ground in the year 135 after the Bar Kokhba Revolt.

New creation myths linked to specific sites therefore had to be created. Cults of saints and martyrs added to the mix, also connecting certain burial sites to places. The Holy Land offered Western European pilgrims something that could not be found at home and exerted a magnetic pull. From 451, it became the seat of the Patriarchate. For zealous Christians, the Holy Land became the "heavenly Fatherland on earth", as the Swiss cultural historian Jacob Burckhardt described it in 1853 in his seminal work *The Age of Constantine the Great*. In countless believers, an irresistible urge grew to visit sites in person which they thought to be holy.

In the year 614, Jerusalem was captured by the Persians, and in 638 by the second Caliph Umar, who then reconstructed the city. From then on, Jews were no longer permitted to enter the old Temple Mount; its western periphery, the Wailing Wall, became a symbol of devotion to Jerusalem and a destination for Jewish pilgrims as the last remains of the former temple. Although the conquerors severely subjugated the Christian population, its community survived and pilgrims continued to visit the country—albeit on suspicion of spying. During this time, pilgrims were mostly noblemen from France and Lotharingia, as well as Scandinavia, who travelled overland to the Holy Land via Constantinople. This gave them the advantage of being able to visit the architecture in Byzantium, even though the city was not considered a pilgrimage destination.

A trip undertaken by the Frankish Bishop Arculf is known to have lasted at least two years, including long stays in Jerusalem, Alexandria, and Constantinople. Arculf came to Jerusalem after it was conquered but before the Dome of the Rock was constructed (687–691). He was praised for his precise descriptions of churches, mentioning, for example, a shroud laid in the tomb above the head of the Lord and the lance of the soldier who pierced Jesus' side while he was hanging on the cross (Adomnán 1895).

It seems odd from today's point of view that Arculf did not include aspects of Islam or Muslims in his descriptions of Jerusalem. However, there is this report: "On the famous site near the eastern wall where the ancient temple used to stand in all its splendour, the Saracens have erected a square prayer house with upright planks and great beams that stands on top of the remains of the ruins. They visit it diligently and it is reported to hold up to three thousand people." Owing to his use of the term "prayer house", this was presumably a mosque; the term "Saracens" was used during that period as an umbrella term for various Muslim groups in the eastern and southern regions of the Mediterranean.

He goes on to describe "never-ending crowds of various tribes" who "gathered on the twelfth of September every year in Jerusalem from all around to exchange, sell and buy goods." Venetian and Byzantine shipping traffic did not intensify until the Arabs lost their strongholds in Italy and France. In the battles of Tours and Poitiers in 732, the French defeated the Moors and restricted their expansion north of the Iberian Peninsula. When Byzantine power was restored in the strategically important Emirate of Crete in 961, maritime transport in this region of the Mediterranean became safer again. Crete, which later became part of the Republic of Venice, was conquered by the Ottoman Empire in the mid-seventeenth century.

The largest mass pilgrimage in the period before the Crusades was probably led by Bishop Gunther of Bamberg from 1064 to 1065, together with Archbishop Siegfried of Mainz and the Bishops Wilhelm of Utrecht, Otto of Regensburg and other religious dignitaries. They travelled to the Holy Land with more than ten thousand people. The Bishop of Bamberg left a report for posterity describing the torturous conditions of this journey which he wrote in the Syrian town of Latakia, shortly before he arrived at their destination. "We went through fire and water, terrified by Hungarians, attacked by Bulgarians, beaten and forced to flee by Turks, suffered tribulations from the arrogant Greeks in Constantinople, and fits of rage by the Cilicians . . . But I fear that the worst is yet to come." (Hochheimer, 1977) His predictions were correct: the entourage of pilgrims was attacked by Arabs just before they reached their destination not far from Caesarea. The bishop managed to reach Jerusalem but then died on the return journey—of natural causes, it seems—and never saw his home country again. It was precisely during this period that Christians, who suffered from constant oppression, began to form a concentrated community in the Christian quarter which was also the seat of the Patriarchate. From then on, Golgotha and the Church of the Holy Sepulchre were considered sacred sites of great importance.

A decisive turning point was reached when in 1071, the Seljuqs emerged victorious from the Battle of Manzikert (Turkey's modern-day eastern Malazgirt region) and Byzantium had to forfeit most of Asia Minor. The Byzantine emperor Alexius I Comnenus appealed to Pope Urban II for military aid and the

Council of Clermont, which convened in 1095, resulted in the First Crusade—a kind of armed pilgrimage, and a consequence that the Emperor surely had not reckoned with. Four years later, in 1099, Jerusalem was stormed by mounted crusaders, and part of the population was massacred. Muslims and Jews were driven out of the city, ending the hitherto relatively peaceful coexistence of Muslims, Jews, and Christians. The mosques were converted into the seats of the crusaders and the Byzantine temples were restored. Further to this, the crusaders perpetuated the old Muslim dhimma system of protection, with the difference that it was no longer Christians and Jews who were obliged to pay per capita tax, but Muslims and Jews instead. The relationship between the Latin Franks and Christians in the region—mostly Greeks and Armenians—was tense.

The complete change in the region's circumstances resulted in a boom in pilgrimages to Jerusalem and the profit made from trade with pilgrims became the most important source of income in the city. As bandits more or less controlled the routes to and within the Holy Land, the journey remained highly risky and required travellers to be armed. During the Easter feast of 1120, 30 members of a party of 700 pilgrims were killed and 60 were taken prisoner. Although the route by sea to Jaffa via the Mediterranean entailed risks of its own and was more expensive than the overland route, demand increased in the twelfth century. Even though the Crusades continued until 1270, and the kingdom was maintained, at least in formal terms, the Battle of Hattin in 1187 ended in defeat for the Crusader states. In 1244, Jerusalem returned to Muslim jurisdiction, and in 1291, Acre was defeated and occupied by the Mamluks. The pilgrims found themselves in enemy territory once more and the flow of travellers ebbed, in part because of the Mongol raids that affected the larger region. It wasn't until the later fourteenth century that Christians undertook pilgrimages to Jerusalem once again.

This city, which was far away from important trade routes in the Judaean Mountains and lacked a fertile hinterland, was the main pilgrim destination, not least due to its important status in Judaism, Christianity, and Islam. When pilgrims arrived, they threw themselves onto the ground, kissed the earth, and began searching for "Biblical atmosphere".

The Holy Tomb, a chamber hewn into a rock massif with adjoining chapels, was always central to the pilgrims' journeys. Despite no complete body ever being recovered in Golgotha, except for a skull allegedly belonging to Adam, reverence for the site where Jesus died and Adam was buried continued unabated. By contrast, the former Temple of Solomon, which was superseded by other structures over time, was an extremely sacred site for Jews. In its incarnation as the second Temple of Herod, it was located on a hill with a raised plateau. When the Babylonians destroyed the temple, the site lay derelict until Muslims laid claim to it in the seventh century, building the Al-Aqsa-Mosque and the Dome of the Rock on it in an impressive, octagonal form. This is where the stone slab with the imprint of the Prophet Mohammed's foot lies, which was made as he ascended into heaven. The western side of Temple Mount is considered one of the holiest sites in Judaism, where the Wailing Wall can be found, the western wall of the former temple complex that belongs to the Jewish quarter of the Old City.

The Temple Mount has been the site of clashes between Jews and Muslims from that time on. By visiting these holy sites, pilgrims wished to absolve themselves of sin, be knighted, and pray that wishes to bear children would be fulfilled, or that sicknesses would be healed. Many, too, wanted to witness firsthand the mystery that surrounded these places.

Occidentals Turned Orientals—The Difficult Relationship Between Christian Faiths

THE ORIENT is the region where Christianity originated, but a fundamental break between Western and Eastern Christendom had occurred at the end of antiquity. The decisive difference was the position held by the Eastern churches. According to them, there was only one nature in the person of Christ, namely the divine; the man Jesus had transformed himself—perhaps based on Hellenistic ideas on deification—into the divine Christ (so-called monophysitism). This contradicted the doctrine of the divine and human dual nature of Christ that had meanwhile emerged in the Western church.

The separation of churches goes back to the resolutions passed in 451 at the Council of Chalcedon (today's Kadıköy district on the Asian side of Istanbul), at which the majority recognized Christ's divine and human natures. From then on, the Eastern churches took on a secondary role in the consciousness of the Roman Church. The Armenian Church, which did not take part in the council and entered into communion with Rome in 1184, stood somewhat apart.

During the time of the Crusades, the hostile tone of Western Christians towards Oriental Christians became more pronounced. The latter were seen less and less as victims to be liberated, but rather as renegades, as apostates. They were oft even accused of having allowed the Holy Land to fall into the hands of the Muslims and of having transferred responsibility for the reconquest to the Christians from the West. The aim now was to make the "heretics" dependent on the Roman Church.

However, a number of crusading knights never returned to Europe and over time intermingled with the local population. These descendants were viewed with little understanding by the pilgrims who arrived later; the "poulains", as they were called, soon resembled the Oriental Christians in their way of life and religious practices.

Fulcher of Chartres, one of the first crusaders, who came to Constantinople via Rome in 1096, soon settled in Jerusalem and later worked in the Church of the Holy Sepulchre, bears impressive witness to his own transformation. For him, there was no going back to Europe:

> "For we who were Westerners have now become Orientals. He who was a Roman or a Frank has in this land been made into a Galilean or Palestinian. He who was of Reims or Chartres has now become a citizen of Tyre or Antioch. We have already forgotten the places of our birth." And how did they live there? "Other Latins are married, not only to women from their former homeland, but also to Syrians and Armenians, even Muslims, but of course only to baptized women." Many of the crusaders were second and third sons for whom

there was nothing to be gained in their European homelands because upon their return they had no claim to any property or office.

The "Christians from overseas" or "Christians of the Orient", in contrast to the "true Christians" of Europe, as they were sometimes called, seemed familiar but also foreign to the travellers. These "other" Christians included Syrians, Armenians, Greeks, Nestorians, Maronites and Jacobites—in the first three cases the name was derived from a country, in the others from specific people with whom they were associated: Nestorius, Maron, Jacob. Despite all the feelings of foreignness they evoked among the pilgrims, they were nevertheless strictly distinguished from the "infidels", that is Jews and Muslims. In Egypt, they also encountered Nubians, Ethiopians and "Indians" (or paraphrased as coming "from the regions stretching as far as India") who were subject to the Coptic Patriarchate in Alexandria and whose exact geographical origin was unidentifiable or even inscrutable to the travellers. These people aroused a particular curiosity in many of the pilgrims, but at the same time caused them considerable confusion which led them to misclassify some of their observed characteristics.

Cardinal James of Vitry, appointed Bishop of Acre in 1214, wrote: "The Ethiopians are black, and we find them ugly. But they consider the blackest to be the most beautiful." The external characteristics of oriental Christians included long hair and beards, which were seen as a sign of their masculinity and authority. At the same time, the appearance of the patriarchs evoked associations with the biblical prophets. In contrast to Muslims, Christians wore a band of different colours. The colour of the turban and the way it was worn provided indications of religious affiliation. An important feature of the priests' way of life was that they were allowed to marry. And Western pilgrims were surprised to find that the Oriental Christians did not use bells to indicate the hours or when to go to mass, but instead chose to strike wooden boards with some iron object.

The fact that many of the Oriental Christians, following the Arab conquests of the seventh to ninth centuries, now spoke Arabic as a liturgical language and also in everyday life, made them—in addition to other characteristics—appear even more foreign. Of course, a sound knowledge of Arabic was essential for missionaries of the Roman Church working in the Holy Land. The locations were also subject to change and, as French philosopher Maurice Halbwachs noted in his groundbreaking work on collective memory (1941), "The Christian memory of the holy places gradually faded, gaps, inconsistencies and confusion arose, even if the building activity in the sixth century, especially under Modestus, gave it new strength. But eventually these sanctuaries also fell into ruins, disappeared from view, and the Christian rites that preserved the local memory could only with difficulty assert themselves in an environment that had been indifferent or hostile to them since the time of Muslim rule."

The Book of a Mysterious Knight—Mandeville and the Consequences

HOW MANY PEOPLE were aware of Egeria's travel diary before it was discovered again in Italy is unknown. It had been ignored for 700 years. Most probably not more than a few monks were aware of its existence. Another work, which made the rounds from around 1357, had an incomparably wider impact: the travel book of the knight John Mandeville, which, albeit in ever-changing forms, remained a topic of conversation for two centuries and had far-reaching consequences such as broadly defining the Orient in the minds of a contemporary readership.

The exact identity of the author is fraught with many questions that defy a definitive answer. The fact that it was probably written in Anglo-Norman French does not contradict its alleged English origin—it was the language in use in aristocratic circles there at the time.

He mentioned the Christians of Turkey, Armenia, Arabia and India as well as black monks who are Christians. "Know that among the Saracens, in several places, many Christian men dwell under tribute; they follow different laws and customs according to the constitution of the realm they dwell in. Nevertheless, they are all baptized and believe in God as Father, Son and Holy Ghost. Still, they differ in some articles of our belief."

And he wrote: "They adduce such authorities in their own language and not in Latin; and because of their authorities they say that men should make confession to God and not to men. And so when they want to make confession, they make a fire beside themselves, throw incense on it, and, as the smoke goes up, they say, 'I make my confession to God and ask forgiveness for my sin.'"

Not everything concerning the Holy Land should be taken at face value though. Does an iron thrown into the Dead Sea really float? And does a feather really sink? Mandeville claimed to have tried it out himself.

It is unlikely that the journey really took place along the lines described in the report; other writings have been identified as sources for many parts of the text. However, this did not hinder its impact. For its contemporary readers, the book had the qualities of an authentic account. Its ideas influenced a whole series of conquerors, not the least of whom is the Italian Christopher Columbus.

The study of Mandeville's book sheds light on a common pattern during the early modern period: travellers' ideas were often based on the writings of earlier pilgrims, which then shaped their expectations and patterns of perception. After their return, they sat down, continued to weave the thread and wrote their own records, ideally, but not always a little more in line with their own experiences. Nevertheless, much was often simply copied from earlier writings, which explains why most of these accounts are rather surprisingly similar.

In the case of Heinrich Bünting's *Itinerarium sacrae scripturae. That is: a travel book about the whole of the Holy Scriptures,* printed

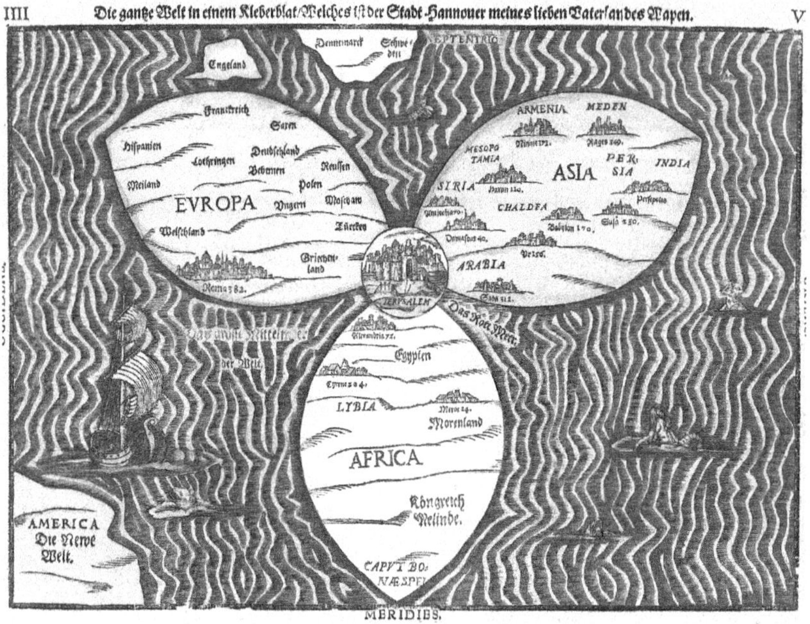

FIGURE 1. The world as a cloverleaf with Jerusalem at its centre as depicted by the German theologian Heinrich Bünting.

in Germany in 1581, there is not the slightest doubt, however, since the Lutheran theologian never made the journey to the Holy Land. This fact still did not detract from his book's success; within a little more than a century and a half, it appeared in at least 60 editions, in German, Swedish, Czech, Dutch, Latin, Danish and English. Bünting is known for his highly imaginative depictions, including symbolizing the continents of Europe, Asia and Africa as three petals connected by Jerusalem, which acts as the hinge and centre of the world. America only peeps out at the edge, as it did not fit with the ideology behind this type of schematic map which showed Jerusalem as the centre of the world and a mixture of geographical and biblical features.

The Digressions of Felix Fabri—A Dominican Pilgrimage

ALTHOUGH THERE are no statistics on the proportion of women among the pilgrims, occasional references do exist that allow for certain estimations. For example, the Dominican monk Felix Fabri from Ulm in Southern Germany recorded the company of his first pilgrimage in 1480:

> "Certain women well-stricken in years, wealthy matrons, six in number, were there together with us, desiring to cross the sea to the holy places. I was astonished at the courage of these old women, who through old age were scarcely able to support their own weight, yet forgot their own frailty, and through the love for the Holy Land joined themselves to young knights and underwent the labours of strong men."

While the references to women often remain vague: In the later Middle Ages, there were apparently so many female visitors to Jerusalem that it was worthwhile setting up dormitories tailored for their specific needs.

The case of the mystic Margery Kempe, the daughter of a merchant from Lynn in Norfolk, is among the few that are well-documented. She travelled to Jerusalem in 1414 accompanied by a group of men and spent the night in the houses of wealthy people. It is known that she regarded herself as a visionary in a lively exchange with Christ and the Virgin Mary. When she spotted Jerusalem for the first time, she asked God to reveal both the heavenly and the temporal city to her. According to the report, she almost fell off her donkey, completely overwhelmed by her emotions. Supposedly, two German pilgrims and a preacher just managed to avert the mishap. Her visits to various well-known holy places were accompanied by her weeping, screaming and praying; it sounds as if she had developed a psychotic condition later referred to as "Jerusalem fever" and "Jerusalem syndrome", a phenomenon in which tourists in Jerusalem develop intense religious delusions. Kempe also described some visions—one example being Christ's crucified body on Calvary—and was convinced she heard voices.

But back to Felix Fabri. He undertook his first journey "eastwards to the lands beyond the sea" in 1480, spending only nine days in Jerusalem and returning dissatisfied. His second journey in 1483/84 took him beyond Jerusalem to the Sinai Peninsula and Egypt. Interestingly, he did not use the word "itinerary", the commonly used term for pilgrimage reports at the time, but rather "evagatorium" ("evagor" meaning, among others, "wandering about").

At first, Fabri seemed to have considerable doubts as to whether he should embark on this journey at all. Count Eberhard the Elder of Württemberg (Reichert/Rosenstock 2018), who himself had already travelled to Jerusalem, told him about the three things a man should unequivocally not do. "The first is to marry, the second is to start a war, the third is to go to the Holy Land. These three I call good, but they can easily come to a bad end. Anyone who asks for advice is like a defendant who should be acquitted and yet it can end badly for him." Apart from that, the count said, success depended on one's attitude; those who undertook the journey with pious devotion and not out of recklessness or base motives would not be taking too great of a risk.

Once they reached the Jordan, the pilgrims baptized themselves, just "in jest", as Fabri noted. And although the Saracens had issued a ban on crossing the river, some defied it and swam to the other bank. Fabri stayed in Jerusalem for a whole month. In the Church of the Holy Sepulchre, he observed the knights as they spent their third night after confession there, attending the Eucharist and receiving their knighthood: "after a hastily completed visit to the holy places, they sat together, ate and drank their fill as if this sacred church were a tavern, and did not stop until the drinking vessels of all their companions had been emptied." In brief: the pilgrims did not exactly present an image of devout Christians, certainly not in the eyes of the "Moorish lords" who were also present. Then there were the nobles who scribbled their names on the church walls, placed plaques with their coats of arms or even, apparently completely unnoticed by the Georgian guard, carved their names into marble pillars on the holy rock under the pretext of devoting themselves to prayer. All of this made Fabri's face "flush with shame". He himself collected small stones on Zion, the Mount of Olives and in the Valley of Jehoshaphat, weaved a crown out of thorn branches—modest relics that nevertheless fulfilled their function and were considered worthy of veneration. He thought nothing of the objects that were sold by Muslims and Christians alike, he had seen through the whole thing: "Because the unbelievers know our burning desire to possess relics. That is why they make pieces of wood like the Holy Cross, nails, thorns, bones and such things to deceive the foolish and rob them of their money."

Muslims in particular came off badly in Fabri's book; he lamented their alleged backwardness in terms of civilization: "The Saracens, the main inhabitants of Jerusalem, are Muhammadans; they are afflicted with the worst heresies, worse than idolaters and more despicable than Jews . . . They practice polygamy and do not shy away from sodomy." But the "Syrians" (by which he most likely referred to Christians) were also "not Christians, but children of the devil, liars, unreliable, thieves and traitors . . . They wear long beards, are effeminate and unfit for war."

Among his fellow travellers, Fabri mentioned a certain Elphahallo, who was presumably over eighty years old, who made his house available to pilgrims and had a reputation as a "reliable counsellor for all Christians": "A simple and sincere Saracen who possessed great moral strength. He knew Italian and a corrupt, bad German, which he had learned from pilgrims with whom he crossed the desert to Mount Sinai forty-eight times. And he was so devoted to the Christians from overseas that he spent his life with them, even exposing himself to mortal danger for them, because, although weakened by age and afflicted with a hernia, he still went through the desert with pilgrims, not expecting a reward, but to be with them."

Occasionally, there were flashes of tolerance and understanding, he had some good things to say, on the cleanliness of Muslims, for example, expressed in the ritual ablutions before prayer and in the bathhouses. Although the exact circumstances remain unmentioned, he reported on a meal attended by pilgrims, two Franciscans, a Saracen, a Mameluke and a Jew, which is said to have taken place in a friendly atmosphere.

Repeatedly, Fabri criticized the behaviour of local Christians. At the Dead Sea, for example, he encountered an oriental Christian at the bottleneck of a rock face, who he suspected of belonging to the monastery of the holy Abbot Saba. The latter pretended that he would throw Fabri into the gorge unless he paid up. Fabri, frightened to death, naturally complied. "From this hour on, I have shunned fellowship with those Christians more than with Saracens and Arabs, and have trusted them even less . . . If an Arab had met me and done that, I would have let myself be amused and declared him a true pagan, but as for this Christian, I can find nothing good."

And he went on to talk about the "blinded" monks of St. Catherine's Monastery: "Once, when they were still in obedience to the Holy See, they welcomed pilgrims with the greatest charity and kindness, served them in whatever was necessary and gave them shoes. That these monks are now schismatics and heretics is because they are Greeks and Greece is chaotic. And they are Orientals to whom the true sun has set . . ." Fabri also mentioned that he and his companions had to refrain from holding their church services "because as members of the Roman Church we are considered excommunicated by them".

Without resolving the conceptual confusion, he noted: "Inhabitants of the desert and wasteland are the Arabs, miserable and poor, an almost animal-like people. Some say they are Ishmaelites, also children of Hagar, who pretend to be Saracens. Others name them after the nearest part of the country and call them Midianites. Still others refer to them as Bedouins. Some also regard them as Zigani [Roma], who came from Chaldea, which is connected to the great Arabian Desert in the north. Usually, however, they are simply called Arabs throughout the region."

Centuries before there were travel guides in the modern sense, Fabri formulated a whole series of recommendations to help avoid disputes with Muslims. These included the request to refrain from drinking wine in public and not to wear white head coverings, as these were reserved for Muslims.

Despite all of this, the pilgrimages were among the highlights of his life. "I firmly maintain that someone gets to know oneself better in forty weeks on this pilgrimage than he would otherwise in forty years. I confess that I have never and nowhere recognized my imperfection and frailty better and more clearly than during this wandering, and this especially in the ship on the sea and under the tent in the desert, because in these places nothing remains hidden in a person."

In 1483, Fabri met another legendary traveller in Jerusalem: Bernhard von Breidenbach, an official of the Archdiocese of Mainz, Germany. Von Breidenbach left behind his *Pilgrimage to the Holy Land* (1486), an opulent work which, despite its interchangeable-sounding title and certainly also because of its many illustrations enjoyed a long afterlife.

The Milanese Cavalier Santo Brasca also made the journey in the exact same year 1480 and provided a report: *Itinerary to the Holy City of Jerusalem* (also known as *Journey to the Holy Land*). His advice on the right attitude: "In the first place, a man should undertake this voyage solely with the intention of visiting, contemplating, and adoring the most Holy Mysteries, with great effusion of tears, in order that Jesus may graciously pardon his sins; and not with the intention of seeing the world, or from ambition, or to be able to boast 'I have been there,' or 'I have seen that,' in order to be exalted by his fellow men, as perhaps some do, who in this case have now received their reward." But Brasca also gave very practical advice, such as about the "overcoat reaching down to the ground to wear when sleeping in the open air, and a thin mattress instead of a bed," not to mention the question of food: "Furthermore, let him take a supply of good Lombard cheese, and sausages and other salt meats of

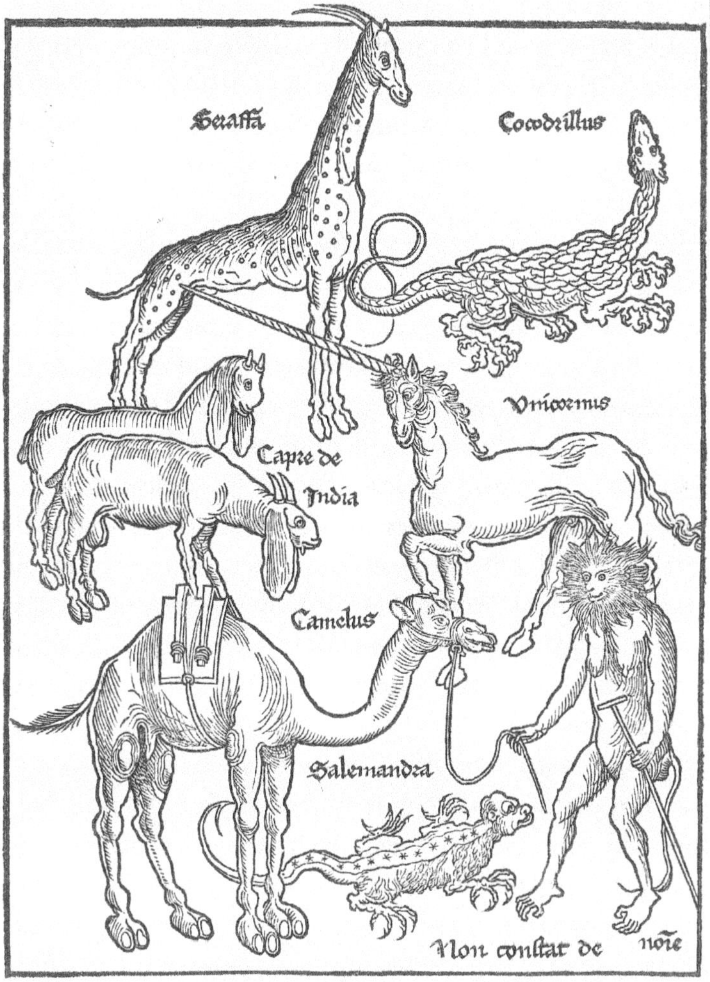

FIGURE 2. An illustration from Bernhard von Breidenbach's book: "These animals are truthfully depicted as we saw them in the Holy Land."

every sort, white biscuits, some loaves of sugar, and several kinds of preserved sweetmeats, but not a great quantity of these last because they soon go bad. Above all, he should have with him a great deal of fruit syrup, because that is what keeps a man alive in the great heat; and also syrup of ginger to settle his stomach if it should be upset by excessive vomiting, but the ginger should be used sparingly, because it is very heating. Likewise, he should take some quince without spice, some aromatics flavored with rose and carnation, and some good milk products."

Pietro Casola, a canon from a respected family who was also born in Milan, studied Brasca's report in detail, so that he did not include the advice himself in his own report. He left his hometown on May 15, 1494, after receiving the archiepiscopal benediction. As Margaret Newett, who translated the book into English, writes, he "recorded the events of his momentous voyage, for the amusement and instruction of his Milanese friends." Casola could not have known that centuries later he would still be reliably cited in literature on this subject. Although he is said to have made considerable efforts to find traveling companions, he ultimately set out on his own. Already in his sixties, he often comes across as a little grumpy in his text, with occasional flashes of humour.

Casola devoted himself extensively to his stay in Venice and the stops on his onward journey, namely Zara, Ragusa, Modone, Rhodes, and finally Jaffa, which, although about 30 miles away, was often understood as a kind of port of Jerusalem. Many things annoyed him, and he observed his fellow travellers with a keen eye during this extremely difficult journey. In particular, the German pilgrims, the "ultramontani" or "Ultramontanes," as they are called in the English translation, were a thorn in his side with their impatience and their quick-tempered behaviour toward the ship's command due to delays that were contrary to the contract. And anyway, the "todeschi impatienti," the impatient Germans, who, against the advice of the shipowner, visited Nicosia (Cyprus), which was suspected of being infected with the plague, and always ran ahead at the holy sites so as not to miss anything: "I always let the Ultramontanes—who trod on each other's heels in their haste to leave—rush in front." Even if Casola shared their displeasure, he did not agree with their form of protest, their many biting words, and distanced himself as an Italian, as a Milanese. His good relationship with the captain, who also accompanied the group on the mainland, ensured that he had fewer problems to contend with.

Bethlehem, the Jordan, and Jericho were also on the itinerary. The highlight of the trip were, of course, the multiple visits to the Holy Sepulchre. Deputies had been appointed to count the pilgrims: "They were ten Moors—men of imposing appearance and not priests—who wore dresses as white as snow and had those large sexule on their heads. It made me feel very hot just to look at them. These men were seated on a certain small platform raised about two braccia from the ground and arranged with mats over the boards, because the said platform was made of wood; and there they were all seated on their legs, like tailors sit at home. They made, however, a fine picture." The pilgrims were initially turned away, but after negotiations in Arabic, they were granted access. Casola, who was in greater safety in the Zion monastery, was always well informed, proved to be a detached observer, and knew how to manoeuvre wisely among the fellow pilgrims, as here in the Church of the Holy Sepulchre: "As soon as I saw that the crowd of Ultramontanes had diminished, I went again with my lighted candle to make all the visitations, and I touched the places and relics with my rosaries without any impediment."

Pilgrims from Various Countries

SOME PILGRIMS even arrived from the Far North. Nikulás Bergþórsson or Bergsson (also called Nikulás of Munkaþverá, after the location of the abbey) reached Jerusalem in 1154 via Norway, Denmark, Stade near Hamburg, Mainz, Basel and Rome. The Icelandic abbot kept a record of the stages of his six-thousand-kilometre journey in a guide; he even indicated the distances between places in miles, a novelty for his day (Werlauff, 1821).

When he finally arrived in the Holy Land, he noted: "There is the centre of the earth, where the sun shines directly down from heaven on the feast of John [June 24]." Nikulás also provided an interesting guide to measuring latitude, which is considered unique in the medieval literature on the Holy Land:

> "Out by the Jordan, if a man lies on his back on level ground and lifts up his knee and sets his fist on top of it and stretches his thumb from the fist, then the Pole Star is to be seen above, that high but not higher."

At this location, the star is only 31 degrees above the horizon. So even in the distance, at the navel of the world, he could feel somewhat connected to home.

The community of pilgrims was not only very diverse in terms of nationalities, all participants brought their own expectations with them. By undertaking this trip, noble pilgrims took the opportunity to achieve particular fame. After three visits to the Church of the Holy Sepulchre and two nights spent there in cramped quarters, they could be made Knights of the Holy Sepulchre—provided they took an oath promising to "uphold law and justice, protect widows and orphans, defend the Christian faith and do their utmost to help reclaim the Holy Land, the Holy City and the Holy Sepulchre", as German historian Folker Reichert wrote in *Experience of the World* (2001).

However, not everyone took advantage of these opportunities: Alexander von Pappenheim, who set out from the Bavarian Alps in March 1563, bluntly renounced his knighthood on the grounds that "among the knights there are priests and cantors, and even shoemakers and tailors." (!)

To be sure, the now predominantly Muslim inhabitants of Palestine did not exactly welcome the travellers with open arms. On the way to Jerusalem, the pilgrims could be pelted with clay and stones by the locals. They could be thrown off their donkeys or shouted and cussed at, while being laughed at by the people escorting them. Unrest and epidemics hardly affected the streams of pilgrims. Even the war between the Ottoman Empire and Venice between 1463 and 1479 could not stop the flow. Meanwhile, the plague would remain a more or less latent danger in the centuries that followed.

Over long stretches of time, Orthodox Christians represented the largest group of pilgrims in Jerusalem and Palestine, although numbers (or statistics) are impossible to come by. Compared to the Western Europeans, these travellers had the advantage of a much shorter route. And unlike the Roman Catholics, they also visited monasteries, for example Mar Saba, founded in 483 and named after St. Saba and located east of Bethlehem in the Kidron Valley. Many of these pilgrims came with the intention of staying as monks for a longer period of time.

The presence of Georgians in Jerusalem dates back to the early Byzantine period. Under the Mamluk Sultanate, Georgian pilgrims in Jerusalem, unlike all others, were exempt from paying taxes and held an important position in the Church of the Holy Sepulchre. The construction of the Monastery of the Cross on the ruins of an earlier church goes back to Georgians in the eleventh century. Since the seventeenth century, however, it had been under the mandate of the Greek Orthodox Patriarch in Jerusalem because the number of Georgian monks had dwindled considerably.

The 18-year-old London Quaker George Robinson was certainly among the more unusual travellers. He came to Jerusalem in 1657, in the aftermath of the English Civil War. Initially, he was not a pilgrim at all, because that would not have been in accord with his theological perspective, as Quakers rejected pilgrimage. He saw himself as being sent by the Holy Spirit and wanted nothing less than to proclaim God's Kingdom to the ruler of the city, thereby also denouncing the Satanic practices of the organized church. Not too surprisingly, Robinson's plans met with little sympathy from the Franciscans: they saw him as a blasphemer. How to deal with him and eventually get rid of him? One of the monks disguised himself as a holder of Islamic rights, received Robinson in the Franciscan's St Saviour's Convent and confirmed to him that his proclamation was legally binding, whereupon the Quaker is said to have left the Holy Land satisfied. Not a single doubt seems to have crossed his mind.

And what about the numerical ratio of the various Christians visiting? In his book *Journey to the area between Alexandria and*

Parätenium, the Libyan desert, Siwa, Egypt, Palestine and Syria in 1820 and 1821, the German catholic biblical researcher Johann Martin Augustin Scholz provided a meticulous count of the Christians who came to Jerusalem at Easter 1820:

> "1400 Armenians, 1200 Greeks, 30 Georgians, 300 Muscovites, 60 Copts, 15 Syrians, 1 Abyssinian, 20 Oriental Catholics of the Greek and Armenian rites, 4 Maronites and 15 Franks". The visitors from Western Europe constituted therefore an almost vanishing minority.

Amulets, Bone Splinters, and Dubious Likenesses—An Endless Range of Relics

THE BUILDINGS and objects in the Holy Land that were considered sacred aroused many desires. Central to this was the idea that primary relics (a corpse or body parts) or secondary relics (material relics such as clothes, tools or other objects allegedly touched by the saints or their remains) were sanctified for all time and contained a supernatural power that could benefit those who simply touched them. Egeria mentioned a believer who, in an attempt to kiss the true cross, was so unscrupulous as to bite off a piece in order to take it away as a relic. The ever-increasing division of objects made it possible to reproduce them almost ad infinitum. If the objects were very small, such as fragments of the Holy Cross, they were sometimes later displayed under rock crystals to make them appear larger.

The relics related to Mary are a chapter unto themselves. Although nothing is known about the appearance of Mary of Nazareth, Empress Eudocia claimed to have discovered an image of her during her pilgrimage to Jerusalem around 435, which is even said to have been painted by the Apostle Luke, with the result that portraits of Mary were produced in such large numbers that they became one of the most common objects in Christian art. And it was believed that certain places could be associated with her: Had the Virgin really rested on that stone on her way to give birth in Bethlehem? Many were firmly convinced of this and as late as 1992, the Byzantine church which was built on the alleged resting place of Mary on her way to Bethlehem and which was destroyed in the eighth century, was rediscovered and later excavated.

The Casa Santa in Loreto, Italy, represents a spectacular case of a relic: After the crusaders lost their last stronghold in the Holy Land in 1291, angels are said to have carried the house of the Holy Family of Nazareth, where Mary grew up, across the west of the Balkan Peninsula to Loreto. The more realistic explanation for this transfer is, of course, that it was built with stones brought from the Holy Land by the crusaders.

Loreto is probably the most striking example of a place that took the place of Jerusalem and developed into a major attraction for pilgrims. A connection with the Holy Land was also celebrated in Walsingham, Norfolk. The myth has its origins in three repeating visions of the Virgin Mary by the Catholic noblewoman Richeldis de Faverches, which showed her the Basilica of the Annunciation in Nazareth in 1061. After her "return", she commissioned carpenters to rebuild Mary's home. Walsingham soon became known as 'England's Nazareth' (Janes/Waller 2010).

From then on, more and more shrines in Europe were regarded as a kind of mirror image of sites in the Holy Land. The Spanish Capuchin historian Matheo de Anguiano believed he recognized "La Nueva Jerusalén" in Madrid, which he justified with the discovery of a crucifix in the city. The story of the crucifix was linked to the speculation that Jews living in Madrid had brought an image of the crucified Christ from Portugal, which they then used to re-enact the suffering of Christ. The alleged culprits were condemned and their house was turned into a monastery.

Some merchants traded in relics on a significant scale. The Venetian Stefano di Bossina, who was active in Damascus in the fifteenth century, left behind a considerable number of them: seventeen small mother-of-pearl crosses, one of which was engraved with the crucifixion, four gilded lead images of Jesus from Jerusalem, eight wooden rosaries from Jerusalem and six ropes, also from Jerusalem, which were typically intended for measuring the Holy Sepulchre—so that it could be rebuilt to scale elsewhere (Carboni 2007). As convoluted and dubious as the creation and journey of relics may have been, the faith associated with them should not be underestimated.

Wherever "authentic" relics were no longer available, objects made specifically for this purpose gained in importance and stimulated business; their sale was the livelihood of many local craftsmen. Amulets, ampoules, crucifixes, rosaries, paperweights, bowls and other small objects were particularly popular, for which mother-of-pearl from the Red Sea, marble from the mountains around Jerusalem, grey asphalt from the Dead Sea or olive wood—taken from trees supposedly growing on the Mount of Olives—were used. Relics enabled a sense of connection with a distant land that remained inaccessible to a vast majority of the people.

Protecting Pilgrims in the Holy Land—Templars and Franciscans

DURING THE time of the Crusades, the organized protection of pilgrims in the Holy Land was in the hands of the Templars. Shortly before 1120, nine French knights joined together and took a vow before the Patriarch of Jerusalem, pledging themselves to poverty, chastity and ecclesiastical obedience. Their headquarters was the site of the Dome of the Rock, built in the seventh and eighth centuries, and the Al-Aqsa Mosque. But barely two centuries later, their order had been disbanded. The Knights Hospitaller (Order of St. John), whose hospital in Jerusalem was founded by merchants from Amalfi at the end of the eleventh century, saw themselves as a service to pilgrims. Their history reads similarly. Clergymen, laymen, monks without the full rights of monks and doctors cared for the sick, including female pilgrims and their children born in the house. When the crusaders' fortress in Acre fell in 1291, the Knights Hospitaller also had to leave the Holy Land. They first found refuge on

Cyprus and later on Rhodes—a hospital building dating back to the fifteenth century can still be seen there today.

As far as Francis of Assisi is concerned, it is certain that the 38-year-old began his sea voyage in Ancona in June 1219, which took him via Cyprus to Acre in the Kingdom of Jerusalem, where he arrived a month later. Brother Elia from Assisi, the Custos of Syria, received him. After a short stay, he sailed, accompanied by a few brothers, to Damietta in Egypt, where the crusade named after this city happened to be underway; the Christians' aim was to reconquer Jerusalem from the Muslim Ayyubids.

However, Francis did not come as a soldier. He was determined to convert Sultan Malik al-Kamil and to bring peace. And he did indeed preach to the sultan, who is said to have been impressed by the monk. Francis, in turn, is said to have discovered a great humanity in the Sultan. Talks between Francis and Islamic scholars took place in a respectful manner as well. These were atypical moments for the age of the Crusades.

The Franciscans' presence in the Holy Land can be traced back to the year 1291. After the fall of Acre, they could establish themselves permanently: in 1333, the Mamluk Sultan al-Nasir Muhammad allowed them to stay in two chapels on the Mount of Olives, in a part of the Church of the Nativity in Bethlehem and in one of the Churches of the Holy Sepulchre in Jerusalem. They were also able to acquire the place of the Last Supper on Mount Zion, where they built their convent.

Finally, in 1342, Pope Clement VI elevated the friars to official representatives of the Roman Church in the Holy Land. From then on, one of their most important tasks became taking care of the pilgrims arriving from Western Europe. Only the Franciscans had the right to read mass at the Holy Sepulchre.

Which places in the Gospels were associated with significant events in the life of Jesus? First of all, Jerusalem, where the sites of the passion and resurrection of Jesus Christ were located. The place of the last Passover meal, the Garden of Gethsemane and the Via Dolorosa, the "way of suffering"—it leads from Pilate's former residence via fourteen stations to the Church of the Holy Sepulchre. The list of important sites also included the Church of the Nativity and its grotto in Bethlehem, Nazareth, Capernaum, the Sea of Galilee and the Mount of the Transfiguration of Jesus, known as Tabor, and finally Sinai. There were many other places of salvation history, as mentioned in the Old and New Testament, as well as springs, hills, trees, caves and graves. The Franciscan monks developed a particularly close relationship with the holy places; they regarded Jerusalem as the centre of the universe and the topography of the Holy Land as central to the past and future of salvation.

Soon, some drastic changes would take place: in 1516, at the height of their power, the Ottomans conquered the Holy Land, restored the walls around Jerusalem, and soon after expelled the Franciscans from their convent on Mount Zion, but allowed them to remain in the country.

As a consequence, the flow of pilgrims ebbed for several decades. After the Jesuits and Capuchins arrived in the first half of the seventeenth century and tensions with the Eastern Orthodox Christians increased, the Franciscans continued to assert themselves. As early as 1560, they set up a new monastery building in Jerusalem and were able to accommodate incoming pilgrims. In return, they had to pay the Ottomans a constant high tribute. They also formulated a whole series of rules of conduct for the pilgrims, in particular regarding their dealings with Muslims. These included avoiding laughter in their presence and the order that they not look at women. Pilgrims were not allowed to carry weapons or even ride horses in the Holy Land—donkeys or mules were always used for the usual route from Jaffa to Jerusalem. Whenever pilgrims died during their journey in the Holy Land, handing over the remaining belongings to the Franciscan convent was customary.

Jewish Pilgrims from All Corners of the Earth

AFTER KING SOLOMON erected a temple in Jerusalem in the tenth century BC, the city became a destination for Jews to celebrate Pesach (Passover), Shavuot, and Sukkot. "Next year in Jerusalem!" became a popular refrain in the Middle Ages when diaspora Jews found it difficult to fulfil the biblical pilgrimage requirements. From this time on, it was commonly used by Jews to express their wish that one day, they would be able to return. Benjamin of Tudela (whose birth name was Benjamin ben Jonah) embarked on a legendary journey in the twelfth century from the northern Spanish kingdom of Navarre, which had been united with Aragon at the time and was one of the first provinces reclaimed from Muslims during the Reconquista. Not much is known about him except that he probably travelled as a commercial trader. He wanted to find out what conditions his fellow believers were living in and wrote reports on the Jews he encountered or whom he had heard about "from credible people". He was also interested in the co-existence of Jews and non-Jews. His matter-of-fact account was written in Hebrew but contains a plethora of words in Arabic. Tudela travelled in

1168 via Italy and Byzantium—rather than North Africa and Egypt, as was usual for Jews living in the Muslim parts of Spain—to Palestine, which was still under the rule of the Crusaders. One of his remarks about Jerusalem was the following: "It is a small, well-fortified town with three city walls. Many people live here—the Muslims call them Jacobites, Arameans, Greeks, Georgians and Franks. One meets people who speak many different languages here. In the town, there is a dye works, for which Jews have to pay the king the purchase price every year anew to reserve the dyeing business in Jerusalem for Jews alone. Around two hundred Jews live here. They live around the Tower of David in a corner of the town." He said of the Church of the Holy Sepulchre: "This is where the man is buried to whom all pilgrims make their way."

Rabbi Obadiah of Bertinoro (Emilia Romagna) set off to the Holy Land in 1485 and several letters addressed to his brother and father have survived (Neubauer 1863, Bekemeier 1993). He arrived during a period of great hardship. "Many of the Jews I saw begging for bread one or two days earlier have starved to death, and there was no one to give them any. People were found dead in their houses and many fed on grasses, going out like deer in search of pasture." About the people he encountered he added: "You find many nationalities here, from Christian countries, from Babylon and Abyssinia. Arabs often go to the temple to pray. They have great respect for this place. No Jews are allowed on Temple Mount. When the Arabs sometimes let in wood turners or money changers for work, no one wants to go there because we are all tainted with impurities. I don't know whether the Arabs enter the Holy of Holies." Obadiah eventually found a house in the quarter close to the synagogue. "In the courtyards surrounding my house, there are five apartments occupied solely by women. Only one blind man lives here, and the women provide for all of his needs." He never returned to Italy.

An anonymous Jewish traveller (Neubauer 1863, Bekemeier 1993) left for the Holy Land a few years later, in August 1495, taking a route via Venice, Corfu, Rhodes, Beirut and Damascus. He left Safed in Galilee "in the company of several Sicilians who joined other caravans of Jews, Christians, and Arabs. They were carrying a great fortune and therefore had to travel in convoy. We all paid 120 silver pieces per person for the trip to Jerusalem for which the leaders ensured we were exempt from all taxes." On the following morning, they reached the environs of Jerusalem. "On Friday 18 Heshvan, when I saw the desolate, bleak city, and the ruins of Mount Zion, where the lions and jackals now dwell, my heart shed tears and I sat down, cried, and as is custom, made two rips in my shift. Turning towards Temple Mount. I prayed that God would soon lead the captives of Israel back to their land, that we may yet see the dwelling place of the Lord, Amen." He remarked on the religious events in the city in the following way: "Jerusalem has some 200 Jewish families who keep themselves free of every kind of sin and fulfill God's commandments with great zeal. There is no difference between them; rich and poor gather in the evening, morning, and midday to pray. Two god-fearing hazzans lead prayers quite reverently and speak each syllable clearly. The entire community rushes twice a day to hear the lectures of the 80-year-old Rabbi Zechariah Sephardi, may God bless him and his descendants. He keeps them to a quarter of an hour after the morning and evening prayers so as not to inconvenience the public." He mentioned his intention to visit the tombs of the patriarchs in Hebron. "On the way is Rachel's Tomb. I haven't visited it yet because the routes through the Bedouins' land are unsafe. Only recently, a Jew from Hebron who came here with his family was robbed of all he owned on the way. I hear that Jews from Cairo and Damascus who come here to celebrate Passover travel in safe company on their way to Hebron. I'll use this opportunity to go there if God lets me live."

A slim volume with the title *Darkhe Tsiyon* (Paths to Zion) was written more in the style of a practical travel guide. Its author was Mose ben Israel Naftali Porges also known as Moses Präger and was published in Frankfurt am Main, Amsterdam or Prague in 1650 in Yiddish. It gives exact details of the cost of certain routes and shows the two alternative paths from Constantinople to Jerusalem, by water or by mule in a caravan, which was estimated to cost "at least 33 Löwentaler coins including taxes, excluding provisions and other individual expenses usually incurred when trekking". But he gives the following warning: "Not everyone can endure the ride, especially women, as one's feet have to be at the same level and it is backbreaking owing to the lack of a backrest, which is why female travellers should have a sedan or a chair made in Constantinople that is tied to the mule. However, this increases costs as someone has to lead the mule." When staying in Jerusalem, Präger recommended that "travellers should not take too much silver and gold, even if one is wealthy, because it attracts a great deal of attention. Gold is also cheaper in Jerusalem than outside the [Holy] Land. Beautiful furs should not be taken due to appearance." Further, he reports on the conditions of Jews living in the area: "Every head of the family, every father, even the poor ones without homes, has to pay 3 Löwentaler coins in land tax, half in the summer and half in the winter. All kinds of food and drink can be found in Jerusalem, but little money. For the rich, everything is cheap but the poor here go without more than in the entire world because the community is in great debt since the great devastation in Poland [1545] from where thousands have come every year." Präger rendered many of the terms in his text in Hebrew too.

The fact that Jews could end up in Jerusalem via very circuitous routes is shown by the example of a certain Mattityahu in the 1890s. He came from the city of Mashhad in northeastern Persia where in 1839, the resident two thousand Jews were forced to convert to Islam and from then on, practiced their own religion in parallel in secret. To prevent suspicion that they were not real Muslims, some of them set off on a pilgrimage to Mecca. Hajj (Pilgrim) Mattityahu was among them, his tefillin, or prayer boxes concealed under his turban. On the route home, he broke away from the caravan and walked to Jerusalem where he found accommodation in housing designed by the Württemberg-born archaeologist and architect Conrad Schick. There, a synagogue was also later erected by his family in his name.

Pious Muslim Pilgrims

PIOUS MUSLIM travellers made their way to Jerusalem, the third holiest city in Islam after Mecca and Medina. The nimbus of al-Quds, or "the Holy"—the Arabic name for Jerusalem—derived not only from the fact that Jesus is an important prophet in Islam but also that it was Mohammed's destination during his Night Journey, when, according to legend, he returned to Jerusalem and finally to Mecca, which was interpreted as proof of his godliness. What's more, one interpretation is that he ascended to heaven during this journey with the help of a ladder from Judea. Jerusalem is considered by Mohammedans as the site where the Last Judgement will take place. In the early period of Islam, Muslims prayed toward Jerusalem. Later the orientation was changed to centre on the Kaaba in Mecca. The splendour of the architecture on Temple Mount bears witness to its major importance in Islam.

Whether the erection of the Dome of the Rock as a holy shrine, finished in 691 under the direction of the Umayyad Caliph Abd al-Malik, was truly linked to an intention to reroute the hajj or annual Islamic pilgrimage from Mecca to Jerusalem—because Mecca had fallen into the hands of insurgents during this period—is not certain. Mecca has always retained its status as the most significant destination for Muslim pilgrims. Jerusalem did not lie along usual pilgrim routes between Syria and Egypt or to Mecca so Muslim travellers always had to make a conscious decision to go there. And some did.

The Franciscan monk Niccolò da Poggibonsi from Tuscany, who undertook a pilgrimage of several years from 1345 onwards, mentioned Saracens who weren't able to travel to Mecca and who went to Hebron instead. "Many of them come from Syria and Egypt and from the city of the sultan which is six days travel away through the desert. Many come for the provinces, some for reasons of piety, others, to see what Christians worship." The latter remark was probably wishful thinking on the part of the monk. In the surroundings of the Al-Aqsa-Mosque, there were several hospices reserved for Muslim groups. In 1326, the legendary traveller Ibn Battuta from Tangiers in Morrocco came to Jerusalem for a week. According to his descriptions, the city's defensive walls lay in ruins and the water supply had to be partially supplemented. "God ennobles [Jerusalem]—the third most important city after the two holy mosques [in Mecca and Medina] and the site of the ascension of the Prophet [Mohammed]—God bless him and give him peace—from where he was taken into heaven." He visited the Al-Aqsa-Mosque and the Dome of the Rock. From Jerusalem, Ibn Battuta travelled on to Damascus where he arrived during the Muslim month of fasting, Ramadan. There, he joined a hajj caravan that travelled onwards to Mecca.

In the Middle Ages, schools, mosques, and centres of instruction attracted scholars from the entire Islamic world. Jerusalem's magnetism for Muslims was emphasized by the high numbers of Sufis who had settled there. They came from Morocco, Crimea, Anatolia, Afghanistan and Uzbekistan. A census in 1670 that was carried out by the Ottoman governor of

Jerusalem, Jawishzadah Muhammad Pasha, found that at least seventy Sufi orders were represented in the city.

The renowned Constantinople-born explorer Evliya Çelebi, who spent a major part of his life traveling the Ottoman Empire and who visited Palestine in 1649 and 1672, even characterized Jerusalem as a "Mecca for dervishes" and as an extremely diverse cultural and religious city. He added to these his impressions of a relatively densely populated country, mentioning hundreds of tombs, shrines, and monuments to holy figures from the Old and New Testament and Islamic history. He also remarked on the "infamous Easter festival", saying that five to ten thousand Christians came to Jerusalem to attend, whom he describes as unbelievers who shall inherit hell. He also wrote about Jewish rituals and dwellings in a similarly derogatory way.

A famous Muslim pilgrim destination was, and continues to be, Nabi Musa, where tradition places the tomb of Moses, one of the most important Muslim prophets. Like Jesus, he is considered a predecessor of Mohammed. The small walled-in mosque lies in Jordan Valley not far from the river. Pilgrimages mostly took place at the beginning of May. The authors of *Through the Eyes of the Beholder*, Judy A. Hayden and Nabil I. Matar, assume that the number of Muslim pilgrims to Jerusalem and wider Palestine outnumbered those of Christians in the early modern period. "The annual pilgrimage caravans to Mecca and Medina, coming from Anatolia or central Asia, or the Maghrib, included thousands of men and women, many of whom visited the prophetic sites in Jerusalem and al-Khalīl (Hebron)".

Travelling to the Holy Land in the Spirit of Martin Luther

WITH THE DISCOVERY of America, the world had become bigger and the European gaze continuously shifted westwards. At the same time, the sea route to India, China and Japan around the Cape of Good Hope had opened up. Overland trade, which had previously been conducted via Asia Minor and Syria, diminished in importance. From then on, Jerusalem was considered much less of a centre. Christopher Columbus had thoughts regarding the Holy Land. In his diary of the first voyage, he recorded that he wanted to find enough gold and spices, which were almost as valuable, to make the conquest of the Holy Sepulchre possible—another crusade with funds from the trade with India. Like many of his contemporaries, he clung to the idea that the conversion of all peoples to Christianity and the reconquest of Jerusalem were necessary prerequisites for the "Second Coming", so that Christ could return before the "end of days". It was no coincidence that Ferdinand II of Aragon adorned himself with the title of "King of Jerusalem", and his wife Isabella subsidized pilgrimages to the Holy Land.

A little later, Luther's teachings began to create a deep rift between the Christians of Europe. In contrast to the reformers Martin Bucer and Huldrych Zwingli, who uncompromisingly regarded pilgrimages and the cult of saints as idolatry, Martin Luther kept at least open the possibility of praiseworthy long-distance pilgrimages as long as they were not associated with the cult of relics and the obtaining of indulgences. According to Luther's understanding, "true Christian pilgrimages" were those in which "we do not walk to God through the holy cities, but through our thoughts and hearts". However, if they are linked to such intentions, they were regarded by him as "fool's work". He formulated clear words—at first—on the veneration of the Holy Sepulchre: "For God asks as much about the tomb where the Lord lay as about all the cows in Switzerland."

He later qualified this sentence and mentioned to a pilgrim on the way to Jerusalem that he would gladly undertake such pilgrimages himself if he were in a position to do so. In any case, he would be happy to be told about it. Luther was of the opinion that God forgives sins without the need for money or a work of penance; only the inner attitude was decisive. Luther's somewhat more "relaxed" view of the phenomenon of pilgrimage was probably influenced by the fact that he himself undertook a pilgrimage to Rome as a monk during the winter of 1510/11 and stayed there for four weeks.

Even the French reformer John Calvin could not object to the pious contemplation of the events of the Gospel *in situ,* i.e. directly on site in Jerusalem and the Holy Land. Protestant pilgrims thought they were getting closer to the Word of God and wanted to deepen their historical knowledge, despite their scepticism about the authenticity of the holy places.

Although Venice had lost its grip on the eastern part of the Mediterranean—including Crete and Cyprus—with the rise of the Ottoman Empire, making travel more dangerous, the Holy Land retained its appeal. In any case, travellers of any motivation were welcome in Jerusalem because they enhanced the city's reputation and the prosperity of its population. At the same time, ideas about the purpose of travel were subject to change. Setting off for foreign climes was increasingly considered legitimate, even if it was solely for educational purposes. This was also an echo of the voyages of discovery to other continents and the reports about them, which were received with interest. The Württembergian Grand Master of the Court Hans Jacob Breuning von Buchenbach, who undertook an *oriental journey* to Turkey, Egypt, Arabia, Syria and Palestine together with the French squire Jean Carlier de Pinon in 1579/80, wrote of the "desire and delight to discover remote countries far and wide, including their inhabitants, life, religion, customs and traditions, I have always had for the Holy Land (but without superstition), because it is commemorated in general and the city of Jerusalem in particular, both in the Old and New Testaments openly and without ceasing".

How could one distinguish between religiously motivated interest and curiosity?

The Protestants had no other option but to place themselves in the hands of the monks, unless they pretended to be Greek or Armenian. The Ottomans obliged all pilgrims coming from the west to stay with the Franciscans. The Protestant guests were welcomed by the monastery brothers in the same way, and their feet were washed and kissed by the custodian, as custom demanded. The Franciscans claimed to be the best judges of what made a good pilgrim; for them, devotion and spiritual enlightenment were the only decisive factors. But it was precisely an excess of curiosity that the Franciscans often noticed in the Protestants.

Mariano Morone da Maleo, who held several high offices among the Franciscans in the Holy Land, mentioned the observation of his friars who accompany the pilgrims visiting the shrines. Some of the visitors, who are "little practiced in the Scriptures and breakers of conscience, not to say heretics", expressed their disbelief that the Holy Land and the Holy City of Jerusalem should have much to do with the way it appears today. "They make fun of it, and they joke about it, saying, 'This is Palestine? This is the city of Jerusalem?'" The friar Francesco Quaresmio, who arrived in Jerusalem in 1616 and was soon appointed President of the Custody of the Holy Land, also observed how Protestants from England, Holland and Germany made fun of Catholic rites and was annoyed by their ingratitude. Apart from points of friction, however, Roman Catholics and Protestants were united by their common geographical origins, not least because it was much easier for them to communicate with each other than with Oriental Christians, who often only spoke Arabic or Aramaic.

The location of the holy places was not always so conclusive; sometimes piety simply changed location, as German theologian Herbert Donner illustrated using the example of Cana, the site of the miracle of the wine—Jesus' transformation of water into wine—in John 2. Since the time of the Crusaders, this was seen as identical to the ruined hill of Khirbet Qana about 14 kilometres north of Nazareth. In 1566, the Greek Orthodox then built a church in Kafr Kanna—about seven kilometres north of Nazareth and nine kilometres from Khirbet Qana, because they located the legendary wedding feast there. Initially, this did not seem to have impressed the Franciscans any further, as they continued to head for the "old" place Khirbet Qana. It was only a few years later, when they acquired a plot of land in Kafr Kanna that they did begin to redirect the pilgrims there, with the result that Khirbet Qana soon fell into oblivion and became deserted.

As far as we know, Michael Oloffson Eneman (Östlund, 2013), who reached the Holy Land in 1711, was the first Protestant Swede and pastor to undertake this trip. Eneman had written two dissertations at the University of Uppsala and had been appointed chief chaplain to the ambassador in Constantinople. While still in Smyrna, he took a clear stance against the removal of antiquities: "Today there is more of ancient Smyrna in Oxford than here on site," he complained, adding that ancient objects should always remain where they were found so that they could be studied in their original context.

In Jerusalem, he showed himself to be a sceptic, but did not want to commit himself to the authenticity of the Holy Sepulchre:

> "I can neither agree nor disagree with their information. Besides I don't care about the earth or stone, but about the matter and the blessing given to us by the one once in the grave."

When he heard the clattering of the monks with their rosaries, it sometimes made him smile, sometimes he was annoyed by the noise and the "superstition". He was at a loss understanding how grace and forgiveness of sins could possibly be linked to holy places and how its blessings would be transferred to rocks or trees. Accordingly, he rejected the kissing of crosses and stones, which raised the suspicion of the monks—his explanations fell on deaf ears. Eneman also had little use for the souvenirs offered for sale in many places.

Nevertheless, he always displayed an admirable degree of diplomacy. He characterized Lorenzo Cozza, the highest representative of the Franciscans, as a "very impressive person" who has acquired a good knowledge of how to "live and deal with strangers".

And he was certainly aware of the difficulties that the Franciscans had to endure: Conflicts with the Orthodox Greeks over the power to dispose of certain locations, attempts at blackmail by the Turks and Arabs. The Swede was also in contact with the Greeks; he had already met the patriarch in Constantinople, who gave him a letter of recommendation for Jerusalem. He mentioned the Jews of Jerusalem, who were often harassed by the Turks, but still did not want to leave the city because of the Wailing Wall and because, as he added, they "believe they have their paradise in hell". Despite all the negative things he heard about the Turks, he still had many a good word for them. This may have partly been due to the fact that they allowed the Swedes to enter the mosques. And a muezzin even let him to climb a minaret at lunchtime so that he could see the vista.

As time moved on, the privileged role of the Franciscans did not remain uncontested. From the middle of the sixteenth century onwards, control of the Church of the Holy Sepulchre alternated between the Franciscans and the Greek Orthodox, depending on who exactly had the permission from the Ottomans at that particular moment in time.

As British historian Simon Sebag Montefiore wrote in his monumental book on the history of Jerusalem: "The Christians hated each other much more than they hated the infidels", mentioning the Franciscan priest Elzear Horn, who once referred to the Greeks as "vomit". In 1757, on the evening before Palm Sunday, violent clashes broke out when the Greeks overpowered the Franciscans from an ambush and seized power over the Church of the Holy Sepulchre (which was recognized by the Sultan). With the aim of ending the dispute, the Sultan had the church divided between the parties in 1767. This decision was reconfirmed in 1852—today, six Christian denominations share the church.

Marie-Joseph de Géramb, a well-known Trappist (reformed Cistercian) from Lyon who set off on a long pilgrimage to the Holy Land in 1831, was accommodated in the Franciscan monastery of the Holy Redeemer in Jerusalem. With several letters of recommendation, including one from the Vatican, he was allocated a room in the monastery itself and not in a separate building, as was usual for most visitors. The furnishings were extremely spartan, so de Géramb had to draw his own water and borrow a broom to sweep the room. The apartment of the Father Guardian of the Holy Land was also modest: "the lowest citizen in Italy would certainly not be satisfied with it."

In his book *A Pilgrimage to Palestine, Egypt, Syria,* de Géramb reproduced a memorable letter sent in 1805 by the superiors of the monastery to Horace Sebastiani, who was the French envoy to Constantinople at the time:

> "The unparalleled acts of injustice, the extortions, the arbitrary imposts, which for some years past have followed one another in rapid succession, on the part of the pachas, the governors, and their subordinate officers, have reduced us to such a state, that, unable to subsist, we shall shortly be obliged to leave the Holy Land, unless we can obtain the means of preventing the Turks from continuing to rob us of a quantity of money, which they do with threats, insults, and even the bastinado." (beating with a stick)

Scientists Discover Palestine

THE SWEDE FREDRIK HASSELQUIST was one of the first European scientists in the Holy Land. As his teacher and editor Carl von Linné noted, "the plants and natural history of the Holy Land had never before been described". Hasselquist set himself the goal of doing so, and in preparation he learned "the Arabic and other Oriental languages".

From Smyrna, where he spent the winter of 1749/50, he first sailed to Egypt, where he turned his attention to the world of plants and animals, locusts, crocodiles, lizards and scorpions. He stayed the whole winter. With the coming of spring, he then set off for Jaffa, Jerusalem and Bethlehem. As the example of a new kind of traveller, he was usually accompanied by pilgrims who still held the traditional view of this part of the world. Once in Jerusalem, he met the Armenian patriarch again, whose acquaintance he had already made in Smyrna, and visited the beautiful church and the large monastery, which had over a thousand rooms. He provides some more detailed information about the monastery of St. Salvator:

> "Franciscan monks from all Catholic nations in Europe have it in their possession. Their number is large, but not always

> the same. On average, you can always count a hundred people. They stay here for three years, and the Spaniards have the freedom to stay for six years. . . . The first post is always held by an Italian, the second by a Frenchman, and the third by a Spaniard. The work of the latter is the most important, because he has to take care of the entire housekeeping of both the convent and the Holy Sepulchre, and thus certainly half a million livres pass through his hands every year."

Concerning the Jewish population, he mentioned that, unlike the Turkish women, the women do not have to cover their faces. And he continued: "The Jews here are largely poor because they do not have the opportunity to engage in activities without which this nation cannot get by anywhere in the world."

Accompanied by monks, he visited a variety of places and locations and became aware of certain contradictions, for example on the journey to Jericho at an old house that was described as "strange": "The most peculiar thing was that they knew the place where something was supposed to have happened that no one knows whether it ever happened."

Hasselquist died of tuberculosis in Smyrna on his return journey.

At the beginning of 1761, six young men boarded the warship *Grønland* in Copenhagen to embark on an expedition to the Middle East, financed by the Danish King Frederick V. They wanted to gain knowledge in the fields of oriental philology, geography and botany. The initiative came from the Göttingen orientalist Johann David Michaelis, who was passionately interested in the *antiquities* of the Orient, but had never had the opportunity to travel to *Arabia felix* himself—meaning the southern part of the Arabian Peninsula, i.e. Yemen, which was to be the focus of the trip. It was assumed that ancient cultural forms could have been preserved there, which would not only be important for science, but would also provide clues for explaining the Bible.

Michaelis knew that his proposal would be well received by the Danish royal family and named the participants: the Danish orientalist Frederik Christian von Haven, the North German geographer and cartographer Carsten Niebuhr (a subject of the English king, who was also Elector of Hanover), and the Swedish natural scientist Petrus Forsskål, who had studied under Carl von Linné. A little later, the learned society was joined by the Danish physician Christian Carl Kramer and the draughtsman and engraver Georg Wilhelm Baurenfeind, who came from Nuremberg but was now working in Copenhagen.

In Constantinople, they were accommodated in the palace of Sigismund Wilhelm von Gähler, Denmark's envoy to the High Porte. "The undisturbed preservation of harmony and peace among them should always be their primary concern" was written down as a directive, but there were a number of reasons for disagreement. Niebuhr, the youngest member, was responsible for managing the travel fund, which annoyed von Haven. Von Haven and Kramer were opposed by Forsskål, Niebuhr and Baurenfeind. The fact that von Haven procured a considerable amount of arsenic while still in Constantinople and that this became apparent caused considerable annoyance. "The portion is so large that it could be the last meal for two regiments," Forsskål, Niebuhr and Baurenfeind state. Von Gähler immediately reports the incident to Copenhagen. It remains unclear what plan von Haven had with the poison, but his continued participation in the journey was not questioned by higher authorities. The friction continued. Although von Haven had been sent to Rome before the journey to Arabia to learn the Arabic language, his knowledge proved to be insufficient for communicating with the locals.

A side trip then took Niebuhr and von Haven to the Sinai. Baurenfeind, Kramer and Forsskål stayed behind in Suez due to Baurenfeind's illness. The ascension of Mount Sinai failed because the porters resisted the ascent. The group was also denied access to St. Catherine's Monastery.

The journey soon took a tragic course, most of them succumbed to illness with Niebuhr being the only one left, so he travelled alone to the west coast of India and made the long journey through Persia and Mesopotamia to Aleppo in Syria and on to Cyprus. From there he finally crossed over to Jaffa. He was in the company of seven Franciscan monks, including "two who had the task of bringing the annual offerings of Malta and the Kingdom of Naples to Jerusalem". As Niebuhr was wearing oriental clothing, the monks mistook him for a subject of the Sultan and asked him whether Denmark was beyond Anatolia. "When I replied that I was a European, they insulted me and called me a heretic. Never before on a pilgrimage had I come across Roman Catholic clergymen who were as arrogant and grumpy as these Franciscans." They also described the French people traveling with them as "bad Christians" and claimed that they were "worse than heretics or Mohammedans". Niebuhr was advised to contact a man named Damiân, an Oriental Christian who worked in Jaffa as a vice-consul for several countries. As it turned out at a meeting with him, the Protestant Niebuhr absolutely needed permission from the local Franciscan Reverendissimo to travel on to Jerusalem. Niebuhr learned that a poor Swedish preacher from Åbo had been refused permission to travel there, so he had set off on foot, but was then stopped by the Franciscans and sent back. Niebuhr later met the man, who felt deeply humiliated, at the French consul's house in Aleppo. The Swede was persistent, apparently making friends with Muslims, Oriental Christians and Jews;

determined to go to Jerusalem via Damascus, but he did not find the support of the Catholics. Tragically, he died on the way without ever having seen the holy city.

Niebuhr arrived in Ramla from Jaffa and was warmly welcomed by the Franciscans, but was not allowed to leave the house. The monks warned him about the Arabs, who were "robbers and barbarians who attacked and beat pilgrims wherever possible", and told him that Arabs had burnt a monk on his way to Jerusalem in an oven, which Niebuhr did not really believe after his many years of experience in the wider Orient: "I later learned that the monks spread such atrocity stories in order to receive the richest possible donations."

In general, Niebuhr was not easily rattled: "After everything I had heard so far, I initially believed that Palestine was home to the very worst race of people. Later I realized that the inhabitants of this country were no more evil than those in other regions. I heard that in some villages between Ramle and Jerusalem a small toll was charged. Those who paid it could travel on unmolested. The monks, however, did not pay this trifle. As they had nothing but their hard robes, so that nothing could be taken away from them, they were often beaten up or had stones thrown at them."

Finally, Niebuhr arrived in Jerusalem, which, as he wrote, is "the most memorable city in the world for both Jews and Christians". His first visit was to a church: "So I went to mass and did not regret it. For here, in the middle of a Mohammedan country, to my great astonishment, I not only saw a magnificent organ, but also heard good instrumental and vocal music. Without exception, the musicians were Franciscans and, as I heard later, mostly Germans." But as much as he liked the music, he thought that Europeans would be wise to do without the music that the Muhammadans despised. And the same goes for the bells with which the churches ring for mass, as Muslims would only see this habit as proof of a false belief that they accuse Christians of having. He put it into the mouths of Muslims: "We only hang bells on cattle."

There were the fees that the Christian visitors had to pay to the governor. "The fact that the Mohammedans benefit from the reverence that the Christians pay to the holy places only proves their cleverness. Moreover, it amuses the Mohammedans when the Christians claim that this or that significant event took place at a certain place and not a hundred steps further south or north."

Niebuhr did not miss the quarrels between the members of the various churches, nor the disparity between the comparatively wealthy Franciscans and the poorer Greeks: "This arouses hatred, and often enough the monks fight in the church or even in front of the Holy Sepulchre. If they get so rowdy that their shouting reaches the Janissary guard, the church is opened and the Janissaries use large clubs to bring both parties to heel. The monks also have to pay a considerable fine."

He was less impressed by the tombs of the prophets on the Mount of Olives and would have liked to have been shown the sites considered holy by the Jews and also to have heard their opinion "about the size and location of ancient Jerusalem", but the Franciscans who hosted him did not want him to seek their company. The journey took him on to Acre, Damascus and Aleppo. In November 1766, Niebuhr set off from there to Anatolia with a caravan consisting mainly of Greek merchants. In his luggage he had some of the souvenirs he had bought "by the ton" in Bethlehem, which he wanted to bring joy to Catholics across Europe.

When Niebuhr, a full seven years later, returned to Copenhagen in 1767, Christian VII of Denmark had just succeeded his father on the throne. Soon a completely new wind was blowing at court, under which a budget for a comparable journey would hardly have been approved. Niebuhr was promoted to engineer captain and received a salary from the military budget for ten years. In 1778, Niebuhr finally moved to Meldorf in Dithmarschen on the North Sea coast, where he worked as a tax official. His son Barthold Georg related the following about his father's latter years:

> "He told us that when he lay blind in his bed, the images of his views of the Orient appeared before his soul; so it was no wonder that he could speak of them as if they were ghosts. In the same way, the starry, deep night sky of Asia, into which he had so often gazed, or its high vault of day and blueness were reflected in the hours of silence, and this was his sweetest pleasure."

Among Muslim Fatalists—Constantin-François Volney in the Holy Land

THE ANGLICAN BISHOP Richard Pococke travelled through Egypt and the Middle East between 1739 and 1743. He devoted the first part of his second volume of *Description of the East and some other countries* to the Holy Land. It does not follow the genre of the pilgrimage report and is written in a sober tone. What is particularly noteworthy are the maps of Palestine and Jerusalem as well as various sketches of buildings, including the Dome of the Rock and Absalom's Tomb. He also discusses the trade in products, such as the soap in Jaffa, which is made from olive oil and ash, and the cotton that is shipped from there. He hardly ever describes encounters with people in any detail; reading the book, one gets the impression that this is a sparsely populated country with a few outstanding architectural monuments.

Constantin-François Volney inherited a handsome fortune and decided to visit Egypt and the Ottoman Empire as a private scholar. Realizing how physically demanding such a journey would be, he spent a year preparing for it: He practiced marching and hardened himself against fatigue and long periods of fasting. At the same time, he began studying Arabic at the Collège de France. He travelled the Middle East for three long years. A journey whose result was *Journey to Syria and Egypt in 1783, 1784, 1785*.

Like few others, Volney imparted his views on the coexistence of linguistically diverse peoples in the wider Syrian region. He spent several months in a Syrian monastery, where Druze teachers taught him Arabic. Turkish, on the other hand, was mainly used by those who belonged to the military or the government, as well as by the "Turkman hordes", as he states. As the language was useful for business, "some natives" also learned it, just as the Ottomans learned Arabic, "but the pronunciation and accent of these two languages have so little similarity that you can tell from the first word whether they are spoken by a foreigner or not". Volney also mentioned the Syriac language [note: he most likely means Aramaic, spoken by Jesus and the Apostles], which is used by the Maronites in the mass and liturgy. Greek was only very rarely understood, even by Arab Christians and Catholic Christians.

He correlated the "difference in worship" between Muslims and Christians with fundamentally different character traits, "as if they were two distinct nations living under two different climates". And he was told: "Travellers, and our merchants, who on account of the habits of intimacy in which they live with both, are still better qualified to decide, agree that the Greek Christians are in general wicked and deceitful, abject in adversity, insolent in prosperity, and especially remarkable for levity and fickleness: the Mahometans, on the contrary, though haughty even to insolence, possess however a sort of goodness of heart, humanity, and justice; and above all, never fail to manifest great fortitude under misfortune, and much firmness of character."

Volney had a monk explain to him that Christians could not "manage the reins of government" because "during their youth they have been continually employed in beating cotton". It is also important, as Volney noted, "that the Mahometans have the prejudices of fatalism instilled into them from their birth, and have full persuasion that every thing is predestined. Hence they experience a security which moderates both desire and fear, and a resignation by which they are equally prepared for good and evil." The Greeks, by contrast, are quite different, they "believe that God may be prevailed on to change his purpose, by vows, fasting, prayer and pilgrimages, live in the perpetual desire of obtaining some new blessing, the fear of losing some good they already possess, or tormented by regret for some duty omitted."

Nevertheless, Volney qualified his statement on the righteousness of members of both religions: For example, the inhabitants of the interior generally demonstrated better morals than those of the towns located on the coast.

By harbouring the view that Jesus did not exist, he offended many of his contemporaries. He saw Christianity as a fusion of different mythologies and considered Jesus to be a purely mythical figure, was even imagining him as a sun god—a theory that first emerged around 1750 and was referred to as the "Jesus myth". He also made reference to the notorious Ahmad al-Jazzar Pasha, who mutilated and murdered people at will. The "Butcher", as he was also known, was a Bosnian Mamluk who had to flee Egypt in 1768 after a dispute with the Mamluk leader and went to Syria. While always remaining loyal to the High Porte, he was nevertheless able to retain a certain independence from Ottoman legislation. In Volney's discussion of the

Ottoman administration, al-Jazzar is an example of pashas who had built up a system of spies and "rogues" that ensured that cities such as Cairo, Aleppo and Damascus were safer than Genoa, Rome and Naples. He attested "barbarism" to Syria (and Egypt) and pleaded for the dissolution of the Ottoman Empire—an attitude that contradicted the doctrine of French foreign policy.

PART II

The Nineteenth Century

Following in the Footsteps of Pilgrims of Earlier Times—Napoleon and de Chateaubriand

IN MARCH 1799, Napoleon invaded Jaffa with a force of thirteen thousand men from Egypt, the Sinai, Al-Arish, Gaza, Ashdod and Ramla, besieged it and had several thousand captured Ottoman soldiers massacred. Napoleon was firmly convinced that he could take Jerusalem within a few weeks, but things turned out differently: the alliance between Great Britain and the Ottoman Empire, the first between a Western and an Islamic country, was stronger and prevented France's advance to the east. The attempt to besiege Acre, which took place around two weeks later, failed. In the end, he was forced to retreat. The outcome was devastating: around a thousand soldiers were killed or wounded in the fighting. In the French camp at Jaffa, the plague claimed hundreds of victims among the soldiers. Napoleon's troops destroyed fortifications and villages and burned crops. The emperor left nothing but a trail of devastation behind.

On March 22, 1799, one day before Napoleon's hasty retreat, the French revolutionary newspaper *Le Moniteur Universel* published a report claiming that Napoleon wanted to restore Jewish independence with his campaign by designating the Jews as the rightful heirs of the country. Revolutionary France had granted its Jewish citizens full citizenship a few years earlier, in 1791, and "the Jewish question" was definitely on his mind. It is possible that this announcement was an attempt by Napoleon to win over Haim Farhi, the Jewish advisor to al-Jazzar Pasha. Later, the "butcher" threatened to murder the local Christians because they had supported Napoleon.

In his memoirs, Napoleon mentioned his encounters with Christians in the Holy Land, how the people of Nazareth, Shfaram, and Safed could finally see people of their own religion after hundreds of years of oppression. He spent one night in Nazareth and visited the Basilica of the Annunciation for a prayer of thanksgiving. Also, he is said to have deliberately left Jerusalem out of his campaign, because he considered it to be outside of his line of operations.

Pierre Jacotin accompanied Napoleon's troops as a cartographer. Among the 47 pages of maps he created are some of Palestine, which is included among the neighbouring countries of Egypt. They are considered to be the first trigonometric maps of Egypt, Syria and Palestine. Jacotin's survey of Palestine took place in the months from February to May 1799 and was necessarily limited to the areas occupied and travelled by the French, i.e. the coastal plain and Lower Galilee, as well as detours to Safed and the Jordan below the Sea of Galilee. How did Jacotin deal with the uncharted territories? In part he left them blank, in part he filled them in with information from hearsay, but did not make it clear whether he had surveyed them at all.

After his return from Egypt, Jacotin began to prepare the plates for publication. However, Napoleon declared them a state secret in 1808, apparently motivated by his efforts to conclude an alliance with the Ottoman Empire. The plates were not published until twenty years later, labelled with explanations in French and Arabic. Despite their shortcomings—many names of places and rivers were missing or incorrect—they were the most complete record of the country's topography at that point in time.

Napoleon's appearance aroused the interest of the European powers in the Holy Land. Until then only France had had a presence as the protecting power of the Roman Christians, while Russia served as the protecting power of the Orthodox Christians with the clergy as their representatives. The Turks had already been losing political power for some time—Constantinople was far away and the local commanders preferred to settle everything among themselves, often evading the payment of taxes to the capital with the result that Turkish punitive expeditions were sent to collect the money. The flow of pilgrims from Europe had clearly lost momentum during the centuries of Ottoman rule; Rome or Santiago de Compostela had long been the preferred destinations for the vast majority, as they were much easier to reach, but gradually more visitors from the West began to arrive again.

François-René de Chateaubriand, the founder of French Romanticism, set off on his journey to the Orient in July 1806, having already travelled to North America fifteen years earlier. He describes himself as "the last Frenchman to leave my country to travel to the Holy Land with the ideas, aim and sentiments of the pilgrims of old, but I have not the virtues that once illuminated the Lords of Coucy, de Nesles, de Chatillon, and de Montfort, at least their faith remains to me; in that respect I could still liken myself to an ancient crusader." He had written off the pilgrimage movement of the eighteenth century and now wanted to set off for new shores. For him, the Orient was one of the memories of a glorious time.

Constantinople initially made an uplifting impression on him, but the tense conditions—he mentioned the thundering of cannons and a revolution in progress—made it easier for him to quit, in fact he was "very glad to leave". As he explains further, "The feelings which, in spite of yon, will obtrude themselves in that city, spoil all its beauty. When you reflect that these regions were formerly inhabited but by Greeks of the Eastern Empire, and that they are now possessed by Turks, you are shocked at the contrast between the people and the country; you think that slaves so base, and tyrants so cruel ought never to have dishonored such magnificent abodes."

While he considered Smyrna (now İzmir) to be "this other Paris", his very first impression of the Holy Land, on the other hand, was sobering: "Jaffa presents itself as no more than a wretched cluster of houses gathered together, and arranged in an amphitheatre on the slope of a tall hill. The misfortunes which this city has so often suffered have multiplied its ruins." However, he was full of praise for the clergy and their reception, "so Christian and so charitable, in the land where Christianity and charity had their birth, this apostolic hospitality, in a place where the first apostles preached the Gospel". One of the priests assured him that he still considered the life he had been leading for almost fifty years "un vero paradiso", and he added: "Would you like to know what that paradise is like? Daily affronts, the threat of beatings, shackles, death!"

A priest warned him not to make his trip appear official: "You don't know these people", he said, "what you take for politeness is merely malicious curiosity. They only welcome you to find out who you are, whether you are wealthy, whether you can be despoiled . . . the Arabs seeing that a wealthy Frenchman is going on pilgrimage to the Holy Sepulchre, will raise the amount of the *caffaro* levy, or attack you."

De Chateaubriand moved in the company of a Bedouin sheikh, a dragoman, two servants and a donkey driver, a Bedouin from Jaffa. They made every effort to give the impression of "poor Latin pilgrims, but we were armed beneath our robes." While de Chateaubriand initially suggested relative serenity, this increasingly gives way to the feeling of having to be prepared for anything at any time.

De Chateaubriand caught his first glimpse of Jerusalem through an opening between the mountains, soon he perceived a heap of rubble and ruins. Beauty only revealed itself to him in the details, for example in the Church of the Holy Sepulchre where the priests of the various Christian denominations live:

> "From the heights of the arches, where they nestle like doves to the depths of chapels and underground vaults, they emit their chants at all hours of day and night; the organ-music of the Latin priest, the cymbals of the Abyssinian, the voice of the Greek, the prayer of the Armenian solitary, the plaint-like chant of the Coptic monk, strike alternately or simultaneously on your ear; you do not know whence these sounds arise; you breathe the smell of incense without seeing the hand that ignites it: you only see the pontiff passing by, vanishing behind the pillars, losing himself amongst the shadows of the temple; the pontiff, who will celebrate the most redoubtable mysteries in the places where they were enacted."

Of course, he wasn't completely free of complaints here either: "I again paid Mahomet for the right to adore Jesus Christ". However, the visit to the sacred sites compensated him for some of the inconveniences that he, the eccentric traveller, had to endure. One highlight was the underground Church of the Nativity in Bethlehem, "enriched with paintings of the

Italian and Spanish schools". In the background of the grotto was the place where the Blessed Virgin "bore the Redeemer of mankind": "Hic de virgine Maria Jesus Christus natus est", said the inscription at this point. De Chateaubriand was deeply impressed by the celebrations held there:

> "I heard an organ, which was very well-played, accompanying the mass with the sweetest and most tender airs of the finest of the Italian composers. These concerts charm the Christian Arabs who, leaving their camels to graze, come, as the ancient shepherds of Bethlehem did, to worship the King of Kings in his crib. I saw the desert dwellers communing at the altar of the Magi with a degree of fervour, piety, religiosity unknown to Christians in the West."

In the Armenian monastery, de Chateaubriand had the chance to meet the patriarch, who was dressed in the regalia of a rich Turk. He was offered coffee, confitures, water and white napkins. He was perfumed with rose essence to such an extent that he almost got sick. The patriarch spoke of the Turks with contempt, assuring de Chateaubriand that Asia was waiting for the arrival of the French.

The Frenchman considered Muslims, their religion and their behaviour to be barbaric, even disgusting; he saw "the Arab" as a civilized man that had reverted to the wilderness,

> "nothing about them would proclaim the savage, if their mouths were always shut; but as soon as they begin to speak, you hear a harsh and strongly aspirated language, and perceive long and beautifully white teeth, like those of jackals or ounces [most likely snow leopards]: differing in this respect from the American savage, whose ferocity is in his looks, and human expression in his mouth."

And he continued with a strange comparison:

> "What particularly distinguishes the Arabs from the tribes of the New World, is, that amidst the rudeness of the former you still perceive a certain degree of delicacy in their manners; you perceive that they are natives of that East which is the cradle of all the arts, all the sciences, and all religions. Buried at the extremity of the west, in a by-corner of the universe, the Canadian inhabits vallies [sic] shaded by eternal forests, and watered by immense rivers: the Arab, cast as it were, upon the high road of the world, between Africa and Asia, roves in the brilliant regions of Aurora over a soil without trees and without water."

He repeatedly referred to the past, defending the crusaders, whom he didn't see as aggressors or as "a mob of pilgrims running to rescue a tomb in Palestine":

> "The point in question was not merely the deliverance of that sacred tomb, but likewise to decide which of the two should predominate in the world, a religion hostile to civilization, systematically favourable to ignorance, despotism, and slavery, or a religion which has revived among the modems the spirit of learned antiquity, and abolished servitude."

From here it was not far-off to demand a conquest of the Orient, to enforce freedom. He saw his mission precisely in this tradition. Not only did de Chateaubriand, in accordance with the traditional custom, have himself knighted in Jerusalem, but also soon had himself immortalized in the cuboid of an Egyptian pyramid, by a messenger, mind you; he left it at that, viewing the pyramids from a distance.

De Chateaubriand did not live to see the Church of the Holy Sepulchre burn down. It only happened two years later. The renovation was carried out by the Greek Orthodox Church. Although the Chapel of the Holy Sepulchre was spared from the fire, it was rebuilt in the Turkish Rococo style.

As entertaining as the lengthy descriptions of this illustrious traveller are to read, it should not be overlooked that critics such as Michel de Jaeghere in *The Magnificent Liar: Chateaubriand in Greece* have expressed considerable doubts about the veracity of many of his details—not only those concerning his 1791 journey through North America, but also his trip to Palestine, which is of interest to us here. Even though de Jaeghere refers primarily to the first part of the journey in Greece, for which he is able to prove the invention of flowery descriptions of stays or visits, this pattern is likely to have continued as he ventured further south. As Pierre Bayard, professor of literature and psychoanalyst, who also deals with de Chateaubriand in *How to talk about places we have never been to?*, writes: "His encounter with countries is fundamentally intertextual, that is, it is at the same time an encounter with books, and these are consulted every time he finds himself forced to omit a stage." De Chateaubriand drew elements from other people's travelogues (perhaps unconsciously continuing a tradition cultivated by countless pilgrims before him?), interspersed long quotations from great classical texts, which he certainly knows how to comment on verbosely, and occasionally even quotes himself from other writings.

A letter de Chateaubriand wrote to a Canadian priest in 1844 contained the following confession: "I have mixed fiction with real events, and unfortunately, over time, the fictions take on the character of the real, which transforms them."

Skeptical Researchers—Edward Daniel Clarke and Ulrich Jasper Seetzen

AS THE nineteenth century progressed, there were more and more voices that no longer paid uncritical homage to traditional ideas. Edward Daniel Clarke, son of a chaplain and professor of mineralogy at Cambridge, with a keen interest in Egyptian and Jewish antiquity, arrived in 1801 as the companion of a wealthy nobleman who made the trip possible for him. Clarke was interested in a true picture of the state of society. For this, only the holy scriptures should serve him as a guide, because "under the name of Christianity every degrading superstition and profane rite, equally remote from the enlightened tenets of the Gospel, and the dignity of human nature, are professed and tolerated . . ."

He made an almost devastating statement:

"The pure Gospel of Christ, everywhere the herald of civilization and of science, is almost as little known in the Holy

> Land as in Caliphornia or New Holland . . . In the Holy Land, as in Russia, and perhaps in Spain and Portugal, the Gospel is only known by representations more foreign from its tenets than the worship of the sun and the moon."

Clarke's assessment of the biblical sites in the Holy Land, to which the monks led the pilgrims, is sobering. For him, the shrines and tombs were evidence of "superstitious trumpery". He could not get his head around the fact that the Church of the Holy Sepulchre appeared to him as an ordinary Roman Catholic church. And he conceded that the monastery church of Nazareth, which is said to have been built over the grotto where the Virgin Mary lived, was a beautiful building, "but it is degraded, as a sanctuary, by absurdities too contemptible for notice". He describes the superiors of the Franciscan monastery of Nazareth as "two meagre little men, in long black cassocks, having hats upon their heads of the size of an ordinary umbrella . . . with their knees quite up to their chins, as they descended the hill towards us."

Clarke was convinced that the real evidence of biblical antiquity still awaits discovery in the landscape. Depending on how critically the pilgrims engage with what they find, he alleged, they "return back to their respective countries, either divested of the religious opinions they once entertained, or more than ever shackeled [sic] by the trammels of superstition." And he ventured a biting speculation about St. Helena, the mother of the Roman Emperor Constantine, who, during her journey to Palestine in the fourth century, made an effort like no other to "obliterate every trace of whatsoever might have been regarded with reasonable reverence." He went on to speculate: "Had the Sea of Tiberias been capable of annihilation by her means, it would have been desiccated, paved, covered with churches and altars, or converted into monasteries and markets of indulgences, until no feature of the original remained; and this by way of rendering it more particularly holy."

He compared the Arabs, which he characterized as "serious and taciturn by nature", to the Roma he had observed in England, who shared their dwellings with their livestock. And he was convinced that the Arabs, as well as the Turks, have in common with the inhabitants of the Scottish Highlands and those of Cornwall the belief in the evil or envious eye. He quoted an Italian-speaking Arab who was full of anger at the tyranny of the Ottoman governors: "Beggars in England are happier and better than we poor Arabs . . . Happier under a good government and better because they will not put up with a bad one."

Ulrich Jasper Seetzen, inspired by Niebuhr's reports to carry out his own investigations, arrived in the Orient shortly after Clarke. Born near Jever, Germany, in 1767, the son of a farmer, he had studied medicine in Göttingen under the important naturalist, anatomist and anthropologist Johann Friedrich Blumenbach and founded the Göttingen Physics Society with no less a person than Alexander von Humboldt, who was a few years his senior. He undertook a series of journeys in Europe and abroad before setting off on his journey to the Orient in December 1802.

As a Freemason, he had committed himself to the ideals of freedom, equality, fraternity, tolerance and humanity, informed himself well in advance about the countries and drew up a broad-based research plan that included botany, zoology and astronomy as well as geography and mineralogy. He spent the first two years in Constantinople and Aleppo learning Arabic, as he wanted to undertake his journey with an Arab identity, so to speak. He did not subscribe to a Europe-centric worldview and approached Islam and the Ottoman multi-ethnic culture with an astonishing openness. He was particularly interested in the Sufi brotherhoods and the dervishes, whom he saw as "the most learned and enlightened people of all classes in the Ottoman Empire". From April 1806 onwards, Seetzen spent a whole year in Jerusalem, which he perceived as largely run-down and claustrophobic. He soberly described his encounters with Christian believers: "It is very rare to meet a monk who takes pleasure in investigations. Their circle of ideas is extremely limited, and their monastery is the center of it. Accustomed to a blind faith, and exhausted by numerous spiritual exercises, the field of reflection is completely devoid of culture. Without any knowledge of the world or of human nature, he pays homage to the most insipid prejudices, and one must place no little distrust in the news that one sometimes still receives from them."

Attempts by Catholic monks to convert him came to nothing, just as he avoided "conversations about religious matters" wherever possible. Otherwise, he was diplomatic: "I assured the clergyman that I too wanted nothing more than for the Catholic religion to be recognized everywhere. However, I understood this to mean, as one must also understand it in the literal sense, a universal religion, and this is indeed my most ardent wish as a cosmopolitan, although I am also firmly convinced by the experience of all times that this time will never take place and can never take place." Seetzen also mentioned the poor reputation of Catholics among the local Muslims:

> "You are, said the Mohammedans, neither Christians nor Jews; Allah may know what faith you have."

In Nazareth, in the "monastery church, which may not be large, but is cute and richly decorated with paintings, gilding and wallpaper, silver lamps and beautiful marble", he was displeased that a silver crown was placed on an image of the

Madonna: "What a tasteless monkish decoration!" Approaching the alleged miracles of the grotto with a critical eye, it did not escape his notice that a column broken off at the bottom was not suspended in the air, but was attached to the vault at the upper end. Shortly before him, Clarke had described this matter as "hocus-pocus". When visiting the bazaar in Acre, Seetzen once again proved to be an attentive observer: "A Méwlewí dervish goes around every day handing out drinking water to Mohammedans, Christians and Jews free of charge and without being asked. In this humane business, however, he gets his money's worth by receiving many a para a day as alms."

He had an interesting encounter in the pilgrimage site of Nabi Musa: "Despite this lonely location, we met a Mohammedan dervish from the Indian border here, from which you can see the reputation of this place of pilgrimage even in the most distant countries. Such a hermit usually stays here for five to six years, as he is then replaced by another Indian dervish. These dervishes are held in high esteem by the Bedouins and receive all kinds of food from them, which they themselves possess."

In Acre, Seetzen mentioned the "music, which is provided by one or a few, usually Egyptian, singers and several musicians. I usually spent an hour in the evening at a busy coffee house to listen to this music, and I must confess that I gradually developed a real taste for it." Finally, he unfolded a small "travel philosophy in the Orient":

> "Make the wicked one your friend, so he may not harm
>   you; and the good for the sake of his goodness.
> Not all Milton's devils are the same. There are also
>   degrees of malice among them.
> Not all wolves are equally hungry.

If you want to learn to appreciate the good, get to know the bad first.
Rudeness only disgraces the one who says it, not the one to whom it is said.
Whatever can be taken for fun, take for fun; what is not: act as if you did not hear it. Return a favour done to you twice, but do not expect double payment."

One might have wished that this advice would have saved him from the worst, but that was not to be. Seetzen never returned to his homeland. After surveying the Kaaba in Mecca in 1811, he suddenly disappeared from the scene. A few years passed before it became clear what had in all probability happened to him. At first there was a rumour that Seetzen had been killed in Africa. A certain J. Buckingham had then learned that Seetzen had supposedly been poisoned after his stay in Mecca in September 1811 in Taes, Yemen, on the orders of the Imam of Sanaa. His botanical, mineralogical and natural history collection, which he was carrying with him at the time, was apparently confiscated in Mecca. Seetzen had wanted to travel on from Yemen to Muscat and Basra, before going to Africa.

Seetzen's journey had a long afterlife, as he regularly sent letters and reports, as well as objects, including botanical, zoological and archaeological finds, to Gotha, which were to form the basis for the Oriental Museum there, which Seetzen wanted to establish after his return. His patron was initially Duke Ernst II of Saxe-Gotha-Altenburg, and later his eccentric son August. The collection, considered as the oldest one of its kind in Germany, was long forgotten and was only rediscovered by Schloß Friedenstein in 2021. In addition to many pieces of writing, it includes a panpipe, a Koran holder, a model of the Holy Sepulchre and a richly decorated feather case used as a hat ornament by a Janissary.

The Sentimental Journey—
A Longing for the Holy Land

THE EUROPEAN perception of the Orient in the eighteenth and nineteenth centuries was influenced by several factors. The Bible had long been the most important document. Here and there, reports from the time of the Crusades played a certain role. With the publication of the *Tales of the Thousand and One Nights* in the early eighteenth century, the perception changed again, and the Orient was romanticized. The tales were made famous by the French orientalist Antoine Galland, who accompanied the diplomat Marquis de Nointel to Constantinople in 1670. In addition to Asia Minor, Galland, who learned Arabic and Persian as well as Turkish, travelled to Syria and the Holy Land. His actual task was to find valuable manuscripts for Louis XIV's library. In Syria, he discovered a collection of texts containing stories of 281 nights, with which he returned to Paris in 1688 after losing a considerable amount of his documents and almost his life in an earthquake in Smyrna (now Izmir). In Paris, Galland was introduced to Hanna Diab, a Maronite Christian from Aleppo, who told him the stories of Haroun al-Raschid, Ali Baba and Aladdin and the magic lamp, whereupon Galland added them to the other stories. He then freely adapted the stories to suit the taste of the public at the time.

The development in Germany: The nowadays mostly obsolete German term "Morgenland" (later to be replaced by "Orient" or, in the later twentieth century, "Naher Osten") goes back to the Luther Bible: "When Jesus was born in Bethlehem in the land of the Jews, in the days of King Herod, behold, the wise men from the East ["Morgenlande" in the original] came to Jerusalem and said: Where is the new-born King of the Jews? We have seen his star in the east ["Morgenlande"] and have come to worship him" (Matthew 2:1). From there, the wise men brought the baby Jesus gold, myrrh and frankincense. Here it is the area to the east of Palestine, where the sun rises. "Ex oriente lux"—light comes from the east. The term corresponds to the Latin *oriens* and the Greek *anatolḗ*.

Contributing to the vagueness of the term was the fact that none of the German thinkers who wrote about it ever travelled to the Orient themselves. Johann Gottfried Herder, Moses Mendelssohn, Gotthold Ephraim Lessing, Heinrich Heine and Annette von Droste-Hülshoff did not venture there, nor did Novalis, for whom the Orient geographically encompassed not only Palestine but also Arabia, Persia, Egypt, even India and China; for him it was a mythical land of origin that allowed a connection with the past. Johann Wolfgang von Goethe, who formulated the demand "we must orientalise ourselves, the Orient will not come over to us", at least came as far as Sicily, which had been in Arab hands in earlier times, in the course of his legendary Italian journey. The poet, who learned Hebrew at an early age, immersed himself in the cultures of the Orient from afar by studying Arabic, Persian and Turkish. The Holy Land—in contrast to Italy, Greece and Asia Minor—did not become the destination of the "Grand Tour", the classic educational journey of the nobility and upper middle classes, until the nineteenth century.

The concept of the "Orient" subsequently found its way into many writings, including numerous travelogues about the Holy Land. Part of the intellectual passion for the Orient in German-speaking countries coincides with the publication of the journal *Treasure troves of the Orient edited by a society of enthusiasts,* which was published in Vienna from 1809, edited by the eminent Austrian orientalist Joseph von Hammer-Purgstall, among others. "In the Middle Ages, when Asia broke into Europe through the conquest of the Arabs in Spain, and Europe into Asia through the crusaders' marches to Palestine, the genius of the Orient first illuminated the darkness of Gothic barbarism with its torch, and softened the harsh exhalation of Nordic customs with its breath," reads the preface to the journal, which "should include everything that comes from the Orient or has reference to it". The spectrum was broad, with contributions coming from all specialist areas.

The journal, which included articles in German, French, Italian, Greek and Latin, appeared in a total of six volumes until 1818 and was an indispensable resource for Goethe, among others. In 1845, the German Oriental Society was founded in Darmstadt and from then on served as a forum for Oriental researchers (as it still does today).

It was not until later in the nineteenth century that the concept of the alleged cultural superiority of the West and the rigid system of thought of Orientalism—the view of the cultures of the Middle East shaped by domination and colonial interests—took hold. The ideas of an exotic, romantic Orient reverberated for a long time and even continued in parallel. As the century progressed, there was a growing number of voices that perceived the Orient as backward, trapped in outdated traditions and more or less incapable of development in the modern Western sense.

North African piracy remained important for Britain's ideas about the wider Orient well until the nineteenth century. The corsairs came from the "barbarian states", i.e. Morocco, which was independent but linked to the Ottoman Empire, and the semi-autonomous Ottoman regencies of Tripoli, Tunis and Algiers. They hunted the ships, confiscated the cargo and enslaved the crews. As early as 1625, Moroccan corsairs captured a merchant ship from the North American colonies. An estimated twenty thousand British and Irish were taken captive from the seventeenth to the middle of the eighteenth century. A very popular genre of narratives, known as "barbary captivity narratives", soon emerged based on accounts of such captives. The first narrative of this kind by an inhabitant of North America is considered to be that of a certain Abraham Browne, who was captured by "Turks" in 1655 and taken to Algiers, but was then able to buy his freedom three years later for a ransom.

But back to the Holy Scriptures. In England, the biblical texts were powerful in a way that differed from other European countries. Identification with the metaphorical Holy Land was particularly strong there. As the Israeli literary scholar Eitan Bar-Yosef shows in his study *The Holy Land in English Culture 1799–1917* (2005), people there had formulated a clear claim to the Holy Land, and they were appropriating it from afar. In fact, the feeling of attachment was so strong among many Victorians that England itself was seen as the Holy Land, the New or Heavenly Jerusalem, and the English regarded themselves as the "chosen people". William Blake

THE PENNY MAGAZINE

OF THE

Society for the Diffusion of Useful Knowledge.

344.] PUBLISHED EVERY SATURDAY. [August 12, 1837.

PILGRIMS IN THE DESERT*.

[Pilgrims in the Desert.]

The long and circuitous journey from Europe to Jerusalem, by Constantinople, through Asia, frequently adopted by pilgrims in the earlier ages, was one of extraordinary toil and danger. After the occupation of Palestine by the Crusaders, it became comparatively an easy task to visit Jerusalem—the pilgrims had only to take shipping for one of the sea-ports; and it was for this reason, amongst others, that the Crusaders held so tenaciously the sea-coast of Palestine. When no longer masters of Jerusalem, they made Acre, which is about seventy miles distant from it, their capital. The fall of Acre was the final loss of the Holy Land. "A motive of avarice or fear," says Gibbon, "still opened the holy sepulchre to some devout and defenceless pilgrims, but a mournful and solitary silence prevailed along the coast which had so long resounded with the world's debate."

Another route was to cross the sandy and generally sterile country which lies between Egypt and Palestine, and which constitutes a portion of the Great Desert of Egypt or Arabia. This desert extends as far into Palestine as close to the walls of Jaffa (the ancient Joppa), the coast-line being covered with sandy hills. The journey from Cairo to Jaffa is calculated as occupying from twelve to fifteen days. With proper care this journey, though attended with some privations, is not a dangerous one. Indeed, Burckhardt says that accidents or misfortunes arising from the want of water, that most grievous of all calamities in "a dry and thirsty land where no water is," must, in general, "arise from a want of proper precaution." But Burckhardt speaks as a hardy and seasoned traveller. Cases must

* A general view of the "Pilgrimages of the Middle Ages" has been given in No. 269 vol. v. of the 'Penny Magazine.'

Vol. VI. 2 R

FIGURE 3. Pilgrimage to the Holy Land became a popular topic in publications geared towards a general readership as this issue of *The Penny Magazine* from 1837 illustrates.

began working on his rhymed prophecy *Jerusalem* in 1804. It states:

> "I will not cease from Mental Fight,
> Nor shall my sword sleep in my hand:
> Till we have built Jerusalem,
> In England's green & pleasant Land."

Even though Palestine was part of the Orient, the hustle and bustle of the bazaars, the slave trade, the hamams and harems were not usually in the writers' focus. Also, cities such as Constantinople, Beirut and Aleppo fulfilled the cliché much better than Jerusalem. But Alexandria and Cairo, from where Egyptomania originated after Napoleon's campaign, should also be mentioned. Egypt was generally known for its hashish, prostitution and the possibility of otherwise illegitimate relationships, which may have attracted some travellers, even if they did not openly admit it or used the expected health benefits of the desert climate as a pretext to travel.

Western travellers to the Holy Land were on the lookout for the Christian past and less receptive to the typical "Oriental". Nevertheless, romantic views had their place here and there. The Viennese Jewish doctor Ludwig August Frankl offers a striking depiction of the colourful juxtaposition of cultures in *On to Jerusalem!* (1858):

> "The Mohammedan strides gracefully in wrinkled robes, the Bedouin in a white and brown striped coat looks around as if for prey, the Polish Jew in a black silk caftan hurries after them. The dark-clad Prussian deaconess walks with her eyes downcast; white and deeply veiled, the Mohammedan woman in yellow slippers shuffles along languidly and shapelessly, accompanied by a black or brown slave carrying her

child or a basket of fruit. The Franciscan with a broad brimmed hat and a rope around his waist looks at an unveiled woman, a Jewess. A Greek priest with a beautiful beard and long hair walks peacefully, as if they were of the same faith, next to a dervish with a yellow round cap; a Muslim with a green turban, the sign of the Prophet's descent, despises them both. In black wrinkled robes, noble figures with fine features, high pointed caps, are men from Persia. We encounter a completely naked man, who horrifies my European eyes, but who is not a nuisance to men or women here. He is a so-called saint who, being poor, is invited to the table in some family's house, even the Pasha's, and whom no one dares to refuse. Next to him strides the richly decorated sheikh, the dainty Effendi, an inhabitant of Lebanon armed to the teeth, Turkish soldiers.

The languages of the world—including those never heard before—sing, gurgle, nasalize, scream and bicker, and the ear is even more amazed and astonished than the eye. The effect is that of a fairy tale suddenly emerging from the Arabian Nights, which only becomes even more fantastic and ironic when people in black tailcoats and round hats, women in a suit they could wear on the Graben in Vienna or on the boulevards in Paris, intervene. Never have I been so disgusted by the tawdry clothes of our salons as in the streets, mountains and valleys of the Orient."

Half a Library in His Luggage—Alphonse de Lamartine in the Holy Land

ALONGSIDE DE CHATEAUBRIAND, Alphonse de Lamartine, one of the most important French protagonists of Romanticism, undertook his 16-month "pilgrimage" in 1832 and 1833. His initial goal was to revitalize his faith. He wrote in good spirits: "Happily the nineteenth century is passing away, and I perceive a better approaching, an age truly religious, in which, if men do not confess God in the same language, and under the same symbols, they will at least confess Him under every symbol, and in every language."

However, his journey also resonates with a political background: he supported the July Monarchy and was once again not elected as a member of parliament in 1831. The long farewell to France helped him to get past those defeats.

De Lamartine set off on his journey with his wife Marianne-Elisa Birch, their daughter Julia, several domestics and a library comprising many volumes.

He decided to travel to Palestine alone due to reports of plague incidences and remained there for two weeks. After visiting the holy places in Jerusalem, he had to take a break and remain silent about the profound emotions that these places have instilled in him. He left Jerusalem at five o'clock in the morning in order to attend mass in the grotto in Bethlehem. His guide was an old Spanish monk with a large beard "wrapped in a macklah (a Bedouin mantle)", who rode on a small donkey. "Although the month was April, a freezing wind—the subsiding gales of the tempest which had raged on the Sea of Jaffa—blew with such violence as to threaten me and my horse with an overthrow."

They were allowed into the Latin monastery, which was actually still closed due to the plague, as there had been no more victims for some time. The fathers of Bethlehem then asked de Lamartine to make their concerns heard in Europe, as the Greeks were laying sole claim to one of the stairs—". . . we had much difficulty in persuading them that, though we belonged to the French nation, we had no power to procure them redress". He goes on to note: "The Greek Churches in the East are much richer than the Roman; humility and modesty are the prevailing characteristics in the edifices of the latter; glitter and ostentation in those of the former; but the rivalry which arises naturally from their respective positions is extremely painful to the observer, who laments to find chicanery and discord in a region, the remembrances attached to which ought to inspire only charity and love."

On the way back to Jaffa, they heard "sounds of wild music" in the distance; the dragoman sent ahead learnt that it was the funeral ceremony for a "chief" who had inhaled the scent of a poisonous flower while hunting. De Lamartine, however, did not believe the explanation and assumed that he "had fallen the

FIGURE 4. Young [Christian] Girls of Bethlehem, photographed by Felix Bonfils.

victim to the jealousy of some rival chief". They watched the procession for a while longer:

> "and the death songs resounded more piercingly; this doleful pantomime, this funereal pomp, these hymns of despair expressed in another language, and attended with other rites, seemed to be a living memorial of those lamentations with which Jeremiah had filled the same valley, and which the biblical world still echoes."

De Lamartine's journey was overshadowed by the tragic death of his ten-year-old daughter Julia, who succumbed to tuberculosis in Beirut.

In addition to his notes directly relating to his stay, his travel diary also contains poems, historical passages and fragments of Arabic poetry. And in stark contrast to his countryman de Chateaubriand, de Lamartine didn't tire to emphasize the religious tolerance of the Turks:

> "Abhorrence and irreconcilable hatred exist among the different Christian communities, much more than between the Turks and Christians. . . . Their religion is a practical deism, the moral code of which is the same in principle with that of Christianity, save the dogma of the divinity of man. The Mohammedan creed is a belief in divine inspiration, manifested in a man more wise, and more favoured with the celestial emanation, than the rest of his fellow-creatures: at a later date some miraculous deeds as to the mission of Mohammed were mingled, but these legendary miracles form no part of the foundation of the religion, and are altogether rejected by the enlightened Turks. All religions have their legends, their absurd traditions, their popular side. The philosophic phase of Mohammedanism is quite free from these stupid admixtures; it contains nothing but resignation to the will of God, and charity towards men. I have known a great number of Turks and Arabs, deeply religious, who only admitted so much of their religion as was human, and according to reason. They did not coerce their reasoning faculties to receive dogmas from which they recoiled in disgust. Theirs was a practical and contemplated theism." Lamartine also emphasized that "Mohammedanism" is used to live in harmony with the Christian cultures.

In general, de Lamartine assumed, "Islamism might be introduced, without effort or difficulty, into a system of religious and civil liberty and thus form one of the elements of a great social agglomeration in Asia."

American Interest in the Holy Land Awakens

INTEREST IN the Holy Land among American evangelical Protestants was fuelled by two developments: the easing of travel conditions, which transformed overseas travel to the region, and the religious revival movement known as the "Second Great Awakening." "True biblical religion and American civilization were understood as being essentially the same thing, with their author being God. The spread of the Bible therefore meant the spread of American institutions and ways of life, the epitome of which was freedom", writes historian Peter Kawerau (1958). The justification for conversion with the help of the mission; the United States was thought of as the tool created by God to convert Jews, Muslims and even some congregations of Christians to "true" Christianity. It was believed that the state of the world indicated that the great pillars of papal and Mohammedan "deception" were beginning to crumble. The conversion of the Jews to Christianity was the highest priority. This would then be followed by the reestablishment of a Jewish state in Palestine. It was the spirit of the time.

Among the American Pilgrims, there were those who believed that the millennium or millennial reign of Christ would follow the second coming *(premillennialism)*, and others who believed that the millennium would precede the return of Christ after which would come the dawn of a golden age *(postmillennialism)*. Traditionally, America's gaze was directed toward the West, because that was where, according to popular belief, the true Israel had been led by God: America was regarded as the new Canaan—numerous places in the New England states and beyond are, after all, called "Salem", "Canaan", "Hebron", "Jericho", "Sinai", "Sharon", "Bethel" or "Goshen"—but Palestine was associated with special expectations. Thus, it was not surprising that the American Board of Commissioners for Foreign Missions—the first Christian missionary organization in America created by graduates of Williams College—turned its attention to Catholic Southern Europe and Muslim-dominated Western Asia as mission areas just a few years after the start of the American world mission. People fervently hoped to find confirmation of their faith there or even to be able to witness in person the events predicted for the turn of the millennium.

However, there were a few stumbling blocks for their activities—apart from the fact that no one was waiting for the missionaries to arrive and unfold their operations there. Convincing Muslims of the Christian faith was futile, as Ottoman law prescribed the death penalty for apostates from the Islamic faith. Religious affiliation was considered a characteristic of a certain population group, which had consequences for jurisdiction, the application of tax law and inclusion in military service. The relatively peaceful coexistence of the different religious and ethnic groups in the Ottoman Empire over long periods of time was based on clear boundaries, which formed the basis for mutual respect. Converting Jews to Christianity would not have been punishable; however, the converts would have risked losing the social and economic ties to their group.

The attempt to influence the indigenous Christians initially appeared to be the most promising: as early as 1819, the Prudential Committee of the American Board wrote in their monthly periodical *Panoplist and Missionary Herald* that "the whole mingled population is in a state of deplorable ignorance and degradation,—destitute of the means of divine knowledge, and bewildered with vain imaginations and strong delusions. It is to be hoped, however, that among the Christians there, of various denominations, some might be found, who are alive in Christ Jesus; and who, were proper means employed for their excitement, improvement and help, might be roused from their slumbers, become active in doing good, and shine as lights in those darkened regions. It is indeed to be hoped, however, that no small part of those, who bear the Christian name, would willingly and gladly receive the Bible into their houses, and do something towards imparting the heavenly treasure, as opportunities should be afforded, to the Jews, the Mohammedans, and Pagans . . ." (1819: 545)

The missionaries' approach was thus similar to that of Western colonial rulers in other countries and continents—even if this was not about the targeted, politically controlled annexation of territories, but "only" about conversion to a different belief system.

Pliny Fisk and Levi Parsons undertook their mission from 1819 to 1828, traveling from Boston via Malta to Smyrna (now İzmir). The trip followed the well-known trade routes. Figs from the Western parts of Asia Minor had been prized in America since the late eighteenth century, and enterprising merchants from New York, Boston, and Philadelphia came to buy ever-increasing quantities of raisins, nuts, and opium. In return, they brought cotton products, tobacco goods, and rum. Parsons' journey to Judea was preceded by his study of Modern Greek on the Aegean island of Chios. He carried the Bible with him in no less than nine different languages—it served as the standard cultural reference. Jerusalem was imagined as a centre of Christian benevolence, from which it would be possible to send the Bible to peoples of every language and nation. In fact, the Armenian Patriarch of Jerusalem allowed Parsons to sell Bibles in his language, but heated disputes between the pashas of Acre and Damascus caused him to leave the country. On the Greek island of Syros, an illness paralyzed him until he finally returned to Smyrna. During the joint journey to Alexandria, Parsons died, leaving Fisk alone. Several others joined the mission, including Fisk's friend Jonas King, who had studied Arabic with the famous oriental scholar Antoine Isaac Silvestre de Sacy in Paris. In January 1823, opposition came from the Catholic monastery in Alexandria, which pronounced the "excommunication" of King and Fisk, who, nevertheless, belonged to the Congregationalists and thus, in a broader sense, to the Protestants.

Jerusalem was now to become a permanent mission station, with a focus on the members of the Oriental churches. However, Fisk and King escaped the summer heat to Lebanon, visiting various monasteries and patriarchs and gathering information about Jacobites and Nestorians. The language barriers proved to be considerable, so that the following year they studied Arabic and Armenian. In February 1824, Fisk and another missionary were arrested by the Turkish police while selling the Bible to Armenian pilgrims in Jerusalem, although the British consul in Jaffa was able to secure their release a few days later.

In short, the planned missionary work did not really progress as intended. In 1825, the three years of missionary service to which King had committed himself came to an end and he went to Smyrna. Shortly afterwards, Pliny Fisk fell ill and died in Beirut. There were considerable attacks on Beirut by the Greek fleet, even fears of war between Turkey and the European powers. The few remaining American missionaries decided to withdraw from the Ottoman Empire for the time being for their own safety. They set off for Malta.

1831 saw decisive political changes: Muhammad Ali, the Ottoman governor of Egypt (and viceroy of the High Porte), brought Palestine and parts of Syria under his control. The background to this was that Egypt had come to the aid of the Sultan of Constantinople during the Greek War of Independence, but the latter owed a reward for his support. For several decades now, Egypt had been awakening from its slumber on the periphery of the Ottoman Empire and acting as an independent player. It was already serving the British as a reloading point for trade with India, even before the opening of the Suez Canal in 1869, which provided a new route for trade between Europe and the Middle East and saved a lot of time compared to the long sea route around the southern tip of Africa.

The occupation of Palestine had far-reaching consequences. Muhammad Ali's son Ibrahim Pasha, who controlled the changes from Damascus, altered several important aspects of the Ottoman administrative system. The entire territory was declared a province, the smaller units were abolished and the local feudal lords lost their influence. Poll taxes, which until then had only been payable by Christians and Jews, were now also levied on Muslims. In a significant move, Ibrahim Pasha allowed the Jewish and Christian inhabitants to repair their synagogues and churches. This decision was preceded by an earthquake in the wider vicinity of the Dome of the Rock, which some Jews interpreted as a divine sign.

The changes enabled Ibrahim Pasha to win over Great Britain and France even further. In general, the Western powers got a foot in the door in Palestine during these years. However, the changes did not go smoothly: in 1834, the predominantly Arab rural inhabitants rebelled violently against the occupation because of the tax regulations and conscription into the Egyptian army. For a short time, even Jerusalem came under their control before the uprising was put down.

That same year, the New York lawyer John Lloyd Stephens came to Europe and the Orient. During his stay in Jerusalem, he visited the Church of the Holy Sepulchre almost every day to observe the pilgrims. According to his observations, there were often between ten and twenty thousand pilgrims who gathered within the walls of the city to visit the Church. He was quite worried about his health as he mingled with the people in his attempt to get a closer look. After describing the conditions near the marble sarcophagus, he continued: "If I can form a judgment from my own feelings, every man other than a blind and determined enthusiast, when he stands by the side of that marble sarcophagus, must be ready to exclaim: 'This is not the place where the Lord lay'". And Stephens added the following astonishing remark: "The sepulchre of Christ is too holy a thing to be made the subject of trickery and deception; and I am persuaded that it would be far better for the interests of Christianity that it had remained for ever locked up in the hands of the Turks, and all access to it been denied to Christian feet."

Stephens' critical observations, which he recorded in *Incidents of Travel in Egypt, Arabia Petraea, and the Holy Land* (1837), were well received in literary circles. Edgar Allan Poe devoted a long and favourable review of his report in the *New York Review*.

Meanwhile, the American Board's missionaries continued their work in Jerusalem. They sold Bibles and tracts in Greek, Armenian, Turkish, and Arabic, and held talks with pilgrims. At least behind the scenes, the tone of the Americans towards the Oriental Christians had become harsher. After visiting the Syrian church in 1824, Pliny Fisk complained about their humiliation and ignorance, while the missionary William Goodell made the bizarre comparison that the members of the Oriental churches knew as much about the liturgical languages as Americans know about the Old Saxon language. After attending the Good Friday service in the Church of the Holy Sepulchre, Jonas King expressed shame of the Christian name, he regarded the worshippers as idolatrous, even pagan, and accused the Christians of desecrating the sanctuary of the Lord.

William McClure Thomson, who came to Jerusalem in 1834, pushed the boat even further out, talking about "the cunning Jesuit", "the pompous Greek", "the gloomy and zealous Armenian", "the poor Copt" and "the shy dark-skinned Abyssinian", adding that he would express his devotions in a pagoda or in the hideous temple of an idol as much as in the Church of the Holy Sepulchre. Such descriptions were then also given for the various churches, without, of course, being aware of the background to the seemingly strange rituals.

Eli Smith, a graduate of Yale College and Andover Theological Seminary, became the spokesman for this type of polemic in the following years. He was convinced that the "superstition" of Oriental Christians had instilled disgust and contempt in the followers of the 'false' prophet [Mohammed]. He regarded Oriental Christianity as absurd and impure. His accusation against the Oriental Christians was that they neglected the Bible, lost their piety and were subsequently subjugated by the "unbelievers". Conversely, only the reformation of the local Christians could lead to the disappearance of Islam. The revival of religion must be brought about by foreign aid, otherwise he expected one generation after another to fall into the abyss.

It was an attitude that became the generally accepted one of the American Board. Smith, who is said to have spoken Arabic, Turkish, Italian and Greek, initially worked in Malta, travelled to Armenia, Georgia and Persia before settling in Beirut in 1833 and transferring the Bible printing works there from Malta. He later supported the Protestant theologian and researcher Edward Robinson in his work in Jerusalem and also worked on the translation of the Bible from Hebrew and Greek into Arabic with native Arabic speakers who had converted to the Reformed faith, although this task was not completed until after his death.

As early as 1824, the dissemination of such writings was overshadowed by a decree of the High Porte addressed to all the pashas of Western Asia, in which the sale of Bibles was prohibited within the entirety of the Ottoman Empire. Jesuits even went so far as to circulate pamphlets against American missionaries in the Orient. The "Luthero-Calvinists" were also a bone of contention for the Greek Orthodox Church. In a circular letter signed by the patriarchs of Constantinople and Antioch as well as several metropolitans and bishops in 1837, the missionaries were accused of preaching the spread of light and only pretending to love humanity. Moreover, the American missionaries were described as satanic heresiarchs, who had resurfaced from the abysses of hell and the depths of the Northern Ocean. Some Armenians, a number of whom had united with Rome from 1830, only began to protest when the missionaries explicitly took a stand against fasting, the veneration of saints, transubstantiation, Marian devotion and the intercession of the saints in their sermons. Shortly before his death in 1830, Sultan Mahmud II instructed all patriarchs to keep an eye on heresies and the possible intrusion of foreign influences—meaning the American missionaries.

Just less than a decade later, the idealism of the Americans had exhausted itself, at least as far as their influence in Jerusalem was concerned. A certain Joel Hawes, who accompanied the missionary Rufus Anderson, reported to the Prudential Committee of the American Board in 1844 that he saw nothing that could give Jerusalem any special claim to their attention as the many pilgrims were not a very hopeful object for missionary endeavours, because they were too taken with their superstitions. Following this, it was only logical that they closed the Jerusalem branch and relocated their activities to Beirut in order to continue their efforts to achieve the ambitiously formulated but ultimately utopian goal of bringing about the "union of all true Christians".

Despite these sobering insights, the writings of the missionaries who made their way to America helped to promote interest in the cultures of the Middle East. For Edward E. Salisbury, who also studied in Berlin and Paris, contacts with missionaries were important in order to obtain Arabic-language documents. In 1841, he became the first professor of Arabic (and Sanskrit) in the United States, at Yale University, and played an important role in the American Oriental Society, which was founded shortly afterwards. Salisbury was also a corresponding member of the German Oriental Society, which had been founded in 1845. He also advocated educational initiatives in Syria and supported the missionaries through his paternalistic stance: "The countries of the West, including our own, have been largely indebted to the East for their various cultures," the scholar

FIGURE 5. A Christian family from Madaba, Transjordan, in festive attire, visiting Jerusalem in 1904/5.

attested, "the time has come when this debt should be repaid." However, Salisbury never visited the region himself.

The rituals that the Americans observed among the local Christians were not compatible with their ideas. Some went so far as to describe Armenians, Nestorians or Copts as "pagans" in need of salvation or redemption. In most cases, travellers were unable to distinguish between the different groups they encountered. The American theologian Edward Robinson emphasized how "thoroughly oriental" the local Christians are. Many visitors could not identify with these "Oriental" Christians. They wanted the Jews, who—to American missionary eyes—appeared more civilized, to play a more important role in the country though they also had considerable reservations towards them, sometimes even bordering on the anti-Semitic.

Many, if not most, of these American Protestants steered clear of the usual pilgrimage sites. They were convinced that direct knowledge of God could only be attained in the nature of Palestine. Ideal for this understanding was the Garden of Gethsemane with its ancient olive trees, where Jesus spent his last night of freedom; this is the romantic place where nature was in dialogue with the God of nature.

Henry Van Dyke, pastor of the Brick Presbyterian Church in New York City and later a professor at Princeton University, elevated Christianity to an "open-air religion"; his book was published in 1908 under the fitting title *Out-of-Doors in the Holy Land* (1908): "How shall we understand Christianity unless we carry it under the free sky and interpret it in the companionship of nature?" As a young boy, Van Dyke imagined, Jesus had gathered flowers on the hills of the Holy Land. Didn't Christ's crucifixion take place outside in nature? It was therefore only logical that Van Dyke did not even want to sleep under a roof; a tent quickly erected next to a spring would suffice as a place to spend the night. He also did not want his first view of Jerusalem to be "mechanically" corrupted by the view from a train compartment, but instead wanted to travel the route as of old. Van Dyke went so far as to disdain modern civilization and saw the lack of comfort and the dirt that many travellers complained about as proof that he was on the right track: "I want to get away from here; to return into the long past, which was also the hidden present, and to lose myself a little there, to the end that I will find myself again."

He not only regarded the Arabs as the exotic Other, but accordingly thought of them as located in an undefined past. They provided vivid evidence of how one could imagine a similar world so familiar from the Bible; thus, it was in them that the "true" Holy Land was revealed. The fact that he considered them both ignorant and uneducated and supposedly opposed to any kind of progress did not detract from his romantic admiration towards them.

Among European travellers, too, there were voices that preferred the numinous experience of Palestine's nature to dark, often overcrowded vaults. One example is the Swiss Protestant clergyman and professor Konrad Furrer, who complained in *Ramblings across Palestine* (1865) that there were more and more books about the country, but that it was not exhaustively described in any of them. "The great mass of pilgrims have been traveling the same roads for centuries, leaving the other parts of the country untouched." He himself ruled out this traditional way of traveling. "I was not driven to the holy land by the longing of the pious pilgrim who hopes to be moved by blissful feelings at the tomb of the Redeemer, such as he never experiences at home. I wanted to see the land of the Bible, if possible the whole land, its mountains and valleys, rivers and lakes, its rocks, its plants and animals, its sky, its people, their customs and traditions."

The undoctrinaire liberal Furrer lamented that "false piety" has turned the Bible "into a relic, as it is shown to us on Catholic altars", and that he would have liked to awaken it "from an artificial torpor". And in view of the dispute over the Holy Scriptures, he was convinced that they "will only emerge more brilliantly from all this dispute". In his book *The Importance of Biblical Geography for Biblical Exegesis* (1870), Furrer further elaborated on the imagined connections. On the Sinai Peninsula, where Jesus—according to tradition—had lived for many years, Furrer recognized the almost ideal ground for his revelation. Why there, of all places, in the desert-like landscape?

"Natural life is extremely simple in this country, with its lack of water and sparse vegetation, and does not have a distracting and confusing effect on the mind with its colourful change of appearances; but the magnificent, majestically silent mountain world in the heart of the peninsula, with its bold, rugged granite, diorite and porphyry masses, has something extremely solemn and serious about it, enhanced by the wide horizon of most of the peaks and the wonderfully pure atmosphere."

Ultimately, however, Furrer was only able to satisfy his intense desire for all these numinous experiences "to a very modest extent".

Arrival in Jaffa and Easter in Jerusalem

MOST PILGRIMS arriving from Europe came ashore in Jaffa. However, there were obstacles to overcome first, most notably a barrier of rocks between the coast and the open sea, which made a direct landing impossible. As there was no pier, arriving ships had to anchor at some distance from the coast, from where the passengers had to be transferred to small, not particularly stable boats via a lowerable staircase or basket before being rowed to the shore. This turned out to be highly dramatic: "The disembarkation took place in the deepest darkness amid shouting, jostling and confusion that was completely bewildering for an Occidental," noted Hermann von Soden, professor at the Berlin Faculty of Theology, in his *Travel Letters from Palestine* in 1898.

Jaffa's cliffs were legendary. "It is almost as if the coast was stubbornly resisting curious strangers setting foot on land here," wrote the German Egyptologist Georg Ebers (1882). Accidents often occurred when crossing the rock barrier, especially when there were strong waves or gusts of wind, and dramatic scenes took place, with passengers drowning time and again. If landing seemed hopeless in winter, the ships headed for Beirut. In addition, the passengers' negotiating skills were in demand under these difficult conditions, as the American Catholic priest Arnold Edward Breen wrote in *A Diary of My Life in the Holy Land in* 1906: "There is no fixed price for the services of the boatmen. From one to two francs will suffice; but the Arabs will always demand much more. The proper way to deal with them is to affect indifference in regard to landing. They are practiced in their profession; and they readily distinguish the cool prudent traveller from the nervous, timid one: the latter is their prey. They often shriek and struggle for no other purpose than to frighten the travellers, hoping thereby to receive more."

The mostly paved road from Jaffa to Jerusalem (distance as the crow flies: a good 30 miles) led through the orchards of the Sharon Plain, past the towns of Lod, Ramla, the Ajalon Valley, Bab El Wad/Scha'ar HaGai and Abu Gosh in the Judean Hills to the outskirts of Jerusalem and the Jaffa Gate. The journey was usually made on a mule and took up to two days. After the inauguration of the railroad connection in 1892, the journey time was shortened to approximately five hours.

During the Easter period, the number of pilgrims in Jerusalem swelled to several thousand. They were able to follow the "Imitatio Christi" step by step from the arrest to the condemnation to the crucifixion and walked in the footsteps of his last days. Volney wrote about the pilgrims who set off towards the Jordan on Palm Sunday: "The reader must consult particular relations of this pilgrimage, to form an idea of the tumultuous march of this fanatic multitude into the plain of Jericho, the indecent and superstitious zeal with which they throw themselves, men, women, and children, naked into the Jordan; the fatigue they undergo before they reach the borders of the Dead-sea; the melancholy inspired by the fight of the gloomy rocks of that country, the most savage in nature, their return and visitation of the holy places; and the ceremony of the new fire which descends from heaven on the holy Saturday brought by an angel." Not too surprisingly, Volney preferred not to watch the spectacle himself.

Marie-Joseph de Géramb arrived in Jerusalem in 1832 in time to observe the stream of pilgrims from many countries. That year, the Easter of the Eastern Christians coincided with that of the Roman Christians. He wrote:

> "I have travelled much; I have seen many fine sights in my life, but never do I recollect to have beheld a more magnificent, a more imposing scene than that presented by the church of the Holy Sepulchre in the night between Saturday and Easter-Sunday. Figure to yourself, my friend, a nave of immense magnitude, illuminated in every part with extraordinary taste and profusion, ten thousand pilgrims, arrayed in their best apparel, carrying torches in their hands, the women and children filling the vast extent of the galleries, also holding torches, and all making the sacred vaults ring with glorious Hallelujahs; while bishops, covered with gold and precious stones, preceded by censer-bearers, perfuming their passage with incense, and followed by a considerable number of priests in white copes richly embroidered with gold, walk in procession round the tomb, in the order assigned to each nation, singing psalms and hymns in honour of Him, who by his resurrection triumphed over death: imagine, I say, such a scene, and calculate, if you can, the impression which it must produce upon the soul of every one who has eyes."

He reported of an "immense concourse of strangers from the Morea, the Archipelago, Constantinople, Russia, Armenia,

Natolia [Anatolia], Egypt, Syria". Nevertheless, his joy at the celebrations was not unclouded, as most of the pilgrims came from countries contaminated by disease. De Géramb was certain that only by a miracle could he escape the plague: "The mere idea of the risks we run makes one shudder, and I perceive that the alarm is extending to all persons who reflect. I am, nevertheless, resigned; and, not only does my faith support me, but it shows me a real happiness in dying on the spot where Jesus my Saviour expired."

A catastrophe of a different kind occurred there two years later, in 1834. Mass fainting spells and clashes between worshippers took place from time to time, but this year, on Easter Sunday, the police had to collect bodies piled up at the entrance to the Church of the Holy Sepulchre. Thousands of people, including many families, had gathered there in anticipation of the Easter bonfire which, according to legend, comes from heaven. For some reason, the lighting of the fire was delayed, causing people to panic, which the Ottomans—so the legend goes—mistakenly interpreted as a Christian uprising. Several hundred believers are said to have died.

The German theologian Friedrich Adolph Strauss arrived in Jerusalem in 1844 at the time of Easter to explore the prospects for a brother house of the Pilgrim Mission. He was convinced that he was the first German Protestant clergyman there and praised the Protestants of the New World, who "to the shame of all Europeans" had first established a mission in Jerusalem and who had finally succeeded "by the grace of God" in 1838, "to receive the first Jewish family into the Christian church through holy baptism". "To whom now the eye of faith is not opened . . . he sees in Jerusalem only a small city of the Orient, covered with ruins of desolation, suffering from want and distress, from which the fleeting traveller has hastened quickly and unsatisfied," he wrote in *Sinai and Golgotha: Journey to the Orient (1848)*. But, he added: "To the believing Christian, on the other hand, the few remaining stones of the temple awaken inspiring memories; on the mountains, on the paths around, he follows in the footsteps of his Redeemer; and an hour on Golgotha transfigures his eye in such a way that he sees everything in the splendour of a new light."

Upon entering the church, visitors were asked about their religion, whether they were "Turco", "Greco", "Armenico" or "Frandji" (Franks, i.e. Western Christians). After sunset, Strauss attended the Roman Catholic celebration in the Church of the Holy Sepulchre and listened to the sermons, which were held in Italian, Spanish, German, English, French, Greek and Arabic. He had no use for the lighting of a candle at the Holy Fire, which he witnessed in one of the Oriental churches; "a beautiful old custom" had been "distorted into the superstition" that the fire in the Chapel of the Holy Sepulchre flowed "by a divine miracle" directly out of the rock. "The more repulsive such celebrations are for us and the more difficult it becomes to put ourselves in the less educated and more childlike position of the Orient, where much of the offensiveness is lost, the more we are inclined to recognize our local and historical kinship with the Western, Roman Christians." This was by no means an exception; it characterizes a view that was widespread in the nineteenth century and beyond. As the German Protestant theologian Maibritt Gustrau notes in her study *Orientals or Christians?* (2016) the travellers hardly "bothered to describe even approximately the diversity and historical development of the churches around the Mediterranean . . . Where not only the Greeks, Armenians, Copts and Maronites but also Jacobites, Ethiopians, Syrians, Nestorians or Chaldeans were mentioned, the readers were not informed about the denominations.

Which of these were churches united with Rome, which were ancient Oriental and which in current terminology belonged to the Eastern Orthodox were barely differentiated. The 'Greek Church' and the 'Oriental Church' were sometimes used as a collective term and the ancient oriental churches were distinguished from them as 'sects' in today's parlance.

His observations strengthened Strauss's feeling that he belonged to the right faction among Christians. He was dismissive of archaeological research: "There has recently been a great deal of controversy as to whether the place which is described as the Holy Sepulchre was really the tomb of Christ and whether the site which is shown to be that of the crucifixion is Golgotha. Although the historical and local proof of the authenticity of the Holy Sepulchre and Golgotha may not yet appear sufficient to some, it has been much less successful in asserting any tenable reason against its authenticity." From this he summarily drew the conclusion that "the probability of authenticity remains even after the most rigorous scientific investigation", and recurred to the artifice of invoking the tradition that has continued uninterruptedly since Christ's death and in this way seeing "with the millions of blessed pilgrims in the aforementioned holy places Golgotha and the tomb of Christ".

Strauss knew that Germans were in great demand as craftsmen in the Holy Land. "But this ease of acquisition also tempts them to indulge in all kinds of vices, and it is unfortunately all too well known how quickly the German transgresses the boundaries of discipline and morality in a foreign country." According to him, it was mainly the poor from Germany who went to Palestine, while many wealthy people from other countries, especially England, took up residence there because of their love of the Holy Land.

He mentioned the Muslim majority only in passing, talked about the alleged "inertia" of the Arab, "who only cares for the moment and does not think about doing anything for the future". "The journey to the Orient was for me a continuing experience of the truth of the divine word," he summarized. After the Jerusalem Association was founded in 1853, Strauss was appointed its secretary, and for more than three decades he was responsible for editing the association's journal *Latest News from the Orient.*

At Easter 1898, Hermann von Soden attended the Greek service at the Monastery of the Cross, which seemed to him "like a sacred spectacle". Von Soden was assigned the seat next to the director of the monastery, where he felt "strangely at home among the venerable gentlemen with their knots of never-cut hair swelling out from under their barrettes". The crowd surrounding them consisted mainly of Russian pilgrims, who, he wrote, stood there "like herrings". The waving of incense, a procession, a donation followed by a "sprinkle in the flat of the hand". Then the singing of the liturgy:

> "The sounds float up and down in constant restlessness, like birds on a perch, over a keynote that changes its pitch from time to time, barely exceeding the range of a fifth, in the character of a recitative, with many suggestions, vibrations and coloratura-like embellishments, mostly moving in half and quarter tones. In between, the epistle and the gospel are read by six different clergymen in brilliant festive robes in Greek, Arabic and Russian."

This was followed by a reception with the highest dignitaries in the audience hall, guarded by a stuffed lion. The Lenten meal posed a few challenges, especially as there was no menu explaining what exactly it was that had been stewed in oil. "Sometimes, with a gourmand's expression, I asked the director for the name of the new delicacy on offer in order to shed some light on the eerie darkness I was about to bite into." Apart from certain "anonymous crustaceans from the bottom of the sea", the culinary secrets were revealed in the end: "An oil soup was followed by mixed pickles and a kind of purée of spicy fish spawn, then, biting into each other like snails, polyps, delicately wrapped in oiled cabbage" and the like. The spook was finally over when oranges and pears were served. "That's how you feel when the train leaves the tunnel and the clear day greets us again."

Although it was not his intention to take part in "the unbelievable game with a puppet hanging on the cross", he was nevertheless drawn to the Church of the Holy Sepulchre. The "flea market" set up in front of it with all its "worthless trinkets" made him want to "cleanse the temple again". "Inside, the dark vaults and the many corners of this conglomerate of sanctuaries and holy places built next to each other according to various layouts and later merged into one grinned at me with so much superstition, so much dizziness, that I avoided the place so as not to upset my Protestant Jerusalem. What is not crowded into the small space by the rampant legend; almost as if it had been necessary to create a Christian panopticon." Von Soden listed the claims: "In that chapel, Abraham wanted to sacrifice Isaac. In another, Jesus was imprisoned; in a third, he was mocked; there, completely in the dark and barred, stands the pillar on which he was scourged. . . . In this chapel Christ was nailed to the cross, in the one next to it the cross was raised. The clothes of the crucified man were distributed there. . . ." And, concluding this part: "No one knows whether there is a real grave underneath at all."

Von Soden was baffled by all the "arbitrary invention of places", so he had no illusions about the starting and finishing points of the *via dolorosa*: "The individual stations, as the pilgrims' reports prove, changed their location even longer. But what does it matter whether these walls or others saw it, whether the path went in this direction or in another, one likes to follow it, the winding line through the narrow alleyways, up and down the steps." And he asked longingly:

> "Where are the ruins of the three temples, of Solomon, of the Jews returning from captivity, of Herod? Where are the remains of Hadrian's Temple of Jupiter that was built in their place?" A quiet, undeveloped hill in front of the city walls, which for a change is not overloaded with dubious meanings, is considered soothing and inviting for contemplation. "Here you can still experience Good Friday in spirit. This is how Golgotha lay in front of the city gate . . ."

He could not hold these ambiguities against Jerusalem, this "marvelous city", which is "built on rubble, sunk in dirt . . . and yet in its history is a mighty sermon of the search of the human heart for that which is above . . ."

Where the Human Species Originated—Ida Pfeiffer and Her Adventures

HER FRIENDS had tried to dissuade Ida Pfeiffer from her plan. As she reported, they were not sure "whether her body could endure the hardships and whether her spirit would have the courage to boldly defy the climate, the plague, the plagues of insects, the poor food, etc.". So the Viennese world traveller Ida Pfeiffer began her first major journey in March 1842, first traveling to Constantinople. In Scutari (today's Üsküdar), on the Asian/Anatolian side of the city, she embarked on a flight of thought: "So now I was standing in that part of the world from which man derives his origin, in which he has risen high and then fallen so low that God would soon have destroyed him forever in his righteous wrath. And here in Asia it was again where God's Son appeared to offer the palm of salvation to fallen man." Pfeiffer was both a pilgrim and adventurer.

She stayed on the Bosporus for six weeks, repeatedly postponing her onward journey, worried by news of unrest in Lebanon and Palestine. A returning pilgrim told her about the death of a fellow traveller and that he himself had been robbed. However, she believed she would be able to dispel these concerns through her own research and prepared herself: "I was advised to make the journey in men's clothing, but I didn't think this advice was wise, as my small, skinny figure would have suited a young man, but my elderly face would have suited a man. But as I lacked a beard, the disguise would have been punished immediately and I would have exposed myself to a lot of unpleasantness. I preferred to keep my simple European costume, which consisted of a blouse and leggings. On my head I wore a round straw hat." Her choice proved to be a wise one, as she was treated with respect everywhere she went.

Via Beirut, she travelled to Saida, Sarepta, Tyre and finally to Acre. Arriving in Jerusalem, she noted:

"It gave me a very special, unprecedented feeling to walk where Christ walked. I looked at every spot, every building with double interest. Perhaps, I thought, I was entering the same place, the same house that Jesus had once visited." As soon as she arrived, she wanted to say a prayer, but was surprised to find that the men were separated from the women in the church and that there were no pews and only a very poor organ. She was also astonished to see that the Christians were dressed "like Orientals". She herself was scrutinized by the people there and prayed in her room. At midnight, she followed the services in the Church of the Holy Sepulchre:

> "The Greeks and Armenians beat and hammer on free-hanging boards or metal poles. The Latins play the organ or sing and pray loudly, while the priests of the other sects also sing and shout. It is a great discordant noise."

Pfeiffer repeatedly had to make detours around villages affected by the plague during her journey. When she encountered sick people, she was asked to cover her nose and mouth. One soldier had painted the lower part of his face with tar to prevent infection. Four hours from Jerusalem, she visited the Greek monastery of Mar Saba, but unlike the masters, servants, Arabs and Bedouins, she was not allowed to enter the building. However, she did not have to spend the night in the open air; a lay brother points to a tower and promised to put her up there: "He fetched a ladder from the monastery and went with me to this tower; there he put it on, and we climbed up about one floor to a very low, iron gate, which he unlocked and into which we crawled. We found a spacious place inside. A wooden staircase led us higher up to two tiny chambers located roughly in the middle of the tower. One of them, furnished with an altar and sparsely lit by a small lamp, served as a chapel, the second as a bedchamber for pilgrims. The latter was furnished with a wooden divan. My guide recommended himself with the promise to come back later and bring me a cushion and a blanket as well as food and drink." She found her sleeping place "kept under lock and key like a kidnapped princess". From the battlements of the tower, she had a sweeping view of the desert landscape.

Again and again, doubts arose in her mind. Had the crucifixion really taken place in the Church of the Holy Sepulchre? She visited the grotto in Nazareth, where Mary is said to have received the Lord's message from the angel. Like other travellers before her, she was not fooled by the claim that one of the three granite pillars that had been destroyed was hanging freely in the air: "If these people had seen further than their noses could reach and only glanced upwards, they would hardly claim a miracle that only exists in their imagination."

During the ten-day and eleven-night voyage from Beirut to Alexandria, a strange incident occurred: a two-master sailed directly towards the ship, but the supposed pirates turned out to be sailors in distress who had broken their compass. "Now the whole scene was transformed as if by a magical stroke of a benevolent fairy. The captains threw themselves back into their former glory, the sailors hugged each other and jumped like children, we poor travellers were released from our imprisonment and allowed to participate in the friendly negotiation of the mutual heroic crew." The foreign ship followed them for the rest of the journey.

After arriving in Alexandria, she had to get through quarantine. The accommodation was extremely spartan and she had to order food. When the delivery did not arrive as requested, she could count on the hospitality of an Arab family. The quarantine culminated in the following procedure: "On the seventh day of our imprisonment, we were all ordered to our rooms at nine in the morning. Doors and windows were closed, large barrels of incense were brought in and a horrible smelling smoke of sulphur, asand [probably referring to the plant resin asafoetida is created from], feathers and the like. We had to endure four or five minutes in this suffocating smoke, then everything was opened up again." With her particular sense of humour she concluded: "A person with lung disease would have found this cannibalistic expedition difficult to endure."

One time, on the way from Alexandria to Cairo, Egyptian women curiously called her "Marie", "presumably believing that as a Christian I must bear the name of the Holy Virgin", whereupon Pfeiffer told them her baptismal name.

The travellers' comments on Islamic culture or Muslims were usually limited to casual remarks about the "followers of the false prophet" or the "Arab strolls". In the case of the German aristocrat and landscape architect Hermann Fürst von Pückler-Muskau, who came to Palestine as early as 1838, astonishment and disappointment at the conditions in the Christian holy sites led to a more intensive study of the Islamic shrines, such as the Dome of the Rock in the heart of the Christian quarter of Jerusalem, which he studied attentively: "If one were to apply merely the aesthetic standard, one would have to confess that the latter is by far the most worth seeing in Jerusalem, picturesque, grand and magnificent in the highest degree," he wrote in a letter to the Prussian consul Roquerbe in Alexandria. Despite such highlights, he was to describe his journey as "the most unenjoyable of all I have made"; the impressions he had previously gained in the Church of the Holy Sepulchre overshadowed everything: "The Christian shrines and everything attached to them seemed to me to be the greatest scandal." On the other hand, the Swiss David Wegelin, who came in 1845, was convinced: "There is a foreboding charm about this church, which should even affect people to whom the interpretation of Christian events would be alien. The most diverse costumes of the earth unite here in pious devotion and cover the meaningful places with their kisses and touching outpourings of worship and fervour."

Until the end of the nineteenth century, access to the Temple Mount was reserved for high-ranking personalities. The enterprising publicist Moritz Busch only succeeded in 1861 to enter because he mingled with the entourage of the Grand Duke of Russia. As the news spread that the Turks had given permission for all Christians to do so, many set off there, including "a large number of Greeks living here", as Busch recorded in his *A Pilgrimage to Jerusalem: Images without Halos* (1861). Chaos was inevitable:

> "It became even more terrible when the procession turned into the narrow alley leading up the slope of the Moriah, and

a Russian priest who stumbled and fell next to me was in the greatest danger of being trampled. But the fighting and choking became worse than anything else when we came to the narrow dark passage that opens up at the north-west corner of the Moriah plateau. Several people fainted here. Repeatedly, the flow of people came to a standstill like ice. The groans of the squeezed people were horrible. I myself was first squeezed so tightly that I seriously feared a broken rib, and then pushed up like a piled-up floe and carried away in this position, with my feet above the ground, probably ten paces."

According to Busch, there were "at least a thousand people" there. Of course, they all had to change their shoes for Turkish leather socks before they were allowed to enter the mosque.

Hot Blood Rushing Through My Veins— Maria Schuber, Pilgrim

MARIA SCHUBER, a Catholic and teacher from Graz, took a whole year for her pilgrimage, which began in October 1847. Her travelogue is a collection of wordy letters she sent to various people back home. Her black veil hat quickly earned her the nickname "monache" (nun) among her fellow travellers, to which she always replied "non sona monache"—"I am not a nun," but she obviously enjoyed playing with her unusual attire.

Via Rome, she first travelled by steamship to Greece. Her itinerary is rather unusual for a pilgrim to the Holy Land as final destination: Egypt is her first stop in the Orient and her emotions ran high: "When I saw the coast of Africa from afar, I was overcome by the feeling the closeness of the fulfilment of all my desires, to tread the ground my Saviour walked, so powerfully moving me . . . A hot sensation flowed through my limbs, as if all the fervour of Africa pour into them." Without hesitation, Schuber joined the funeral procession of Boghos Bey, the governor of Alexandria, and was surprised that, as a single woman, she was allowed to walk at least as far as the mosque. "The whole thing doesn't seem strange at all. I didn't think I would feel so at home in a Turkish city." She continued: "You walk among all kinds of people of all nations, white, black, brown, Europeans, Turks, Arabs, distinguished and common, completely unnoticed and uninhibited. My European black nun's habit with a long veil is probably as conspicuous here as a red sock with a blue fez in our country, which people stare at as I were a camel here, but no one cares about me, except when I ask someone to show me the way, which everyone is willing to do with the greatest kindness."

Maria Schuber went to Mass at the Franciscan Church. An encounter with two Italian Jews surprised her, as she perceived "their speech and actions" as "edifyingly Christian." She combined this with a wish that sounds strange to today's ears: "All that remains for me is my wonder and my wish that soon all Jews would be indistinguishable from Christians!"

Upon arriving in Cairo, Schubert's interest was focused on Christian sites. With the help of an Arab, she rode to a garden with the tree under whose shade Mary is said to have rested with her child when she arrived. "It is truly unique in its entirety, as it stands, no tree like any other. From the root to the canopy, there is a life of its own within it, and its entire is mysterious." She was deeply moved, her tears flowed. When another Arab man approached her and asked her to carve their names into the trunk of the tree, she did not want to, instead she took a twig with her. Her next stop was the grotto where Jesus, Mary, and Joseph are said to have stayed during their flight. It is "in the middle of the old town in a house, up stairs and down stairs. . . . In an ordinary house in the narrow alleys, you go up narrow stairs into a structure full of wooden latticework that makes you feel uncomfortable and strange, that is the Coptic church.

A stone is lifted from the floor, you are given a small wax candle, and you descend a narrow staircase as if into a crypt. It is a sparsely furnished room with a sleeping niche, a stone "workbench" for Joseph, and a stone washbasin, divided by six small columns, with an empty old board serving as an altar. Schuber appeared disillusioned, as she probably expected something more impressive. This is followed by another tirade against the "schismatic heretics," as she called the Copts. "Why should it not be possible for a Christian power to free the grotto from the hands of the Copts, that is, to buy it and consecrate it for Christian use?"

The visit to Alexandria and Cairo was, of course, only the prelude. With the "Arab bed" (a straw mat) in her luggage, accompanied by a dragoman named Ignaz and riding a camel she called "Herr Bruno," she set out on the arduous journey through the desert. After five days of quarantine in the plain of Ashkelon, north of Gaza City, a Turkish guard approached her: "He made the sign of the cross over himself in a very friendly manner to welcome me as a Christian; I smiled at him, took my crucifix, and asked him indicating whether by the cross he meant Christ, the crucified one. He kissed it reverently and showed his veneration with his forehead. I offered him my hand in friendship, he kissed it and placed it on his forehead. I pointed to heaven to show that we are one in Christ." After some back and forth, she managed to enter a "Turkish prayer sanctuary," even though women were actually denied access there—"For ten para I bought myself [the services of] a gentleman." Everywhere, she was surrounded by curious people, and Schuber was annoyed that she cannot speak to them. "In general, I wish I knew the Arabic language and had a missionary vocation, with the support of the country, and I would have an easy and rewarding job."

In Jerusalem, she was irritated by the Greeks with the splendour of their churches and their "sniffling singing", "their kissing of all the images in turn, the countless crossing of themselves from head to toe, the incessant burning of incense, the tireless ceremonies, so that one cannot even make out the mass among them, the completely visible lack of devotion inside . . . I would gladly call upon the entire Protestant protest against it [which, as Schuber mentions, is directed against the Roman Church] if it had not protested itself out of Christianity." She praised the Turkish guards for their serenity and even says: "In general, the Mohammedans of today seem to be increasing in their secret love and respect for Christianity . . . "

She only noticed the Copts in the Church of the Holy Sepulchre in passing, describing them as "quiet people" who keep their "incense offerings" very modest and have no part in the entrance to the Holy Sepulchre. She remarked that the Russians are "very good people". With regard to the Jews, her comments repeatedly boiled down to the recommendation that they should "all together" convert to Christianity because they are "waiting in vain for their Messiah."

The differences between the Latin and Eastern Churches were then manifested to her in the chants and sounds, which she found "unpleasant to the ear": "The holy church of God called with its friendly, solemn ringing of bells, the Greeks and Armenians with a noise of wooden beats, which in time turned into metallic sounds, and when it went further, into a similarity to our Lower Styrian triangles."

Schuber learned from the Austrian consul general that he has promised his support "if colonists from Württemberg want to cultivate that fallow garden of God." The conditions for this seemed favourable to her: "Throughout Syria, an infant can put its hand into the hole of the adder; it has lost its venom. The power of hatred against pilgrims and strangers from the West has been broken."

Maria Schuber belongs to the 'old school' of pilgrims who are still completely untouched by the doubts that have repeatedly gripped many other visitors to the Holy Land. For her sense of connection, it was ultimately irrelevant whether an event described in the Bible actually took place at the place where it is commemorated. She does not ask herself questions. She simply believed.

After the Egyptian Occupation of Palestine

IN 1841, the Ottoman Turks—supported by England, Russia, Austria and Prussia—regained control of Palestine. It was not a complete regression to the time before the Egyptian occupation; many of the rules introduced in the meantime were retained. Around the same time, the phase of *Tanzimat* ("New Order"), which entailed far-reaching reforms based on the model of European societies, had begun in the Ottoman Empire and was implemented in various stages over the following decades. Modern universities, newspapers and tax reforms were introduced. From then on, people living there were considered citizens, no longer just "objects". The reform of 1856 put non-Muslims living in the empire on an equal legal footing with Muslims. The previously applicable poll tax for non-Muslims was abolished and replaced by a fee for which non-Muslims were exempted from military service—although there were both Jews and Christians who volunteered for service.

After the Crimean War, the Ottoman Empire was integrated into the European system of powers with the Treaty of Paris of 1856, whereby the contracting parties France, Great Britain,

Sardinia and Russia guaranteed its independence as a state. (Prussian and Austrian diplomats were also involved in the negotiations). Among many other points, the treaty included a commitment to improve the situation of Ottoman citizens who were not of Muslim faith. The Sultan had the official recognition of all faiths and the prohibition of religious coercion enshrined and solemnly declared by the governor of Jerusalem. Although some forms of discrimination continued, the situation of religious minorities was fundamentally improved. This was also due to the fact that thousands of Christians and Jews now benefited from the protection of British, Austrian, Prussian, Russian, French, Spanish and American diplomats in the country. Any offense against a person associated with one of these nations triggered the intervention of the consul concerned, who could then exert his influence on the Ottoman Empire.

As early as 1841, a Protestant diocese was established in Jerusalem on the joint initiative of Queen Victoria and the Prussian King Frederick William IV. The intention was to coordinate the activities of British and German missionaries, as it was still assumed at that time that Jews could be converted to Christianity. The powers agreed to appoint one bishop each in turn. The first bishop was Michael Solomon Alexander, appointed by Queen Victoria. He was followed in 1845 by the Swiss-born Calvinist Samuel Gobat, who had studied Arabic in Paris with Antoine-Isaac Silvestre de Sacy and had previously served as a missionary in Ethiopia. He was appointed by the Prussian King, had to report regularly to him on his activities and held this office for more than three decades. The conversion of the Jews was a matter close to his heart, as he wrote, "since the time when I sat as a child on my mother's lap, who often spoke with deep emotion of the desolation of Israel, and especially since it pleased the Lord to reveal himself to my soul . . .". Gobat felt himself to be a "debtor" not only to the Jews, "but also to the Greeks and the barbarians, the wise and the ignorant, Papists, Armenians, Turks, etc., whose miserable spiritual and earthly condition I had already noticed twenty years earlier, on my first visit to Palestine . . ."

Missionary work among the local Christians was difficult, as Gobat explained in his annual report for 1851: "Here in Jerusalem there are many, Latins, Greeks and Armenians, who seek the truth more or less earnestly, but they are almost all poor, and their dependence on the monasteries is a terrible obstacle for them: for where any one begins to read the Bible seriously, or to send his children to my school, or to attend the Arabic Bible and prayer classes . . . he is immediately threatened by his priest, and if he does not yield at once, expelled from his home, which is generally the property of a monastery . . ." Nevertheless, small Arab-Protestant congregations emerged, for example in Reineh near Nazareth.

Against this backdrop, it's easy to see why missionary efforts were marked by disagreements, jealousies, and intrigue. The Swiss doctor Titus Tobler, for example, accused the English missionaries of having no true love for Christians. Criticism from the Catholic side was sparked by the "dual nature" of the bishop, who represented both the Anglican and the Prussian Protestant national churches, which followed different dogmas and were not really compatible with each other. In fact, Gobat was accused of proselytizing among the Christians by parts of the Anglican Church, which was striving for harmony with the Oriental Church, as Gobat was able to record a number of conversions among the Arab Christians.

In 1857, Gobat noted that the country was suffering "under the curse of a bad, negligent and tyrannical government", although the head of the empire was actually benevolent and the prejudices of the Muslims against the preaching of the Gospel were diminishing. "Some regions are covered with thorns and hedges, and generally groan under the curse of a godless population, which ekes out its miserable existence in want and misery despite the abundant harvest of this past year; nothing to be said of the blood that is shed so abundantly every year in all parts of the country. . . . It is true we can sometimes talk about the truths of the Gospel with individual Moslems; but at best they hear the word of God with coldness and indifference; in general, their hatred of Christians, whether European or native, has been on the increase during the last few years; and since the outbreak at Nablus in April, 1856, it is not unusual to hear them speak of a total extermination of Christians."

Gobat alludes here to the uprising of the local Muslim population against the Ottomans. Nablus was particularly feared by Christians and Jews (along with the predominantly Muslim Gaza, by the way), and Ottoman punitive expeditions had repeatedly taken place there in order to curb the misconduct of the inhabitants, who were considered particularly fanatical. Although the reforms taken during the Tanzimat, which included the equality of Christians and Jews in relation to Muslims, also applied to Syria, the Ottoman governors often proved powerless to implement them on the ground and the old conditions continued. At the same time, Prussia began a comprehensive commitment: a hospital, a hospice, a library and a girls' school were built—the first of their kind in the country.

In the 1870s, Anglicans and German Protestants finally decided to end their cooperation. Britain went its own way, opening the Suez Canal in 1869, annexing Cyprus in 1878 and occupying Egypt in 1882. In the Levant, it intensified its involvement through the Palestine Exploration Fund, whose task was to explore the archaeological remains, geography, topography, botany and zoology of Palestine. At the first public meeting, held in 1865, the Archbishop of York, who remained President of the Society for many years, made an impassioned plea:

> "We mean to walk through Palestine in the length and in the breadth of it, because that land has been given unto us. It is the land from which comes news of our Redemption. It is the land towards which we turn as the fountain of all our hopes; it is the land to which we may look with as true a patriotism as we do to this dear old England, which we love so much."

Religious, scientific and political, even imperialist interests complemented each other in the work of the organization. The detailed map produced for the Palestine Exploration Fund—the result of surveys carried out from 1871 to 1879 and 1912 to 1914—proved to be of great value decades later, when Palestine was taken over. The British did not establish settlements such as those created by the Americans, Germans and Swedes (none of whom, however, made any territorial claims to Palestine).

The tasks of the Palestine Exploration Fund were largely congruent with those of the "German Association for the Exploration of Palestine", which was founded in 1877 by the Swiss Carl Ferdinand Zimmermann and still exists today. A number of members, including scientists, rabbis, pastors and merchants, were associated with both organizations at the same time.

The construction of a German Protestant church was still a long time coming. Although in 1869 Sultan Abdülaziz had given Crown Prince Friedrich Wilhelm the "Muristan" site in Jerusalem's Old City—where the first hospital of the Knights of St. John stood at the time of the Crusades—funds still had to be raised for three decades before the plan to build the church could be realized.

Samuel Gobat died in 1870 and was laid to rest in the Protestant cemetery under an olive tree on Mount Zion: *The Observation Post of the Temple,* the organ of the Württemberg settlers in Palestine, reports in detail on the funeral, "which moved a large part of the inhabitants of the Holy City and will certainly be heard with participation in the West as well. . . . Apart from the bereaved families, the funeral procession included the Protestant schools of Jerusalem and Bethlehem, the German, English and French consuls, the kawasses (honor guard) of these consulates as well as those of the other consuls and the patriarchs with the exception of the Latin ones, an escort of the Turkish military, then the members of the Protestant communities and many Arab Christians as well as Jews and Mohammedans."

Forerunner of the Zionists—Moses Montefiore

FOR A LONG TIME, throughout the Middle Ages, emissaries, especially in Holland and Germany, had been collecting money for the elderly and infirm Jews living in Tiberias, Safed and Jerusalem or those who lived there for religious reasons. Among these were descendants of the Sephardic Jews expelled from Spain following the Edict of Expulsion of 1492. Officially, the administration of the "Chaluka" was established in Amsterdam in 1809. However, only a few European Jews took a more pronounced interest in Palestine in the first half of the nineteenth century; this was soon to change. Moses Montefiore, the son of a Sephardic Jewish family of Italian origin, had, after a short career as a stockbroker in London, campaigned for the removal of civil law obstacles that made public life difficult for Jews in Great Britain.

In 1827, he and his wife Judith undertook their first journey to the wider Orient and the Holy Land. Their route first lead via Rome, Naples and Malta to Alexandria. In Cairo, they were received by Muhammed Ali Pasha. In Palestine, they were accommodated in a Greek Orthodox monastery and were apparently unaware of the affront this represented in the eyes of the local Jews, who were not on good terms with the Greeks. They expressed "their grief at the sight of Jerusalem lying in ruins, as mourners do when they lament the loss of a dear relative". They said a prayer, thanked God for bringing them safely to Jerusalem, the great long-awaited destination of their journey, and asked for his blessing. Their secretary, the orientalist Louis Loewe, kept the diary. A personal butcher was hired to ensure that they always had kosher meat at their disposal.

In Palestine, they encountered a much more religious Judaism than they knew from their British homeland. They were surprised to find that secular knowledge was alien to most Jews in Palestine and was even rejected by them. Moses Montefiore did not speak Hebrew and, unlike his wife, an Ashkenazi Jew, did not know any Yiddish either. In addition to the well-known sights, the two visited the synagogue and received representatives of the Spanish-Hebrew and German-Hebrew communities, who told them about the oppression and the governors' constant demands for money: "There are fifty Portuguese families, consisting of about 200 individuals; forty German families, or one-hundred-sixty persons, and near two-hundred elderly widows in great distress".

While Judith Montefiore, accompanied by several women, travelled to Rachel's tomb near Bethlehem, Moses Montefiore, feeling weak, stayed in Jerusalem, taking some "terra santa", or holy earth, from the Jewish cemetery as a souvenir. Eventually, he underwent a profound change as a result of this journey: "I was in better spirits than I had been for months . . . No city in the world can have a finer situation than this; nor is there a better climate", he commented in his diary: "This day I begin a new era. I fully intend to dedicate much more time to the welfare of the poor, and to attend Synagogue as regularly as possible on

Monday, Thursday, and Saturday". In the time ahead religion was to play a much more important role in Montefiore's life. On their way back to Alexandria they were hailed by seven large boats, full of Turkish soldiers, who apparently took them for Greeks, came alongside, entertaining great suspicion of them until they were convinced of their mistake.

Their later trips to Palestine were often accompanied by dramatic circumstances. During their visit in 1837, the plague was raging in the country and Galilee had just been shaken by a strong earthquake. In Tiberias and Safed, the houses that had been laid out in an interlocking pattern, collapsed on top of each other, and appeared to them as a field of ruins. They set up camp on the Mount of Olives and helped the people with aid wherever they could.

In 1839, Montefiore met with Zvi Hirsch Kalischer, an East Prussian Orthodox rabbi and a pioneer of early Zionism, who wanted to convince him that Palestine should be a new homeland for the Jewish people. Kalischer did not want to await patiently the arrival of the Messiah, but proposed to start creating agricultural settlements as early as possible. The funds were to be collected from Jews of all countries. To guarantee the security of the settlers, Kalischer proposed that a Jewish military guard be set up. And indeed, Montefiore later agreed with the Egyptian ruler Mohammed Ali Pasha to establish a joint stock company to finance this project. However, as the Egyptian occupation of Palestine came to an end just a short time later, the matter came to nothing. Kalischer had already approached the Frankfurt banker Amschel Mayer von Rothschild in 1836 with a request to acquire Palestine, Jerusalem or at least the former Temple Mount from Egypt.

Nevertheless, Montefiore did not abandon the basic idea. Progress was made in small steps: after his American friend

Judah Touro, also a Sephardic Jew, bequeathed him funds, Montefiore first acquired an orchard on the outskirts of Jaffa in 1855, where he also provided training. Then, in 1860, he had the first Jewish housing estate and a poorhouse built outside the Old City of Jerusalem (today Mishkenot Sha'ananim), where it was considered dangerous to live. Sephardic and Ashkenazi Jews were to live there together. Two more neighbourhoods founded by him followed in the area, each reserved for Sephardic or Ashkenazi Jews.

Over the course of half a century, Montefiore travelled to the Holy Land seven times and became a philanthropist for the Jews who were subject to persecution in many places. After some high-ranking foreigners had been granted access to the Temple Mount, he infuriated his co-religionists by climbing the Mount in 1855 together with his wife Judith, Mohammed Kamil Pasha, the Turkish governor, and James Finn, the British consul in Jerusalem. This was strictly forbidden to Jews as long as the Messiah had not returned. Montefiore was apparently of the opinion that he could elegantly circumvent the ban by having Muslims carry him across the grounds in a palanquin and not setting foot on the Temple Mount itself. However, it is not certain whether this really is what exactly happened.

There were other pioneers of early Zionism. Laurence Oliphant, a British author and occultist, founded a group called "Christian Lovers of Zion" in the 1850s, which laid the groundwork for Jewish immigration to Palestine and tried to persuade Jewish organizations that had previously advocated emigration to America to shift their focus to Palestine. Oliphant was taken with the idea that England would eventually take over Palestine and leave it to the Jewish people. Baron Edmond de Rothschild then acted as a patron of Jews coming from Russia in 1882, after

Tsar Alexander II had been murdered by terrorists in 1881, triggering anti-Semitic pogroms.

For Great Britain, supporting and protecting the Jews in Palestine also had the effect of creating a counterweight to the Catholic Christians protected by France and the Orthodox Christians close to Russia and strengthening its own presence and position. In 1840, half a century before Zionism emerged in an organized form, the British Foreign Secretary Lord Palmerston wrote to his ambassador in Constantinople: "There exists at present among the Jews dispersed over Europe a strong notion that the time is approaching when their Nation is to return to Palestine; . . . I have to instruct Your Excellency strongly to recommend [to the Turkish government] to hold out every just encouragement to the Jews of Europe to return to Palestine."

A dazzling example for the proto-Zionists is the American Warder Cresson, who was initially a devout Quaker before he began to take an interest in the Shakers and the Mormons. However, he received decisive impulses for his further career through his contact with *Mikveh Israel* (Hope of Israel), the leading Jewish community in Philadelphia, as well as the consul Mordecai Manuel Noah, who worked in Tunis and wanted to establish a Jewish refuge named after Mount Ararat in Grand Island in the Niagara River in 1825 (which very quickly came to nothing). Incidentally, Noah was one of those who, curiously, harboured the belief that the American Indians were descendants of the lost tribes of Israel.

Cresson supported Noah's new idea of pushing for American involvement in the restoration of a Jewish homeland in the Middle East. Convinced that God had created the United States primarily to deliver the Jews of the world from their exile and oppression, Cresson set his mind on becoming the first American consul in Jerusalem, arguing that American pilgrims and missionaries would benefit from his diplomatic representation in the region. His appointment in May 1844 was facilitated by his promise to perform this function without financial remuneration. Determined to leave, Cresson said goodbye to his wife and six children, "I left all these in the pursuit of truth, and for the sake of Truth alone." However, critics soon appeared on the scene and accused Cresson of being mentally confused. In short: they considered him unfit for his position.

In the meantime, Cresson had already long been on his way to Palestine. On his arrival in Jaffa, he is said to have held the American flag in one hand and a cage with a dove of peace in the other. Once in Jerusalem, he assured the Jews that they would enjoy the reliable protection of the American government in the future. Although his appointment was revoked shortly afterwards, Cresson continued to present himself unimpressed as an envoy of the American Republic—at least he was far enough away for anyone to seriously get in his way!

Five years after his arrival, Cresson finally converted to Judaism and henceforth called himself "Michael Boz Israel ben Avraham". When he travelled to America a few months later, he received a cold reception: his wife Elizabeth had taken the property and, together with other family members, sued her husband for "lunacy". The court case functioned like a litmus test for religious freedom in America. Even if many took offense at this, he couldn't be accused of converting to Judaism; there was no further legal recourse. In 1852, Cresson returned to Jerusalem with the intention of establishing agricultural colonies there, and he acquired two pieces of land for this purpose—one near Jaffa (now part of Tel Aviv) and another outside Jerusalem's Old City.

In 1856, Herman Melville paid a visit to Cresson, who was now married to a Sephardic woman. As usual during his trip to the Holy Land, Melville was sober, and in Cresson's case even deeply sceptical: "The idea of making farmers of the Jews is vain. In the first place, Judea is a desert with few exceptions. In the second place, the Jews hate farming. All who cultivate the soil in Palestine are Arabs. The Jews dare not live outside walled towns or villages for fear of the malicious persecution of the Arabs & Turks. Besides, the number of Jews in Palestine is comparatively small. And how are the hosts of them scattered in other lands to be brought here? Only by a miracle."

Developments would later prove Melville's assessment wrong. Cresson died a few years later—in his honour, all Jewish stores in Jerusalem remained closed on the day of his funeral. Melville was also unequivocal about the attempts of American missionaries to convert Jews and Muslims to Christianity: "Might as well attempt to convert bricks into bride-cake as the Orientals into Christians. It is against the will of God that the East should be Christianized."

Jews in the Holy Land

BEFORE JEWISH immigration from Europe gained more momentum during the last two decades of the nineteenth century, only a few thousand Jews lived in Palestine, with around half concentrated in Jerusalem and the rest in the cities of Safas and Tiberias in the north and Hebron in the south. In Jerusalem in 1836, there were around 2,200 Sephardic Jews, born in the North African-Near Eastern region, and 650 Ashkenazi Jews, who felt connected to their origins in Russia, Galicia, Germany, Hungary, Bohemia and Moravia and had retained their respective citizenship, which, in turn, weakened their rights in the Ottoman Empire. Within these groups there were further ethnic and linguistic differences due to their respective origins, with the Sephardim being subject to a locally elected chief rabbi and, as Turkish citizens, to the "Millet" system, the legal system under which this religious community (and others) had relative autonomy. The religious leaders of the Ashkenazim, on the other hand, were mostly located in Europe.

Joseph (also: Yehoseph) Schwarz from the Upper Palatinate was an early Jewish emigrant. After studying in Pressburg, the stronghold of Jewish orthodoxy, and in Würzburg, he initially worked as an accountant for the landowner and rabbi Mendel

Rosenbaum, who was the spokesman for the Jews of Lower Franconia and Bavaria. From an early age, Schwarz had planned to research the history and natural history of Palestine. After an arduous journey he reached Jaffa in 1833 and shortly afterwards Jerusalem, where he soon married the daughter of a rabbinical family. From the Mount of Olives, he diligently noted the times of sunrise and sunset, as these were of particular importance to the pious sect to which he belonged, published in 1843 as *The Cycles of the Sun.*

During this time, he also travelled throughout the country and wrote his book *Tvu'ot Ha'aretz,* which was published in Jerusalem. It is a catalogue of names of places, mountains and bodies of water mentioned in the Bible, Talmud and Midrash and contains explanations of the climate, animal and plant kingdoms, geology and climate as well as descriptions of the religious customs of the Jews in Jerusalem, sections on the history and stories of the Jews in Palestine.

In 1849, Schwarz went to America to arrange the publication of an English version, which appeared in 1850 as *A Descriptive Biography and Brief Historical Sketch of Palestine* and was well received. Schwarz returned to Jerusalem in 1852 and from then on devoted himself to the study of rabbinical writings and the Kabbalah.

The previously mentioned Jewish doctor Ludwig August Frankl was a literary rambler who liked to dress up his experiences in little stories. He told of a strange incident near Jerusalem:

> "Near the walls of the town, a man whom I had not noticed earlier suddenly approached me, gripping the collar of my outer garment with his left hand while his right brandished a long knife. I was torn out of my deep thoughtlessness by

the sudden apparition and its silent attack, and when I almost automatically pulled the pistol from my holster—at least the attacker was able to get ahead of me with his weapon—the man quickly let go of my dress, lowered both arms and, pale to the lips, shouted: 'Shema Yisrael! What do you want to accomplish?' All this had happened in barely a minute, and recognizing my fellow believer, I, who had just been pale with shock, laughed out loud. But he explained to me that every Jewish pilgrim, before entering the city, had to tear his clothes in mourning for its destruction as if for a blood-related dead person. So I asked Mr. Mosche Kural, who has a meagre income from this business, to tear the garment, while I said the usual saying after him: Zion has become a desert, it lies destroyed."

Frankl described the Ashkenazis and Sephardim as follows: "The Sephardi in the picturesquely pleated costume of the Orient makes the impression of nobility through the decorum of his gait and gesture, through the noble formation of his face. Climate and example have made him resemble his Mohammedan fellow-citizen outwardly by dignity, inwardly by calmness, perhaps by indolence. The Ashkenazim, especially the Russians and Poles, are hasty, restless in every movement, grimacing, subtle in speech and counter-speech. Their appearance is uncomfortable due to the well-known ugly Polish costume and the dirt clinging to it." He also mentioned other Jewish groups in Jerusalem in detail, such as the Karaites, "who only hold the text of the Bible sacred as law". And he mentioned the Perushim, "the separated ones", who were born in Lithuania or Russia, and the Hasidim from Austria.

Together with Elise Herz, Frankl founded a Jewish school in Jerusalem. His contemporary Constantin von Wurzbach praised Frankl's report as "an important book for the knowledge of Israelite conditions in the Orient" and described it as "the first work to reveal the prosaic side of the Orient, which had previously only been poetically glorified, with statistical evidence and an unsparing depiction of the great evils".

Marie Joseph de Géramb was among those who took a closer look at the Jews. The first thing he noticed was the wretched state of the synagogues. "No sooner had I set foot in this dismal temple, than an old Jewess, perceiving me, exclaimed: when an old Jewish woman, catching sight of me, exclaimed: 'Aha! one of our people!'—'Not exactly so, daughter of Abraham,' I replied, by no means flattered by the mistake that caused her joy. The other Jewesses fell a-laughing at her blunder: they had perceived that I was a monk."

Despite de Géramb's displeasure at the neglect of the Jewish sites, in which he perceived a contradiction to their religiosity, he expressed his admiration: "No people entertain a higher veneration for the books that contain the doctrines, the moral laws, and the history of their religion. I felt shame for certain Christians, alas! too numerous, in whose libraries the sacred Scriptures, frequently from indifference, sometimes from a sacrilegious combination, are placed beside an impious or an obscene book."

In addition, de Géramb perceived an important differencc in mentality: "The Jew is a stranger to that slothful fondness for rest, so common among the people of the Levant, whose indolent and useless life is the principal cause of indigence."

And he observed a "civility" that, in his eyes, distinguished them from the other inhabitants of the country: "Have you lost your way? are you seeking a street?—a Jew, be sure, will offer to conduct you; he will even accompany you for a considerable distance; and, too proud to ask for pay, too fond of gain to make an absolute sacrifice of it, when you have reached the place to which you are going, he will look at your hand, he will cast an eye at your pocket—if you choose to take the hint, well and good."

The hopes of the Jews for a "new revelation", after which Palestine would be brought under Egyptian sway, were not hidden from him: "They consider Mehemet Ali as destined to rescue them from slavery, and to ensure them brighter prospects."

The two missionaries Andrew A. Bonar and Robert Murray McCheyne, who explored the situation of the Jews on behalf of the Church of Scotland, repeatedly heard German (possibly meaning Yiddish) during their stay in Palestine in 1830, especially in Galilee, where they encountered the most Jews outside of Jerusalem. They are also said to have spoken some Italian for their dealings with the "Franks". In any case, Hebrew apparently had the function of a *lingua franca* for the Jews living in Palestine and the visitors who knew the language, as Bonar and McCheyne noted in their *Narrative of a Mission of Inquiry to the Jews from the Church of Scotland in 1839*: "The Hebrew is the most necessary language for one who labours among the Jews in this country, and it is spoken chiefly in the Spanish way . . . Arabic is not as absolutely necessary as Hebrew. All Jews in Palestine speak Hebrew, but then they often attach a meaning to the words that is not the true meaning or grammatical sense, so that it is absolutely necessary to know the vernacular tongue in order that you and they understand the same thing by the words employed."

In his book *Eight years in Africa from 1846 to 1855* (1858) the Moldavian-Jewish writer Israel Joseph Benjamin documented his attempt to "shed some light on the ruins of the descendants of a people whose centuries-long exile appears only in the yearbooks of history". Benjamin, who had worked in the timber trade until he began traveling and had to give up his business, prefaced his book with an expert opinion from Julius Heinrich Petermann, the Prussian consul in Jerusalem in 1868/69, as well as from Alexander von Humboldt, who had given Benjamin's "noble purpose" to "fathom the conditions of a dispersed and oppressed people . . . They describe conditions of degeneracy in the oppressed, of arbitrary power in the oppressors, which are little known in Europe and will certainly and rightly provide their book with many readers."

With the records of his wanderings in the Orient, which he began in 1845, Benjamin wanted "to arouse the sympathy of my co-religionists in Europe for their unfortunate brothers who have been exiled to those inhospitable lands which the foot of a European has rarely, almost never, set foot on. Under the centuries-long yoke of fanaticism, of barbarism, despite all persecutions and oppressions, despite robbery and murder, they have nevertheless remained steadfast in the faith of their fathers."

In contrast to the Jews he had seen in other parts of Asia, Europe and Africa, he emphasized that the Jews of Palestine, who are always threatened by reprisals, find themselves in a particularly miserable, even unbearable situation, as they are subject to the orders and whims of the sheikhs and pashas.

And Friedrich Adolph Strauss remarked on the Jews: "Despite their dispersion, despite their separation, they have remained one people, unmixed, separate from all other peoples; there is no end to them. . . . Is it not Jews, converted sons of Israel, who occupy the first places in the sciences as well as in the arts? Are not Jews in our day among the richest and most educated? Is it not Jews, whose mighty influence in the most important states of the world rises higher and higher with each passing day?" And he knew of their hope for a new kingdom:

"Almost half of all Jews, about three million, are therefore on the shores of the Mediterranean Sea, waiting for the moment when they will return to the seat of their fathers at the call of the Lord over the waters of the sea." As much as one can hear his understanding for their concerns here, Strauss was pleased about the few cases in which it was possible to "convince orthodox Jews of the truth of the Christian faith".

Many visitors emphasized that the Jews in the country are generally very poor, dependent on donations from abroad and hardly active in trade and crafts. John Lloyd Stephens first had contact with the rabbi of Hebron, then with the rabbi of Jerusalem. He had seen Jews "in the cities of Italy, everywhere more or less oppressed; at Rome, shut up every night in their miserable quarters as if they were noxious beasts; in Turkey, persecuted and oppressed; along the shores of the Black Sea and in the heart of Russia, looked down upon by the serfs of that great empire of vassalage; and, for the climax of misery, I had seen them condemned and spit upon even by the ignorant and enslaved boors of Poland. I had seen them scattered abroad among all nations, as it had been foretold they would be, everywhere a separate and peculiar people . . . waiting for, and anxiously expecting, the coming of a Messiah, to call together their scattered tribes, and restore them to the kingdom of their fathers; and all this the better fitted me for the more interesting spectacle of the Jews in the holy city."

The Dutch naval captain and cartographer Charles van de Velde noted the following about the Jews living in Hebron:

> "It is true that their number has sometimes been small, even as low as one or two families; but this number has gradually increased. Families from Spain and Portugal, the so-called Sephardim, or from Germany, Poland, and other places, the

Ashkenazim, have gradually settled there, and at present there are about sixty families of the former, and about fifty of the latter residing in it. They have each a synagogue." (Today, Jews who do not come from Europe are divided into Mizrahim, "eastern" Jews from Arab countries, and Sephardim, although these categories are not clear-cut because the Sephardic Jews, who were expelled from Spain and Portugal at the end of the fifteenth century, often settled in areas of the Near and Middle East and are also Arab in their culture. There are also Jews who come from Ethiopia, who are called "Falasha").

In relation to the six to seven thousand Muslims, "who are of a more fanatical and Christian-hating character than are to be found anywhere else in the country", they only made up a small proportion of the total population. Charles van de Velde nevertheless considered Hebron and its surrounding predestined for further Jewish settlement: "If only converted Jewish colonists were able quietly to settle here, what could be thought more desirable!", he wrote in a letter to a friend.

The Franciscan priest Alessandro Bassi, theologian of the Apostolic Delegation of Arabia and Egypt, gave a harsh judgment in his *Historical and descriptive pilgrimage to the Holy Land* (1857). The Jews were "all foreigners or descendants of foreigners", and part of the "landscape", but they had no legal authority or independent role, and their presence there did not follow any easily intelligible logic:

> "A strange force holds them together there: a mysterious attraction drew them from the remotest regions, not as Christian pilgrims to visit their old homeland, but to settle there and prepare the grave. It can be said that they are forever condemned to witness the fulfilment of the prophecies

about Christ who was killed there and to hear the fierce curses that their fathers uttered at his slaying *His blood be upon us and upon our children.*"

Catholic travellers sometimes claimed that the Jews were responsible for the murder of Jesus. Although it is considered a fact that Pontius Pilate ordered the crucifixion of Jesus and that the prefect's soldiers then carried it out, this prejudice is not easily overcome. This complex of topics, justifying the alleged superiority of Christianity over Judaism, which includes the shameful accusation of Jews carrying out ritual murders of Christian boys, can be traced back to the Middle Ages.

The so-called Damascus Affair made international waves in 1840. After a Sardinian-born Capuchin monk and his Muslim servant disappeared and were murdered, several members of the Jewish community of Damascus were arrested, although there was no direct evidence that they had committed the crime. They were accused by Christians of murdering the men in order to use their blood to bake unleavened bread (matzah) for the Passover feast. Benoît Ulisse de Ratti-Menton, the French consul in Damascus, known for his anti-Semitic stance, ordered an investigation in the Jewish quarter and asked the Egyptian governor at the time to look into the matter.

As a result, there were riots by Christians and Muslims against the Jewish population. Confessions were forced under torture and some of the men accused of the crime were killed. Thanks to the intervention of Moses Montefiore the remaining prisoners were released. And after the Turks regained control of Syria towards the end of the year, the accusations of "blood libel" were declared null and void by Sultan Abdülmecid I in an edict, as it was slander against the Jews and forbidden throughout the Ottoman Empire.

Hillel Jaffe, born in 1864 in a small village not far from Yekaterinoslav (then Russia, now Dnipro, Ukraine), came to Palestine in 1891. In a letter to a former fellow student, he wrote: "I have now spent three years of my life in the holy and blessed land, which, strictly speaking, is not in the least holy, but desecrated and afflicted by all kinds of diseases, not blessed but cursed." Jaffe came to terms with his circumstances, initially working as a medical officer for the Ottomans, but soon accepted an offer from Baron de Rothschild to work in the Jewish settlements He continues: "I no longer have any longing for Russia, while Europe seems so cold, so foreign. Here we are at home, so to speak. If only there were a little more order and less fever, and fewer scoundrels in the local administration, things would gradually improve." (For Jaffe's papers see Ya'ari, 1947 and the Central Zionist Archives in Jerusalem).

Encounters in the Harem

MUSLIM WOMEN in Palestine were subject to the provisions of the Koran, according to which they were to stay at home and avoid any contact with the outside world. If they did go outside the home, then only in the company of a man from their own family. In principle, these and many other Sharia rules of conduct also applied to women from other ethnic groups in the country, but the travel reports conveyed a more complex picture. While in Muslim-dominated cities such as Nablus, Hebron and Jaffa, women were typically clad in blue dresses and often only their eyes were visible, the situation in the Christian-dominated cities of Nazareth and Bethlehem and also in the countryside was more flexible and tolerant, according to the study by French literary scholar Guy Galazka, although this does not mean that they were equal to men there.

However, a certain amount of caution was required, as the travellers tended to idealise villages and rural life. "Nothing is so fresh, lively and picturesque as the costume of the women of Bethlehem. The brightest colours are artfully interwoven, and the way they arrange their coiffure, their headbands of silver coins and their abundant jewellery has a wonderful effect," wrote Monseigneur Pierre-Louis Péchenard in *From Reims to*

Jérusalem (1893). In Nazareth, women and men could apparently show themselves together in public in a relaxed manner, as Louis Lortet reports in *Syria of Today* (1884): "The young men of the city come around this fountain to court their fiancées. Nazareth is the only city in Syria where the mixing of the sexes is tolerated in a public place. Although this approach is strongly rebuked by Turkish purists, it is obvious that the morals here are far above those of the neighbouring population, whose women are rigorously shielded."

Even if such descriptions may have been exaggerated, voyeuristic and orientalist, and most likely may have been erotic fantasies that fired the imaginations of those who recorded them, the accumulation of such observations in certain Christian-dominated places points to a certain tolerance.

The English author Mary Eliza Rogers, who came from the literary circles of London, had a keen eye for people who are missing from the vast majority of other travelogues. In 1855, at the age of 27, she travelled to the Holy Land with her brother Edward, who was in the British diplomatic service.

It was the year of a détente in relations with Europe. At dawn on September 27, the news of the Ottoman Empire's victory over its arch-enemy Russia, achieved with the help of France, England and Sardinia, was accompanied by twenty-one cannon blasts in the Holy City. The peace treaty signed in Paris the following year ended the Crimean War and sealed the Ottoman Empire's integration into the European power structure.

Rogers stayed for three years. In the company of her brother she travelled all over the country and was warmly welcomed everywhere. Although Rogers had no missionary intentions, she learned Arabic, which helped her to gain the trust of the people. In her book *Domestic Life in Palestine* (1860), she documented everything in a sober tone. In Arraba, a walled city in what is now West Jordan, she was received by female members of the household of the local governor Mohammed Bek. The women—Abyssinian slave girls dressed in purple and silver and Arab women clad in purple and gold robes—welcomed Rogers to the harem. "They pounced upon me as if I were a new toy for them. They kissed me one after the other, and stroked my face. They had never seen a European, and told me that no daughter of the Franks had ever entered their town before. They said, 'Be welcome oh sister from a far country, this house is yours, and we are your servants.'" The hookah-smoking Sit Habîbî, the eldest wife of the governor of Arraba, introduced Rogers first to two other wives, then to the three wives of Saleh Bek, the governor of Haifa. When the Englishwoman told them that she happened to know Saleh Bek, they were very surprised, because women in their environment never used to meet men outside the family.

The Englishwoman took the women's many questions in her stride: they wanted to know whether the people in her home country are all white, and how it is that she can live without "her" women when traveling and why they weren't wearing headdresses. They were astonished when Rogers made portrait sketches of the women, as they had never seen anything like it. When she neatly wrote down all names, the governor's two young sons Selim and Saïd said: "Mashallah! The stranger knows the writing of our language". She answered the question of whether she is a Muslim in the negative, but she has read the Koran and explained her position as follows: "I'm not called a Muslim. but I am your sister, made by the same god, who is the one and only god, the god of all, my father and your father." The women were impressed by Rogers' words, consider her "a true believer". "She is indeed an angel," the Abyssinian slaves added.

The young women didn't let up. They asked her if she is married, which Rogers denied, why she left her parents, and if she would marry an Arab, to which Rogers replied, amused: "My mother is not here to find a husband for me. How can I marry?" and Sit Sâra replied: "I will be your mother, and bring you to a husband. My brother is a Cadi, a great Judge of Nablus; he looks for a wife, he has only three. He will love you because you are white."

Rogers got even more involved in the hypothetical game and was asked about camels in her possession: "My father has no camels. In my country there are only three or four living camels kept as curiosities, in a house in a beautiful garden, with servants to watch over them and take care of them. We have a few stuffed camels also, in a large glass house." Of course, she also had to answer the question about the fertile olive trees in the negative. Sit Sâra had precise ideas about the dowry: She said that Rogers' father had gold and would give her some of it along with precious stones, a red box of clothes and cloths, some silk cushions, a red wooden cradle and lots of soap. Sit Sâra also claimed her brother had great wealth, and would give Rogers' father camels and gold coins according to her share.

Rogers did not criticise the polygamy she was confronted with. Her curiosity was piqued in any case. She asked some of the men who were her guests one evening: "Is there any law (which you regard as sacred and binding) forbidding you to see and converse with women out of your own individual families? If there is such a law, I will not cause you to disobey it, but will help you to keep it, by hiding myself from you." They referred to a customary law that kept women in their harem. Rogers quoted Mohammed Bek who believed he could justify the practice with the following reference:

> "If we gave them liberty, they would not know how to use it. Their heads are made of wood. They are not like you. When you speak, we no longer remember that you are a girl: we think we are listening to a sheik. To live in the world knowledge and wisdom are necessary. Our wives and daughters have neither wisdom nor knowledge. Give them wisdom, and we will give them liberty."

As surprising as this may seem to us, Rogers continued her contact with the men, apparently still trusting them to have insight despite these categorical-sounding assessments: "I think I gave them some new ideas on the capabilities and capacities of women which may in time be turned to account."

Rogers' comments on Christians and Jews were brief; she mentioned having sought contact with them, for example with the Christian Sakhali family and with religious Jews who explained the laws, fasting and celebrations to her. Her conclusion was sobering:

> "Sadly, The Oriental Christians are very bitter in their hatred of the Jews. They generally treat them with great contempt, and make a merit of avoiding association with them, but they agree with the Moslems in admitting that the Jews throughout the East are, as a body, remarkable for the purity of their lives, the simplicity of their manners, and the strictness with which they observe their religious services. They are, however, notorious for the quarrels which take place among themselves, and for the noisy disputes which sometimes arise between the representatives of the different congregations or communities.

The Jewesses, especially of the Ashkenazi communities, are renowned for their domestic virtue and industry."

There are generally not many references to Roma in reports about historical Palestine. Did travellers possibly confuse them with Bedouins if they took notice of them at all? At the beginning of the nineteenth century, Ulrich Jasper Seetzen specifically sought out "gypsies" or "Náuar", as he also called them, in the east of Nablus. For a small tip, he asked a member of this "troop" to help him compile a list of words and numbers. "Judging by this list of words, the language of the local Gypsies or Náuar is a gibberish of several languages, and I find many Arabic and Turkish and some Greek words in it. It seems to me, however, that they borrowed a lot from a fourth language, which I cannot specify because I have no dictionaries at all, and this language may be their actual mother tongue." He understood them as "wild" and "raw", unable to read or write.

Mary Eliza Rogers also came into contact with the Roma who she called a "mysterious race of people". At first, it was their tents made of black goat hair that she noticed outside a village—the dwellings of tinkers and blacksmiths who move from place to place, they reminded her of their brothers in England.

"The men had rather a sullen and stern expression of countenance, and were clothed in sack-cloth, girdled with leather straps. Black shawls were fastened on their heads with ropes made of camel hair, in Bedouin style. The women and girls seemed hardy, bold, and daring, but good-natured. Their features were strongly marked. . . . Broad silver armlets adorned their tattooed arms, and clumsy cabbalistic rings were displayed on some of the swarthy hands, to protect the wearers from harm."

Rogers noted that the Roma did not use the name of Allah in their greetings and spoke Arabic, but also had their own language. She related that they are known for their tricks, often consulted for fortune-telling and dream interpretation, and for sleight of hand. One time, she observed a boy being called from the middle of the audience and apparently being cut into six pieces to be reassembled a few minutes later. "The Arabs generally, and especially of the lower classes, firmly believe in the occult power of the gypsies. They are hated and feared, yet patronized and encouraged to a remarkable degree," reported Rogers. And she added the following warning, according to the clichéd ideas: "These people are very mischievous, and when they are in the neighbourhood, it is necessary to look well after the fowls, lambs, and kids, and to set a double watch in the orchards and vineyards, and the gardens of cucumbers."

Given the composure she showed in her encounters with members of other groups, her judgment is surprising. Her warnings are in line with prejudices that go far back into the past. For example, the Roma were long accused of being spies for the Turks and traitors to the Christians; and because of their mobility they were often also considered to be carriers of disease.

Ida Pfeiffer also had the opportunity to visit a harem in the home of the Pasha of Acre. "I did not see many excellent beauties, if one does not consider the much-revered corpulence here as such, but I did see a one-eyed woman, a phenomenon not uncommon in this country. I saw slaves of all shades. One had a ring through her nose, the other had blue-painted lips. But all of them, women and slaves, had black-coloured eyelids and eyebrows, and their nails and the inner surface of their hands were dyed light brown by the sap of the henna root." Pfeiffer had the impression that they do not pursue any activities and spend their time smoking nargileh and drinking coffee. Her communication with the women was limited, "pantomimic", as she wrote. The women touched her head, marvelled at her thinness and short hair. Pfeiffer went on to visit other harems, where she encountered "the same ignorance, curiosity and indolence", followed by an astonishing conclusion: "On the whole, they may be happier than us Europeans, I conclude this partly from their corpulence and partly from their calm facial features."

The prominent New York women's rights activist Frances Willard, one of the founders of the Women's Christian Temperance Union, visited a whole series of girls' schools during her stay in Palestine in the 1870s and was impressed by the dedicated work of the teachers. She hoped that her donations to Western aid organizations working on the ground would provide some relief to the wretchedness of the conditions under which women lived and worked. Nevertheless, she identified a group of women that she described as modern Rebeccas with bright faces. She was soon shocked by Jerusalem, which she characterized as "the most disagreeable, dismal, ugly city I have ever, anywhere seen." In vain, she embarked on a search for the "mysteries" described by some travellers.

The American settler Clorinda Minor also felt compassion for the women's toil and complained in the book *Meshullam! Or, Tidings From Jerusalem* (1851), published under her pseudonym A. L. Wood, that the women of Jerusalem had to get up at midnight in order to turn the millstones until morning and thus not be exposed to the heat of the sun. Interestingly, at a time when it was common to squeeze upper bodies into corsets in the West, some American women perceived the wide pants they noticed in Palestine as liberating, soon making them a fashion among women's rights activists. And Western men were flirting with exotic ideas of oriental masculinity when they clad themselves in typical garments, immortalized themselves in paintings or had themselves photographed as fearless warriors, perhaps in the hope of giving themselves the appearance of knights.

Even though women were much further away from equality than in Western societies, the situation was still complex. Londoner William Henry Bartlett, who visited the Holy Land three times, paid a visit to a Jewish family during his second stay in 1842 and noted that the women—in contrast to their native Christian and Muslim counterparts—were largely equal, and was also pleased at how relaxed and humorous they were in his presence. On the one hand, the Jewish population was very poor and therefore dependent on handouts and hardly involved in trade and crafts. During his last visit, Bartlett noted that a Jewish pharmacy had been opened in the meantime, which Bartlett attributed to the efforts of Moses Montefiore.

In Nablus, some travellers met Samaritans, members of a religious community that had not been considered part of Judaism since the Babylonian exile. Rogers noted that they were sometimes forced to move their festivities to secret locations so as not to be disturbed by fanatical Muslims. Since the English stood up for the persecuted, they could feel safer. Although they maintained friendly dealings and business relations with foreigners, they did not engage in exogenous marriages. Nevertheless, their relationship with the other groups was complicated, as Rogers observed:

> "The few native Protestants in Nablûs are on a very intimate footing with the Samaritans; and native Greek Christians, and many Muslims, are on good terms with them. But their Jewish neighbors do not like them at all. They accuse them of heresy and even of idolatry, and avoid them as much as possible, saying that they are worshipers of pigeons! This is a very anciently-founded calumny. The Samaritans, on the other hand, declare

that the Jews neglect the Law of Moses, and have departed from purity of life and worship, and follow the Talmud."

Rogers recalled the persecution of the Samaritans in 1842, when Muslim religious scholars threatened to murder the entire community because the Samaritans did not believe in the Law of Moses, the New Testament, the Psalms, the Prophets or the Koran and did not want to become Muslims. The situation could only be defused after the Chief Rabbi of the Jews in Jerusalem had certified in writing to the Samaritans that their people were a branch of the Children of Israel who recognized the truth of the Torah (Pentateuch).

With the Bible, a Telescope, and a Compass—Archaeology in Palestine

THE FIRST excavations carried out in Palestine are associated with Lady Hester Lucy Stanhope, the eldest child of the statesman Charles Stanhope, 3rd Earl Stanhope and his first wife, Lady Hester Pitt. Born into the British upper class, she broke free from all social expectations at an early age. The death of her favorite brother in the course of the Napoleonic Wars is said to have been an important trigger for her break with tradition. In addition, she experienced a decisive encounter in the London psychiatric institution Bedlam. One of the inmates was firmly convinced that it was Lady Hester's destiny to lead the Jews of the world to the land of their ancestors and return Jerusalem into their hands—with the Messiah through the gates of the city. This prophecy developed a pull for her from which she could release herself. In 1810, she set off via Athens and Constantinople, initially suffering shipwreck off Rhodes. After losing all her luggage, she put on the typical clothing of a male Turk in the form of a coat, turban and slippers; and from then on, she refused to wear a veil.

At a chance meeting Johann Ludwig Burckhardt in Nazareth is said to have convinced her to go into excavations. When Franciscan monks gave her an Italian document containing references to a treasure of gold buried by Christians below a mosque in Ashkalon during the Middle Ages, her enthusiasm was aroused. After the British ambassador in Constantinople rejected her written request for support for her project, she was even more motivated to obtain permission directly from the Ottoman government. She promised the Turks the hoped-for gold find, as she was probably only interested in strengthening the relationship between Great Britain and the Ottoman Empire. She obtained permission and the Pasha of Jaffa accompanied her.

In 1815, she had hundreds of locally hired fellahs carry out excavations in the port city on the Mediterranean coast north of Gaza. Instead of gold, however, she only discovered the headless marble statue of a Roman ruler, which she had destroyed and entrusted to the waves of the Mediterranean. In short, the whole thing turned out to be a fiasco. The governor spread the rumour that she destroyed the statue in order to get hold of the gold hidden inside and share it with the Pasha of Acre. An ironic footnote is that the pashas themselves were cannibalising ruins at this time in order to reuse parts of them in mosques and other buildings.

For three decades, Lady Hester Stanhope entrenched herself in mountain monasteries in Lebanon, where she is said to have offered refuge to persecuted Druze. She renounced her Christian faith and embraced the role of the heroine who fearlessly rode through the Syrian desert at the head of Arab tribes—or so the legend goes. Her cunning and confident demeanour earned her the reputation of a queen: "Malika". Others regarded her as "the mad nun of Lebanon".

De Lamartine eagerly awaited his meeting with "this extraordinary woman, the modern enchantress, recalling the famous magicians of antiquity—the Circe of the deserts", who was always surrounded by thick clouds of smoke. "It appeared to me that the religious doctrines of Lady Hester were a clever though confused mixture of the different religions in the midst of which she had condemned herself to live: mysterious as the Druzes, whose mystic secret she, of all the world, perhaps alone knew; resigned as the Moslem, and like him a fatalist; with the Jew, expecting the Messiah; and with the Christian, professing the worship of Christ, and the practice of his charity and morality. Add to this, the fantastic colouring and supernatural dreams of an imagination tinctured with Oriental extravagance, and heated by solitude and meditation, the impressions perhaps of the Arabic astrologers, and you will have an idea of this compound of the sublime and ridiculous, which it is more convenient to stigmatise as madness, than to analyse and comprehend."

However, de Lamartine was quick to dispel any misconceptions based on his glowing description of Lady Stanhope, to whom he attributed a "truly superior intellect": "No; this woman is not mad. Madness, which displays itself in the eyes, so as never to be mistaken, is not expressed in her mild and straight look; madness, which is always betrayed in conversation by the interruptions it gives to the chain of discourse by sudden, disordered, and eccentric bursts, is not perceptible in the elevated, mystic, and obscure, though sustained, connected, and powerful conversation of Lady Hester. If I were called upon to decide, I should rather say it was the voluntary and studied madness of one who knows what she is about, and who has her own reasons for appearing insane."

In any case, according to the poet, she fitted perfectly into this environment: "To the men of this land of prodigies, to these men of rocks and deserts, whose imagination is more vivid and wreathed in mist than the horizon of their sands or seas, the words of Mohammed or Lady Stanhope are necessary! They require the knowledge of the stars, prophecies, miracles, the second sight of genius!"

De Lamartine would not be surprised, he remarked, if she were given "an empire in Arabia", even a "throne in Jerusalem".

The Ashkalon burial site is, of course, only a rather insignificant side-show. Several decades had to go by before archaeology was able to gain a real foothold in the Holy Land. After Charles Darwin and Charles Lyell ushered in a whole new era characterized by skepticism towards the generally accepted principles about the past and it no longer seemed plausible that the world had been created from nothing a few thousand years ago, the question increasingly arose as to whether and how what was recorded in the Holy Scriptures could be reconciled with what was still found there and what architectural traces could be found in Palestine at all.

Do the "holy sites" mark places where biblical events actually took place? Or are they merely places of remembrance that have acquired their significance over the centuries and have been "weighted down with the weight of the divine", as the French philosopher Maurice Halbwachs put it in *The legendary topography of the Gospels in the Holy Land* (1941)? The matter is even more complicated by the fact that there were or are different names for the same places: "The Christian community comprised various groups, each of which had its own traditions and also its own writings. Christians, recently converted Jewish-Christians, Greeks, Latins, pagans.". He refers to "the fabrication of Christian tradition", and offers a sobering insight: "The holy sites are therefore not reminders of facts authenticated by contemporary witnesses, but of beliefs that may have originated not far from these places and were reinforced by taking root in them."

Among the early archaeologists in the country such fundamental doubts and questions were not popular, of course, but things slowly changed. The American Protestant theologian Edward Robinson is regarded as the founder of biblical archaeology. After studying theology in America, he studied oriental languages in Paris, Halle and Berlin, followed "an impulse from on high", crossed the Sinai Peninsula from Egypt and arrived in Jerusalem in 1838 equipped with a Bible, telescope and compass. Although a convinced Christian, he did not want his scientific judgment to be affected by his faith. And Robinson did indeed discover some of the places mentioned in the Old Testament. At the southwest corner of the temple precinct, he found a spectacular relic that can be dated to the Second Temple period around 515 BC. He identified the wall projection as the remains of an arch that once spanned the road running along the foot of the Western Wall. Robinson was concerned with the question of whether the location of the Church of the Holy Sepulchre—as had been generally assumed until then—actually corresponds to the place where Jesus was crucified and buried. This would require proof that it was outside the boundary of the second city wall, because Jews were not allowed to be buried inside the city wall. However, Robinson was unable to resolve this question and considered the current location to be unlikely the correct one, but did not completely rule out its authenticity. The question remains unresolved to this day; a number of other locations have also been considered.

Robinson extended his activities beyond Jerusalem and investigated the connection between the Arabic and the Hebrew place names. Almost all places in Palestine were named differently by Jews and Arabs. For example, he finds the village of as-Samu (As Samu) and the biblical Eshtemoa, al-Jish, which was previously called Gish, and the former Gibeon, the remains of which can still be found in part of the present-day Palestinian settlement of al-Jib. His travel diary was published as *Biblical Researches in Palestine, Mount Sinai, and Arabia Petraea* (1841).

Fourteen years later, he returned to Palestine to investigate Galilee, Samaria, the Lebanon Mountains and Damascus. All in all, he provided some insights for a more profound understanding of Palestine and prepared the ground for further investigations. What Robinson did not address directly, perhaps because he still had a certain idealism, was that there was never anything of very great significance to find. Jesus and the first Christians were very poor people and not rulers. The Jews had lost their temple a long time ago, before they had to work as slaves for the Pharaoh in Egypt and became subjects in Palestine.

In the meantime, Titus Tobler, a proven expert on medieval travelogues of Palestine, had also begun a comprehensive survey, the results of which he published in 1853 under the title *Topography of Jerusalem and its Environs.* He listed churches, mosques, synagogues, walls, gates and other important buildings, supplemented by sketches and historical background information. Like Robinson, Tobler also assumed that Jesus was buried outside the current city wall.

Born in the German territory of Württemberg, Conrad Schick, who came to Jerusalem as a young man in 1846 with the aim of proselytizing Jews and Arabs, soon became an expert on the architectural history of the city (Silberman, 1982). On behalf of the Russian Orthodox Palestinian Society, he carried out excavations near the Church of the Holy Sepulchre and discovered parts of large marble columns and a large staircase that were apparently connected to the original Constantinian basilica built there in the fourth century, which earned him an award from Tsar Alexander III, for which Schick in turn earned the disfavour of some Protestants. He also worked for the Palestine Exploration Fund and was even granted permission to carry out research on the Temple Mount, which was otherwise reserved for Muslims, and made two wooden models of it, which were exhibited at the World Exhibitions in Vienna in 1873 and in St. Louis in 1904. As an architect, Schick designed hospitals, schools and private buildings, in which he always tried to merge Middle Eastern and European architectural styles and methods. The Mea Shearim neighbourhood, until this day inhabited by ultra-Orthodox Jews, was also built under his leadership. The fact that Schick spoke Arabic and was familiar with the customs of the local population certainly contributed to his assertiveness and success. He was the ideal liaison for the British, highly regarded by the European community.

However, the archaeological excavations met with little understanding from the locals, Muslims and Jews alike, for whom the disturbance of the peace of the dead was a thorn in their side. Researchers were often forced to conceal their true identity and give other reasons when they worked here or there. Operating outside Jerusalem, they were often less exposed to the scrutiny of the locals.

The aforementioned Charles van de Velde was one of the pioneers of Palestinian archaeology. In the 1850s, he traversed the length and breadth of the country several times and produced a map that was published in eight sheets and was considered the best before the Palestine Exploration Fund published an even more detailed one in 1876. Van de Velde's doubts about historical attributions also arose again and again on a small scale. He makes a note about a large oak tree near Hebron, which is said to have been left over from the Mamre oak grove:

> "Meanwhile, I do not believe that there are any instances of oaks, even of this sort—namely, the oak with thick drooping bunches of foliage, and with a small prickly leaf (Quercus coccifera, holy oak), that go back to such a remote antiquity as tradition here asserts; but it is highly probable that this elegant and majestic tree is an off-shoot from the group under which Abraham received the Lord at the door of his tent (Gen. xviii.)."

However, his doubts did not abate:

> "Is the place where the Lord appeared to Abraham, a piece of ground in no respect different from all around it? Yes, such is Mamre; such is this holy spot. With what difficulty do I realise it! I am now living in the Bible country, and yet I cannot familiarise myself with the idea. Is this not a proof of the corruption of our imagination, which pictures to us the events of Scripture as if they belonged not to this world but to some other planet."

Van de Velde's doubts related to the tree were indeed justified: The actual tree died off, while the growth of the young shoots is sustained to preserve the relic.

What makes it difficult to identify certain places and regions were not only the oft-confusing explanations given by the guides, but also the fact that the same areas were often described in different ways by earlier travellers. Van de Velde believed to have identified the reason:

> "The different seasons, as they come round, make hills and villages, valleys and towns, wear totally different aspects. Has this been so at all periods?"

Louis Félicien de Saulcy (1854), a wealthy amateur archaeologist, senator and confidant of Emperor Napoleon III, who travelled to the Middle East several times around the middle of the century and supplied the Louvre with all kinds of objects, came to Palestine for the first time in 1850. He learned Hebrew and Arabic, but was not considered a scholar of the Orient in the classical sense, which repeatedly led to disputes with the Académie Française. He was the first person to be granted an official excavation permit for Jerusalem, which the French ambassador in Constantinople, Marquis de Moustier, obtained for him from Sultan Abdülaziz.

When de Saulcy visited the previously violently looted Tomb of the Kings north of Jerusalem in 1863, which he believed to be the necropolis of the kings of Judah, David and Solomon, this provoked an outcry from the local Jews, who knew that the Prussian consul and orientalist Georg Friedrich Wilhelm Rosen (who held this position there from 1852 to 1867) was on their side.

Resistance also came from some Muslim families who lay claim to parts of the site and demanded money, which de Saulcy harshly countered with the reference to "a few hundred whacks with my walking stick". De Saulcy wanted to disprove Edward Robinson's theory that the burial place of the early Judean kings was on Mount Zion, on the other side of the city.

Determined to carry out the excavation, he gave his cartographer Charles Gelis a small pistol with instructions to use it should anyone oppose further progress. Two Sudanese were assigned to secure the entrance. He later admitted that he had succumbed to "a moment of insanity". All in all, he discovered five sarcophagi in the Tomb of the Kings. When some Jews bribed one of the guards to see for themselves what is going on in the tomb and then discovered with horror that human bones were lying on the floor, this fueled the unrest even more. The situation put Mehmed Khurshid, the governor of Jerusalem, in a tricky situation, as he had to keep the peace but also respect the permission that de Saulcy has received from the highest authority in Constantinople. De Saulcy arranged for Edmond de Barrère, the French consul, to come and officially confirm the significance of the find.

In order to silence the resistance of the locals, de Saulcy had the Aramaic inscriptions on one of the sarcophagi concealed with clay, arguing that these were "only" the graves of Romans. However, the locals were hardly impressed, let alone convinced. With the rather reluctant support of the French consul, de Saulcy finally succeeded in retrieving the mentioned sarcophagus and another one and having them brought to Paris, where he presented them along with his real theory of their origin—because that was precisely the reason he was there. However, it soon became clear that it was not the "Tomb of the Kings", but the tomb of Queen Helen of Adiabene—as the analysis of the signs written in various Aramaic scripts revealed. The three other sarcophagi are still in Jerusalem today. Although not a pilgrim in the classical sense, de Saulcy did not miss the opportunity to receive the Order of the Holy Sepulchre in Jerusalem. In 1868, a law was passed in Constantinople making it illegal to take antiquities from the Ottoman Empire out of the country.

Scottish travel writer John MacGregor combined sport with the utility during his 1869 trip. Using a canoe modelled on an Inuit kayak, he navigated the Nile Delta, the waters of Palestine and explored the sources of the Jordan River, assisted by a dragoman named Hany and two helpers. "The name of no other river has been known so long and so widely as this, evoking a host of ancient memories in the Mohammedan on the plains of India, in the last Christian settlers in the Rocky Mountains of America, and in the Jews in every part of the globe." And so

MacGregor could hear "the suppressed murmur of secret water dammed up . . . under a mass of fig trees, reeds and creepers, the water comes freely to light and fills a round basin, a hundred feet wide to the rim." What he describes as the "new-born Jordan", the river Dan, is one of the three sources of the Jordan, albeit the strongest.

MacGregor's expedition by water caused quite a stir among the local population, who had never seen such a means of transportation before. One time, he was detained by villagers on the River Jordan, to be released shortly afterwards. MacGregor's notes, *In a Canoe on Sacred Rivers*, were useful to the Palestine Exploration Fund in mapping the region. MacGregor was irritated by what he perceived as the Jews' lack of interest in the archaeology of the Holy Land: "I wonder how with all their love of their people and their land they leave it to us Christians to search for their records among the rubbish—how they never ask the world for what the world would give them free, their own beloved Palestine." The excavations continued albeit under different conditions all the way to the present day. According to the American journalist Rachel Poser "Archaeologists reconstruct the past based on whatever material has happened to linger in the ground for thousands of years—a tiny percentage of what existed at the time. Turning that partial record into a narrative about people and events takes a deep knowledge of history and some degree of imagination." More than in many other countries, researchers here were always driven by the question of who could use certain discoveries to gain legitimacy for the past and territorial claims to the present, an extremely existential and politically explosive matter.

Among the travellers to the Holy Land mentioned so far, the Frenchman Ernest Renan plays a special role. He was not only an archaeologist, but also an orientalist, ethnographer, and folklorist. Renan undertook his first journey and archaeological mission to the Middle East in 1860/61 on official assignment from Napoleon III to explore Phoenicia, the ancient Mediterranean civilization. Renan, a romantic positivist, fulfilled this mission (and published several books about it), but his main focus was on researching Semitic languages, the history of the people of Israel, and the origins of Christianity. These topics were truly close to his heart. Already in Lebanon, which he considers to have a "magnificent charm," he feels he is on biblical soil, where he can empathize with the places and the person of Jesus. In *Phoenicia Mission* (1864) he writes:

> "I am increasingly grasping the eminent personality of Jesus. I can clearly see him traveling through Galilee amid perpetual celebration. His love for children, his taste for flowers, for wedding festivities, the idyllic and rustic nature of his imagination are all well explained to me. There are few scenes in the Gospels whose truth I have not seen."

After mentioning the places he visited in the Holy Land, he continues with restrained enthusiasm:

> "Palestine offers the bizarre contrast of a country where you encounter the world's most famous sites at every turn, yet where monuments are rare and puny. Palestine bears the burden of the main flaw in the Jewish spirit, namely its lack of taste for the visual arts. Two thousand years later, countries once inhabited by artistic peoples still benefit from their past. It takes months to get to know Rome or Athens; in a few days, one has exhausted Jerusalem."

Statements such as this hinted at his early reservations about Judaism. He reduced it to a precursor of Christianity, which earned him accusations of anti-Semitism, against which he spoke out strongly and distanced himself from contemporaries such as the influential Arthur de Gobineau. Nevertheless, he remained in the memory of many with his statement that "Semites" were alien to military, political, scientific, and intellectual progress, and he generally lamented the "terrible simplicity of the Semitic mind." Also, Renan understood Islam as being in contradiction to modernity.

In a letter from Jerusalem written in May 1861 (addressed to the chemist Marcelin Berthelot), he sounds more conciliatory:

> "Jerusalem is truly the most unique place in the world, currently a mixture of comedy and odiousness that nothing else can compare to; and behind all that, the past is translucent at every turn. The topography here is very precise. . . . A few small parts of the walls and the underground passage of the Al-Aqsa Mosque are true Hebrew monuments. As for Jewish monuments, they can be found everywhere.
>
> In short, the past is very visible here to penetrating eyes. The tombs of the Valley of Jehoshaphat and the Golden Gate are monuments far above their reputation. All in all, I am delighted with my stay here. I will not hide from you that I am very tired. The climate of Palestine, with its strange alternations, does not suit me."

A few months later, Renan's year-long mission came to a dramatic end with the death of his sister Henriette, who succumbed to malaria in Lebanon. She had been a reliable support in all his endeavours over the years. Ernest Renan also fell ill and is said to have narrowly escaped death.

He continued to work on his book with determination. In 1863, his book *La vie de Jésus* was published, and the following year it was published in English as *The Life of Jesus*, soon also in Spanish, Dutch, German and other languages. Renan viewed

Jesus as a charming, itinerant preacher and a somewhat naïve shepherd of souls. He saw Jesus as a cheerful friend of the people who had freed himself from his "Jewish traits" and was only declared "God" after his death. Renan rejected the miracles of the Gospel. It was an interpretation that was celebrated by many, but heavily criticized by others for its humanizing, historicizing view of the person of Jesus, including by the Episcopal Conference. Oscar Wilde (whose father William Wilde had, in charge of an invalid patient, sailed through the Mediterranean for nine months and also visited Egypt and Palestine), on the other hand, described it as "the gracious fifth gospel, the gospel according to St. Thomas."

Renan later revised his critical stance on Judaism. In the 1880s, he wrote: "The Israelite race has in the past rendered the greatest services to the world. Blended with the different nations, in harmony with the diverse national unities of Europe, it will continue to do in the future what it has done in the past. By its collaboration with all the liberal forces of Europe, it will contribute eminently to the social progress of humanity."

Renan's career progressed in waves: although his appointment as professor of Oriental languages at the Collège de France was initially suspended after the publication of his biography of Jesus, he was later rehabilitated and elected a member of the Académie française. From 1883 until his death, he served as director of the Collège de France.

In the Babel of Languages—On the Role of Tourist Guides

EDWARD ROBINSON had recognized the basic problems: "In the first place, travellers simply followed the footsteps of the monks. It made little difference if they were Catholics or Protestants. . . . The monks served as their guides; and from that great storehouse of the monasteries they obtained their information. The majority of them were also rather credulous as regards the things that were told them. Thus it comes that their accounts are substantially alike. . . . The other mistake was that travellers were ignorant of the Arabic language and could hold intercourse with the people only through interpreters; accordingly, they never stepped off from the well-beaten paths, which all their predecessors had trodden. In this way, the valuable traditions, which still continued to live among the people, escaped them."

Unless they were in the company of Franciscans, travellers depended on dragomans who mediated between a European language and Arabic or Turkish to communicate with the locals and find their way around. Their assets were letters of recommendation, which they could present as proof of their expertise in order to win new customers. Those who had built up a good reputation were even listed in travel guides later. The relationship between dragomans and travellers was often characterized by tension. If the visitors were specifically led to certain shops, the suspicion quickly arose that the dragoman was profiting from this through a commission. When the foreigner was ripped off by a dragoman (or at least had this feeling), this sometimes became part of the travel report. The fact that many dragomans deliberately cultivated a picturesque oriental habitus was part of the "program" so to speak. The American John Ross Browne even went so far as to name his report on his trip to Lebanon in the early 1850s after his dragoman Yusef Simon Badra, who had advertised himself with the following words:

> "Gentlemen, I am Yusef Simon Badra, the dragoman for Syria. This is my book of recommendations. I have taken a thousand American gentlemen through Syria. Yes, sir; the Americans like me; I like the Americans! I hate Englishmen; I won't take an Englishman; they don't suit me; can't get along together; I know too much for 'em. But the Americans suit me; always ready; up to everything—fun, fight, or frolic. There are other dragomans here, gentlemen. Emanuel Balthos is my friend; I won't interfere, if you wish to take him. I don't say he's afraid of robbers; I don't say he hires guards in all the bad places on that account. I speak only of myself. The robbers know me. The name of Yusef Badra is guard enough in any part of Syria. Courage is a great thing in this country; courage will carry a man through where a thousand guards daren't show their faces. The last time I was out I killed six Bedouins. I sometimes kill such fellows for fun. They know me; they know it's a habit I have, and they always keep clear when they can. But you can choose for yourselves,

gentlemen; there's my book; look over it. Of course you'll smoke some chiboucks. Ho! there—Hassin—chiboucks!"

Conversely, Browne described him as follows:

"Face open and intelligent, eyes round and full of fire, moustache fierce, temperament nervous-sanguine, age twenty-eight, costume rich, careless, and dashing; figure well-knit and of medium height; manner frank, self-relying, and chivalrous; whole tone of character imposing, captivating, and Oriental."

And it is not without humour that Browne outlined the high demands placed on a dragoman:

"He is responsible for the name of every village and town on the route; he is responsible for every assertion made by Robinson and other authorities, and if there be any incongruity in the name or location, it is the dragoman who is compelled to answer for it; he is responsible for every moral and physical defect in the horses and mules; for every shower of rain that interrupts the journey; for every headache and fit of indigestion suffered by any member of the party; for the amount of fleas that infest every stopping-place; for the sterile and unsatisfactory character of the scenery in certain stages of the journey; for the roughness of the roads; for the uncivilized appearance of the Arabs throughout Syria; for the bad state of repair in which the bridges are kept; for every extreme of heat and cold; and all the discomforts of the climate and country; in short the dragoman is responsible for everything. He must be a man of courage, of energy, of patience, of good temper, of intelligence, of learning, of everything under the sun, moon, and stars. He must know all that the Howadji [foreign traveller] doesn't know, and all that the Howadji ought to know; his brains must act for himself and the Howadji, and for the muleteers, and for the horses, mules, donkeys, and every living thing in the company; if they don't, they are very poor brains indeed. He must be dragoman, tutor, lexicon, valet, cook, caterer, comforter, warrior—all in one; always ready for duty, night and day, never tired, never at fault in any emergency. In effect, the dragoman has a pretty busy life of it, and Yusuf is a good specimen of the best class."

More detailed insights into the career of a dragoman are provided by the booklet with collected evidence from Solomon Negima, which the British archaeologist Rachel Mairs bought at auction on Ebay and analysed. Negima was born a Syrian-Roman Catholic in Ramoth-Gilead, his father came from Nazareth and his mother from Moab. He attended a German Protestant missionary school in Jerusalem and initially worked as a translator for the British army in Egypt and Sudan before returning to Palestine in 1885. From then on, Thomas Cook and other travel agencies commissioned him as a dragoman for tourists. Specifics of his working life are revealed in the 65 letters from clients, photos and other notes that he collected over the decades—they form his portfolio so-to-speak. Negima was often praised in the letters for his reliability and honesty, as well as for his sense of humour. Many travellers particularly appreciated the fact that he was able to point out the connections between certain places and the Bible. Some mentioned his ability to negotiate favourable prices. The fact that he was a Christian himself stood him in good stead.

Negima was recommended to the English author Ellen E. Miller. Extremely adventurous and determined to travel off the beaten track, she definitely did not want to be part of a group. During the two months they spent together, she repeatedly presented Negima with challenges due to her unconventional demeanour. Magically attracted by everything that corresponded to the oriental cliché, she once burst into a Muslim wedding celebration in Jericho: "On my appearance, I, instead of the bride, became for a moment the centre of the demonstration! The wild creatures joined hands and made a circle round me, performing a kind of dance to the music of harsh yells, among which the word "bakshish" was easily distinguishable."

Negima then had the task of getting her out of this uncomfortable situation: "I was secretly rejoicing in the good luck which had led me into this novel scene, when cautious Solomon came up, whispering that I had better get out at once, before the cordon became too tight round me!"

On the banks of the Jordan, Miller insisted on being left alone by Negima for an hour. To his relief, however, she did not follow through with her announcement that she wanted to bathe in the river. If something had happened to her, it would have ruined his reputation. With some persuasion, he even managed to get Miller access to a Roman Catholic monastery under false pretences, as Protestants were actually forbidden to enter. Although she was unable to convince him of her faith, she is positive about their exchange on religious topics. Despite the fact that she was always traveling in Negima's company, she published her book under the title *Alone Through Syria* (1891).

Negima's clients also included the preacher Charles T. Walker, who was born a slave in 1858 and was sent by the African-American Tabernacle Baptist Church in Augusta, Georgia. He undertook his three-month journey in the spring of 1891. Negima and Walker apparently got on very well. After his return to America, Walker wrote a letter to Negima to ask him for help in sending souvenirs. Walker took this opportunity to remind him that they had swapped hats: Walker had worn Negima's fez.

Evidence of a particularly good relationship with a dragoman can also be found in the work of the English writer Muhammad Marmaduke Pickthall, who travelled to Syria and Palestine in the mid-1890s. Pickthall was only a Christian on paper and harboured the "sneaking wish" to "fraternise with Orientals", had learned Arabic fluently and is remembered by posterity primarily as a translator of the Koran—he only converted to Islam later. Pickthall did not write any of the usual travelogues, and the locations are usually not precisely identifiable. He published his collection of incidents under the title *Oriental Encounters*. For a while, he stayed at the inn of the German colony in Jaffa, but soon found it boring. He quickly became a thorn in the side of the English because he sometimes dressed in Arab costume, which his fellow countrymen found inappropriate.

Pickthall wrote at length about the Syrian dragoman Suleymân, whom he quickly befriended:

> "His wisdom and his independent way of airing it did not please everybody as they did me; and reverence in dealing with a fellow-man was not his strong point. By travellers, I gather from innumerable testimonials which he showed me, he was either much beloved or the reverse, though none could say he did not know his business." About his language skills Pickthall remarked: "His English, though voluminous and comprehensive, was sometimes strange to native English ears. He had read the Bible in a German mission school, and spoke of 'Billiam's donkey' and 'the mighty Simson' where we should speak of Balaam's ass and Samson. He called the goatskins used for carrying water 'beastly skins,' and sometimes strengthened a mild sentence with an expletive."

Suleymân only became dangerous if he was distrusted, then he played tricks on people.

> "One Englishman, with a taste for management but little knowledge of the country, and no common sense, he cruelly obeyed in all things, with the natural result in loss of time and loss of luggage, sickness and discomfort. . . . 'And yet the man was happy, having had things his own way, even after the most horrid and disastrous journey ever made,' he told me with a sigh. 'Some men are asses.'"

The dragoman is said to have had a special attitude towards clergymen: "For clergymen he kept a special manner and a special store of jokes. When leading such through Palestine he always had a Bible up before him on the saddle; and every night would join them after dinner and preach a sermon on the subject of the next day's journey. This he would make as comical as possible for their amusement, for clergymen, he often used to say to me, are fond of laughter of a certain kind."

Isabel Burton, author of *The Inner Life of Syria, Palestine, and the Holy Land* (1875) and wife of the famous adventurer Richard Francis Burton, described Hanna Misk, the chief dragoman of the British Consulate in Damascus, as "remarkably clever man, one of those curious specimens of equally balanced good and evil one so frequently sees in the east . . . I have seen him blush with pleasure when detected in a lie or an intrigue." Burton was nevertheless well-disposed towards him: "he used to teach me scraps of Arabic, and amuse many a dull half-hour; he always saw the comic side of a situation, and was ever a welcome guest." The downside of his personality was that he never was "faithful to any master or employer, and he betrayed his friends." Burton assigned an indispensable role to these intermediaries when they are in the higher spheres of the social hierarchy:

"The country is governed by Dragomans. . . . All Turkish authorities, Consuls, and other officers, have several of these Secretaries. Their masters are mostly puppets. If a great man wants to see another great man, A's Dragoman goes to B's Dragoman, and arranges the visit."

Apart from linguistic communication in the country, travellers had to decide whether they preferred European clothing—in the nineteenth century this typically meant long coats, veils peeking out from under their sun helmets, sunglasses and umbrellas—or whether they wanted to appear in oriental garb. If they chose the latter option, they had a much better chance to be granted access to mosques and were usually spared the insults and harassment of beggars. But because the Ottomans were notorious for their aggression towards the Arab population, "disguised" Western visitors run the risk of being mistaken for Arabs here and there and treated badly. Therefore, the decision had to be weighed up carefully, since both had their pros and cons.

Seetzen, for example, usually dressed in Muslim garb; in Aleppo he walked like a Janissary. Later, when he was traveling east of the Sea of Galilee, he pretended to be a beggar in order to be spared by the Bedouins who roamed the area and were considered particularly predatory. To avoid misunderstandings and to be able to travel more freely, he adopted the name Musa al-Hakim—according to him, his family name often sounded like "Seïtun" (olive) or "Seïtan" (devil) to the Arabs.

With the increasing presence of Western nationals, especially through the establishment of diplomatic missions, the atmosphere relaxed and the locals no longer perceived the European-dressed travellers as "foreign" as they used to do. Similar to the dragomans, the ethnic affiliation of former consuls and consular agents—although they held the position for a particular country (or even several) and were primarily responsible for safeguarding local trade interests—was not always apparent to travellers. The country representatives also benefited from the movement between languages, cultures and identities and knew how to use them to their advantage here and there.

A colourful person in this context is Bernard Damiani, who acted as honorary consul for both France and Austria in Jaffa around the middle of the nineteenth century and is mentioned in several travel reports. He was part of an entire dynasty of consuls of the same name in Jaffa, which continued after him well into the twentieth century. Ida Pfeiffer, for example, was welcomed by Damiani and his family who were all dressed in Turkish clothes. She noted the following about the evening's dinner conversation:

> "Some of the family spoke a little Italian, and even that with so much Greek dialect that I had to guess what they wanted to say. They certainly felt the same way about me. The consul claimed to know French very well, but for this evening it seemed to have slipped his memory. There was a lot of conversing, but little actual understanding."

The French author Auguste Romieu commented on Damiani's appearance: "The excess of his clothes, like his language, is half-Muslim and half-European. In a word invented by a contemporary, he resembles the opera Turks, whose name will forever be celebrated in the world of carnival." And de Lamartine remarked, thereby describing him in more detail: "The grotesqueness of his costume made us smile: he was dressed in an old sky-blue robe, lined with ermine, and bound by a sash of crimson silk; his bare legs issued from wide pantaloons of dirty muslin; and he was crowned by an enormous three-cornered hat, worn smooth by time, and greased with sweat and dust, attesting numerous services during the Egyptian campaign."

The apparent Turkish style cultivated by Damiani was continued in the interior design, while the food served was European in character, albeit "with the opulence of Muslim meals", as other guests pointed out. Also, rumour had it that European wines had always flowed freely in his house. As Damiani's son explained to de Lamartine during his visit: "Ours is an Italian name; our family is originally from Europe, but from time immemorial has been established in Arabia. We are Arabs, but we have French hearts, and should regard it as a disgrace and an insult to our feelings if you accept hospitality in any other house than ours."

The Land of Milk and Honey

AS PART of the eastern Levant—bordered by the Mediterranean coast to the west, Lebanon to the north and open to the Syrian desert to the east—Palestine offers great scenic contrasts, even extremes, in a comparatively small area. The fertile valley, which extends to the edge of the desert, is crisscrossed by the Jordan River, the Sea of Galilee and the Dead Sea. Travellers had long been interested in the natural conditions of the country. The Franciscan Paul Walther von Güglingen, who undertook his pilgrimage in 1481 and spent a whole year in Jerusalem, said that it was the land of milk and honey and that grain grew faster there than anywhere else, even though it rarely rained.

His brother in faith Francesco Suriano, who was writing a travel guide to the Holy Land at this time, was convinced that the "most temperate, clearest and healthiest" climate could be found there and that diseases such as gout, diarrhoea and fever were much rarer. Also, he assumed the quality of the water to be the best in the world, excluding that of the Nile. Nevertheless, he did not fail to notice that the country is very dry due to infrequent rainfall. What mysterious forces are involved in the ripening of the melons? "It is a true wonder to see the large and juicy watermelons growing in the bare sand without irrigation and only with the help of the perfect air, and in such quantities that they are there all year round. They also have many other things that we don't have, such as eggplants, coconut, bamboo, sugar cane and many other things." With these characteristics, Suriano saw proof "that the land of promise is holier than any other part of the world because it is the richest in all temporal things" (van Eck and Ritsema, 2019). Suriano located Jerusalem at the centre of the universe, as was typical for Franciscans at the time.

In addition to the fertile areas, some of the land consisted of very dry stretches of land where not even water flowed—let alone milk and honey, or wine and olive oil. Could these stony hills and deserted valleys really be the land of promise? Was this perception of the fertility of the land possibly only due to the "Western view", as the Scottish theologian and Old Testament scholar George Adam Smith suggested in *Historical Geography of the Holy Land* (1894), a highly regarded work that represents the high point of nineteenth century exploration of the Holy Land?

> "To a western eye it must, at certain seasons of the year, seem singularly meagre and uninfluential—incapable of stirring the imagination, or enriching the life of a people. Yet come in, with the year at the flood, with the springing of the grain, with the rush of colour across the field, the flush of green on the desert, and in imagination clothe again the stony terraces with the vines which in ancient times trailed from foot to summit of many of the hills—then, even though your eye be western, you will feel the charm and intoxication of the land."

Scientifically inclined people suspected that changes in the climate had caused the water sources to dry up. The British clergyman Arthur P. Stanley, who had travelled to Palestine in 1852 and again a decade later, wrote in *Sinai and Palestine: In Connexion with their History* (1856) that it was "an island in a desert waste . . . as compared with the whole surrounding country in the midst of which it stands, it is unquestionably a fertile land in the midst of barrenness."

Nevertheless, he wondered why it could not compete with the banks of the Nile, which were much richer in vegetation, or the river Kebar mentioned in the prophetic book of Ezekiel, whose banks are said to have been densely covered with carpets of flowers. He saw the reasons for this in the destruction of the forests that once stretched across the mountains and which were home to wild bee colonies, and the neglect of landscape terraces that were created by farmers centuries ago on the slopes, adapting to the shape of the mountains and helping to consolidate the soil. Vines and maize plants grown on slopes are now easily carried away by the rain. In addition, the composition of the population and other methods of cultivating the land have changed.

It was often emphasized in travel reports that Palestine was a poorly developed hinterland of the Ottoman Empire and an appendage of Syria. Sometimes a comparison was made with Lebanon, the region around Damascus and the banks of the Nile. According to the British officer Claude Regnier Conder in *Tent Work in Palestine* (1878), Lebanon was under better administration, was rich in vineyards and gardens and had a "cheerful population". As Eitan Bar-Yosef writes in *The Holy Land in English Culture* (2005), the arid lands of Palestine caused the negative perception of the country as a whole: "The mere presence of a desert, that most non-European feature, signified inefficiency, laziness, and bad government".

On the other hand, there was indeed ample evidence of exuberant fertility. The British diplomat William Turner, who worked at the embassy in Constantinople, recorded on his way from Acre to Jaffa in 1820:

> "For the last half hour we rode along a narrow lane, bordered on each side by the city gardens which abound in orange, lemon, almond, mulberry, olive, and fig trees; sycamores, prickly pears, &c., and produce large quantities of tobacco."

In fact, Citrus plants are frequently mentioned. However, the famous sweet orange, which became Jaffa's trademark, only appeared in the later second half of the century. Quite a few chroniclers became entangled in contradictions when they described lush plantations on the one hand, but then criticized the poor economic situation on the other. These assessments were typically combined with criticism of the local inhabitants, who supposedly were incapable of working the land effectively. The British diplomat John Bowring wrote in 1840 in *Report on the Commercial Statistics of Syria*, giving such assessments an official touch:

> "The agricultural produce of Syria is far less than might be expected from the extensive of tracts of fertile lands and the favourable character of the climate. In the districts where hands are found to cultivate the fields, production is large and the return for capital is considerable; but the want of population for the purposes of cultivation is most deplorable".

Ida Pfeiffer remarked just along these lines:

> "It is a pity that the inhabitants of these countries do not contribute anything to the culture and improvement of the natural resources, how well and wonderfully many things could then flourish. Indeed, they do not even know how to

> treat properly what nature often offers them in abundance and of a good variety, as is the case with olives, for example. You can't easily get a worse oil than in Syria. . . . It is the same with wine. They could have very good varieties if they knew how to cultivate the vine and treat the wine."

Of course, olive oil was only one part of the agricultural production; grain, sesame, wine, almonds and cotton were among the most sought-after products in Europe. There have been vineyards near Jerusalem since the late nineteenth century, with winemaking most likely solely in the hands of Christians and Jews. And although Islam actually forbids the consumption of wine, there are contemporary indications that Muslims were also fond of it here and there; however, they were not offered the alcoholic beverage on official occasions out of decency.

Clarke also mentioned millet, linseed and small fields of barley. Many travellers were of the opinion that the country would experience a great upswing under a different administration. Charles van de Velde, for example, emphasized that the gardens were "a miracle of fertility", and added:

> "What, then, shall it be when the day of salvation shall have dawned on this land? Oh Israel, what a glorious destiny is reserved for you!"

These assessments reinforced the idea that establishing a new power in the country was necessary to improve conditions. In other words, it was a subtle call for Western intervention. Although this criticism refers specifically to Palestine, it is difficult to separate it from the complaints of Western visitors about the neglect of the Middle East during the last decades of the Ottoman Empire, which could be heard everywhere.

Contemporary research shows that there were in fact strong local economic structures and businessmen involved in lively trade with foreign countries in many places. During the American Civil War, when cotton supplies from the South were blocked from reaching the North, imports from Palestine (and other areas of the Ottoman Empire, such as western Anatolia, where cotton cultivation increased during this period) filled an important gap. However, the small boom was already over by the time devastating swarms of locusts destroyed the harvest in Palestine in 1866. Research by the Palestinian-American historian Beshara Doumani, who has analyzed Nablus as the economically most important city in Palestine, confirms the existence of an extremely vital trading hub for the eighteenth and nineteenth centuries, whose businessmen were closely interwoven with the rural structures. Also, with the help of consular reports from the second half of the nineteenth century for the ports of Jaffa, Acre and Haifa, the German oriental scholar Alexander Schölch was able to prove that exports exceeded imports and that Palestine even helped to reduce the otherwise negative trade balance for the whole of Syria.

In any case, many inhabitants benefited from the economic upturn that was due to the newly arrived settlers—Templers and Jews alike—and the skills they brought with them. "For the first time since the Crusades, European Christians had succeeded in gaining a foothold in the Holy Land and laying the foundations for a modern settlement in this region that had been neglected for centuries," wrote the historian and bridge-builder between Germany and Israel Alex Carmel, which was perceived as a provocation by some Zionists because Carmel was shaking up the myth that only Jews were responsible for the upswing.

As far as Jaffa is concerned, oranges, soap and wine played the most important role as export goods in the late nineteenth century, with England long being the main market for Jaffa oranges. According to statistics from the Anglo Palestine Company, exports of these fruits doubled between 1903 and 1911 to 870,000 crates. Lemons only play a certain role in the Etrog variety because it is used for ritual purposes during the Jewish Feast of Tabernacles. Tobacco was also initially grown in the Upper Galilee colonies with good yields. However, as the taxes levied on it by the monopoly authority under French administration were too high, it was soon abandoned.

Geological and Botanical Curiosities

"FOR THOUSANDS of years, no part of Palestine has been viewed more with the distorting glass of prejudice, countless are the stale fables that have been spread about Palestine. European travellers, pilgrims and especially monks vied with each other to preserve ancient legends that would otherwise have long since crumbled into nothingness," wrote Ulrich Jasper Seetzen, capturing something of the fascination that repeatedly draws travellers to explore the Dead Sea and its surroundings. At 425 meters below sea level, the Dead Sea is the lowest lake on earth that is accessible from the shore.

Although Seetzen had been advised not to do so, he was curious, wanted to get a picture of this legendary part of the country and follow in the footsteps of the "terrible natural phenomenon"—caused by fire, volcano or "earth fire"—that is said to have once ravaged this area. One of the geological curiosities is a limestone mountain that looks like a volcanic cone, called "el Pherdéis", "Frankenberg" or "little paradise". The Bedouins lead him to a labyrinthine cave that was visited by Franciscan monks every few years. "The ground became more and more bare, gritty, stony and barren." There are only a few wild pigs and a "gasalle" [presumably meaning a gazelle]. In the middle of the seemingly ghostly landscape, the scree of hornstone and flint, lies a pile of stones that marks the grave of a Bedouin. In the oasis "Ain Dschíddy" (today Ein Gedi), located on the western side of the sea, Seetzen studied the plant world. He is considered to be the first European scientist to have circumnavigated the Dead Sea.

De Chateaubriand had been advised to give the Dead Sea a wide berth, but he wanted to go there. The possibility of seeing the place where the Jordan flows into the lake, which he had read about in Hasselquist, awakened the naturalist in him. Even though the Arabs refused to take him there, he found ways to get there and spend two entire hours on the banks of the lake. He could not bring himself to drift on the water lying down and then emerge from the salt water like a white ghost with matted hair, like many travellers after him. But de Chateaubriand could not resist the temptation to scoop some water out of the Jordan with a leather vessel and taste it:

> "I then drew water from the river in a leather jug: to me it did not seem as sweet as sugar, as a good missionary has said; I found it, instead, somewhat salty; but though I drank a large quantity, it did me no harm; I think it would be very agreeable if it was purged of the sand it carries."

Even Hermann Fürst von Pückler-Muskau was not impressed by all the gossip he heard during his journey and stuck to his decision to camp for a few days on the shores of the Dead Sea. "The mare mortuum lay as black and immobile as a metal mirror at our feet. Seen from here, no description could be more fitting in every respect, for sea and land at the same time, for hardly a single tree was visible in the immense stretch of land that surrounded us, nothing but black cliffs and an endless grey stone range, constantly rising and falling in monotonous uniformity, stretching to the farthest horizon." In keeping with his status, he treats himself and his companions to a few carefully chilled bottles of champagne, "while further away, soldiers, slaves and horses pêle-mêle, in their southern costumes and adventurous equipment, provided the most animated genre picture for our evening feast".

Hasselquist was already pondering the question of what the special fruits that grow around the Dead Sea, the Sodom apples, were all about. These were already mentioned by the Roman-Jewish historian Flavius Josephus. According to him, fruit grew in the vicinity of the "asphalt lake", in which he recognized the biblical Sodom, the contents of which dissolved into smoke and ashes after being picked. Hasselquist was certain that the plant bearing them was *Solanum melongena,* so named by Linné. But was the "apple of Sodom", as it was also called, actually an eggplant? Seetzen developed a different theory; he identified the Sodom apple with a fruit similar to the pomegranate, in which a type of cotton grows. De Chateaubriand was certain that he had discovered the mysterious fruit:

> "I am now somewhat embarrassed, for I believe I too have found the desired fruit: the shrub which bears it grows eight or nine miles from the mouth of the Jordan; it is thorny, and its leaves are thin and slender; it looks much like the shrub described by Amman; its fruit is very similar in colour and shape, to the small Egyptian lemon. When this fruit is not quite ripe, it is swollen with a salty and corrosive sap; when dried, it yields a blackish seed, which might be compared to ashes, and which tastes of bitter pepper. I picked half a dozen of these fruits; I still have four

dried specimens, well preserved, which may merit the attention of naturalists."

Scientifically, the Sodom apple or "Dead Sea apple" is known as *Calotropis procera*—and is the fruit of the oscher or fat-leaf tree. Adding to the confusion was the fact that there is also a fruit known as "Sodom apple" among the nightshade family.

The so-called Rose of Jericho, with the scientific name *Anastatica hierohuntica,* which can also be found in the wider Dead Sea area, is less associated with questions, but all the more with numinous associations. With its little branches that gather together to form a dry ball that is easily carried away by the wind, it has been popular with pilgrims for centuries, who could easily carry it with them as a souvenir. As soon as the seed capsules attached to the herbaceous plant come into contact with sufficient liquid, it awakes to new life, hence its name "Resurrection flower".

Other sights cast a spell over visitors to this region. There is the fortress of Masada, which Herod had built shortly before the turn of time and around 70 AD became the scene of a fierce battle between Romans and Jews that dragged on for months and culminated in the mass suicide of the inhabitants, which became part of Jewish commemorative culture. Van de Velde spotted the desert fortress: "I stood wondering at the mind which could have conceived the idea of constructing a fortress on this isolated rock that rises perpendicularly to a height of a thousand feet above the Dead Sea."

The aforementioned Scottish theologian George Adam Smith formulates an uninviting conclusion about the Dead Sea and its surroundings:

"Perhaps there is no region of our earth where Nature and History have more cruelly conspired, where so tragic a drama has obtained so awful a theatre. In many other parts of the world the effect of historical catastrophes has been heightened by their occurrence amid scenes of beauty and peace. It is otherwise here. Nature, when she has not herself been, by some volcanic convulsion, the executioner of God's judgments, has added every aggravation of horror to the cruelty of the human avenger or the exhaustion of the doomed. The history of the Dead Sea opens with Sodom and Gomorrah, and may be said to close with the Massacre of Masada."

The American naval officer William Francis Lynch, who, bored with his mission in Mexico, came to Palestine in 1847 on behalf of the United States Naval Hydrographic Office with a crew of 16, was more interested in the more remote Jordan region and the Dead Sea from the outset. As he wrote in his *Narrative of the United States' Expedition to the River Jordan and the Dead Sea* (1849), Lynch believed the Jews were destined to "civilize" the Arabs. His plea for the targeted resettlement of Jews in Palestine is therefore only logical. Firmly convinced of the country's economic potential, Lynch also proposes settling black Americans in the Jordan Valley, where they should work on plantations. His team soon suffered from a fever and one of the officers died. After Lynch's return, the financial outlay for the expedition came under fire—the whole thing was a waste of public money, according to critics. His book presumably found a sympathetic audience precisely because of his racist proposals.

After the legendary British traveller and secret service agent Gertrude Bell spent a few weeks with her friends Nina and Georg Friedrich Wilhelm Rosen, then German consul, in Jerusalem in early March 1900—intensive Arabic lessons demanded her full attention—she undertook a ride on her Arabian stallion to Jericho and along the eastern shore of the Dead Sea, together with a cook and a few muleteers. In the Jordan Valley, she found herself surrounded by waist-high flowers. "The wilderness had blossomed like the rose", it was an unforgettable sight. On her return north, she crossed a pilgrimage road that leads to Mecca: "Road of course it is not: it is about one-eighth of a mile wide and consists of hundreds of parallel tracks trodden out by the immense caravan which passes twice a year."

Writers Joining in and a Community of Fanatics

NIKOLAI GOGOL, an Orthodox Christian, undertook a pilgrimage to Jerusalem in 1848, a few years after the publication of his book *Dead Souls*. In a messianic mood, he reached the city on a donkey in February. However, Gogol did not encounter the paradisiacal city he had expected, but rather dirt, beggars and traffickers; he found the atmosphere anything but hospitable and was denied the spiritual experience he had longed for. The sight of the run-down religious sites worsened his depression and he returned to Russia disillusioned. His pilgrimage was to have a memorable aftermath. In Moscow, the restless writer came under the influence of the fanatical priest Matvey Konstantinovsky. The latter strengthened Gogol's conviction that his works were sinful, ultimately the cause of his misery and that a pilgrimage was not sufficient to prove his devotion to God. One evening, Gogol burnt the manuscript for his second volume of *Dead Souls*. His condition continued to worsen and in February 1852 he starved himself to death near Moscow during a strict fasting regiment.

When the young Gustave Flaubert together with Maxime du Camp, boarded the ship which took them on a week-long voyage to Egypt in Marseille in November 1849, he was actually travelling on behalf of the French Ministry of Agriculture and Trade; among other things, he was to find out the quantities of certain products. The sometimes more, sometimes less elegant bon vivant confided in his diary just how serious he was about this, that he cared as little about this mission as he did about the King of Prussia. Flaubert's stay in Egypt is best known for the freedom from European conventions that he claimed for himself in the sexual sphere, it is often overlooked that he also travelled to Palestine and Lebanon. It was a trip he had long desired to undertake. Flaubert had spent a lot of time researching the origins of Christianity and the early saints for his *The Temptation of St. Anthony,* the first version of which was published in 1849.

Although, as literary scholar Anthony Zielonka remarks, "thought of as an unambiguously anticlerical individual, as a lifelong agnostic and sceptic who was always interested in the diversity of religious beliefs and practices, but who rejected adherence to any one faith, and often expressed his doubts and his cynicism in matters of religion", Flaubert was overwhelmed emotionally when he saw and experienced the Holy City. Of course, he realized the significance for Christians and Jews.

> "How clean it is! The walls are all preserved—I think of Jesus Christ entering and leaving to go up to the Mount of Olives—I can see him there through the door in front of me. The mountains of Hebron behind the city, to my right, in a hazy transparency; everything else is dry, hard, gray; the light seems to me like that of a winter's day, so harsh and white is it—yet it is very warm in tone, I don't know how that is."

However, time and time again, his stay provided him with strange situations and lead him to unexpected observations: "A Christian asked my dragoman if I wasn't the Pasha." And a few pages later: "It's the Turkish Pasha who keeps the keys to the Holy Sepulchre. When you want to visit it, you have to get then from him. I find that quite striking. On the other hand, it's the most humane solution. If the Holy Sepulchre were given over to the Christians, they would unfailingly massacre each other. Such cases have been known." He returned from his visit "bone-tired" and "disgusted". All in all, he finds the holy places "ridiculous", his verdict is devastating: "It's all whorish to the last degree: hypocrisy, cupidity, falsification, impudence, yes: but as for holiness, go fuck yourself."

Thousands of travellers to Jerusalem in the nineteenth century alone saw their journey to the Holy Land as so important and incisive that they wrote about it, but no one is likely to have reached more readers with his statements than the American Samuel Langhorne Clemens, who arrived there in 1867 as part of a broader European trip in the company of predominantly religious passengers. The letters of Mark Twain, as he called himself, are also a reckoning with other chroniclers who, in his opinion, portrayed the country in too beautiful colours and did not prepare the travellers at all for what they actually got to see. He initially wrote them for the newspaper *Daily Alta California*, which had sponsored the trip, and later published them as *Innocents Abroad, or The New Pilgrim's Progress.*

"Of all the lauds there are for dismal scenery, I think Palestine must be the prince. . . . It is a hopeless, dreary, heart-broken land." Of course, Twain did not fail to mention the animosities among the pilgrims crowded together in the Church of the Holy Sepulchre, the proof "that they cannot worship together at the tomb of the Savior of the world in peace". And he pokes fun at the American pilgrims who have brought their verdicts with them:

> "I am sure, from the tenor of books I have read, that many who have visited this land in years gone by, were Presbyterians, and came seeking evidences in support of their particular creed; they found a Presbyterian Palestine, and they had already made up their minds to find no other, though possibly they did not know it, being blinded by their zeal. Others were Baptists, seeking Baptist evidences and a Baptist Palestine. Others were Catholics, Methodists, Episcopalians, seeking evidences indorsing their several creeds, and a Catholic, a Methodist, an Episcopalian Palestine. Honest as these men's intentions may have been, they were full of partialities and prejudices, they entered the country with their verdicts already prepared, and they could no more write dispassionately and impartially about it than they could about their own wives and children."

Unquestionably, Twain, who loved to present himself as an original, unspoiled American, gave his readers impressions of the Holy Land that are less embellished than what they knew from the Bible and *Arabian Nights*. He skilfully encouraged their sympathy, for example when he transferred the dimensions of Palestine to those of the United States: "When I was a boy, I somehow got the impression that the river Jordan was four thousand miles long and thirty-five miles wide. It is only ninety miles long, and so crooked that a man does not know which side of it he is on half the time. In going ninety miles it does not get over more than fifty miles of ground. It is not any wider than Broadway in New York."

This was, of course, a carefully calculated polemic; Twain wanted to make the country appear smaller than it already is.

But does this also make it less important? Even if he repeated himself with this and similar comparisons, they were certainly good for a smile from his readers. Like many others, Twain deplored that the people were enslaved by inhuman tyranny. He had every sympathy for the country's inhabitants:

> "These people are naturally good-hearted and intelligent, and with education and liberty, would be a happy and contented race. They often appeal to the stranger to know if the great world will not some day come to their relief and save them. The Sultan has been lavishing money like water in England and Paris, but his subjects are suffering for it now."

In view of the history crammed into a very small space, he hoped that readers will understand:

> "How it wears a man out to have to read up a hundred pages of history every two or three miles—for verily the celebrated localities of Palestine occur that close together. How wearily, how bewilderingly they swarm about your path!

Whatever the situation, he took on the burden of continuing to travel from one place to the next because he wanted to complete his newspaper assignment. Despite his aversion to tourism, Twain was also a diligent traveller who collected souvenirs—at least in this respect he conformed to the cliché. In Jerusalem, he bought a Bible for his mother. Not just any Bible, mind you; its cover was supposedly made from such precious materials as balsa wood from the Jordan, oak from Abraham's tree near Hebron and olive wood from the Mount of Olives. He even stole a stone from Solomon's tomb for his mother. And as an established Freemason, he did not want to return to America empty-handed; he had a log of Jerusalem cedar carved to resemble a hammer, which he gave to his lodge's president.

The American colonists from Maine with whom Twain met were probably far worse off than the locals. They had arrived the previous year under the leadership of George J. Adams, a former actor who had become the prophet of a fundamentalist Christian sect. Their aim was to wait in the Holy Land for the return of Christ and to help prepare for the return of the Jews to the Holy Land; they saw themselves as practical benefactors of the land and the people. They had even brought dismantled wooden houses from America so as not to waste any time. The settlement on a dune outside Jaffa, built shortly after their arrival in September 1866, soon turned out to be a complete fiasco. The crops didn't thrive, the inhabitants struggled with vermin and disease. In order to get alcohol, Adams defrauded the participants of their money. After some of the settlers asked the American consul for help, a number of them were able to return to America in the spring of 1867. When Twain arrived in Jaffa, only 86 of the original 157 people were still there. He helped 44 destitute colonists to leave the country and embarked them with him on the *Quaker City* from Jaffa to Egypt.

Six months after Twain, the American landscape painter Frederic Church and his companion David Stuart Dodge (Chernik 2019) visited the colony and were welcomed by Adams. Dodge noted: "Such a tirade of ignorance, coarseness, vulgarity, and well-nigh blasphemy, I never heard. . . . I fear his method of helping forward the restoration of Palestine will have to join the list of failures." Some of the settlers sold their land to the soon-to-arrive Württemberg Templers.

After his return to America, Adams exploited his experiences in a *Palestine Museum* and presented himself to the public in "Arab" clothing: Wearing wide pants, a long robe and a turban trimmed with tassels, he smoked his hookah with a stem a full fourteen feet, or four meters long. The advertisement read as follows: "Among his collection may be seen Jewish unleavened bread, Pomegranates, Olive Berries, Bread Fruit, Simsim [sesame], Banana Leaves five feet long, Olive Branches, Water from the Dead Sea, Wood from the Banks of the River Jordan, Scorpions, Centipedes, Lizards, Crabs, &c, &c, A collection of Minerals from every place of note throughout the Holy Land." It was certainly an impressive collection!

There were other American settlement attempts. As early as 1852, the Dicksons from Massachusetts established a farm, also in the Jaffa area. Their motives were similar to those of Adams later on: they too wanted to speed up the return of the Jews. Herman Melville paid a brief visit to the small colony in 1857. Shortly afterwards, it fell victim to an attack by Arab raiders. Melville used this as a model for Nathan's death in *Clarel: A Poem and Pilgrimage in the Holy Land,* his epic about spiritual search and expulsion in Palestine.

All in all, Palestine brought together a wild mix of visitors from the Western world: evangelistic Protestants, unorthodox Protestants, sceptical romantics, even humourists.

> "Jerusalem is full of cranks. This sounds a little coarse, perhaps, but it is the only expression which I know adequate to convey the precise thought. The Holy City, while it is the object of the most solemn and tender regard by all Christians, is at the same time an attraction for all the religious driftwood in this great world . . . The majority of these religious cranks hail from the United States, which has produced so many and such strange religions",

wrote the commentator named 'Ichabod' on July 6, 1844 in the Chicago newspaper *The Daily Inter Ocean*.

The *American Colony* in Jerusalem goes back to Horatio Spafford and his Norwegian-born wife Anna. In August 1881, both led a small group of Chicagoans, called "the Overcomers", whose aim was to bear witness to the second coming of Christ. The Spaffords' initial motivation was to escape the grasp of creditors to whom they owed 100,000 dollars. When they reached Jerusalem by late September, they rented a residence understood as a "religious household while awaiting the fulfilment of biblical prophecy" (Vogel, 1993). Anna Spafford took the helm of the Jerusalem commune. By offering accommodation to tourists, the couple put the enterprise on a solid financial footing and came to terms with the local Muslims, Christians and Jews, especially as they did not try to convert them and proved to be charitable towards the poor. Towards the end of the century, the colony counted about 150 members.

The downside, hardly known at the time, was that the children of the colony were exploited. However, the Spaffords excluded their own daughters from these tasks. The extremely restrictive, even dubious rules that governed life in the community remained hidden from outsiders—Anna Spafford derived them from messages that she claimed to have received directly from God. These initially included celibacy, the separation of children from their parents, the restriction of meals and the redistribution of beds. Spafford also limited teaching and forbade children to read for pleasure. From time to time, members managed to escape the colony and bring information to the American consuls, but they didn't really receive attention. Protestant missionaries avoided the colony. Anna Spafford regarded death as God's punishment for the sins a person committed in their life and was firmly convinced that she would never die.

Contrary to her expectations, however, she in fact did meet her fate in 1923.

Among the prominent visitors of the colony was the deeply religious British General Charles "Chinese" Gordon (Vogel, 1993) who had fought in the Crimean War, had taken part in the Anglo-French expedition during the Second Opium War, was involved in the storming of Beijing in 1860, served the Khedive of Egypt and became Governor-General of the Sudan. In 1882–83, he came to Jerusalem to study biblical history and antiquities, accompanied by Reverend Herbert Drake, a young chaplain. Even though Gordon harboured reservations about the "extravagant American sect", they supposedly established friendly relations with the Spaffords. When Drake got seriously involved with the colony, things got difficult and Gordon tried to separate him from the cult—unsuccessfully so, and Drake became responsible for the education of the colony's children. Gordon, in any case, had his own eccentricities. He is associated with the so-called 'Garden Tomb;, discovered in 1867, which he observed from the roof of the colony's house. He concluded that the tomb, a Roman-era burial chamber carved into a rock face several metres high beyond Jerusalem's Old City, was the true sepulchre of Jesus. The site became known as "Gordon's Calvary", and some Anglican and Free Church Christians still believe it to be the tomb of Jesus today. A few years later Gordon got killed in Khartoum, Sudan, after a conflict with the country's religious leader and self-proclaimed Mahdi, Muhammad Ahmad.

The Swedish future winner of the Nobel Prize in literature Selma Lagerlöf also visited the colony. Together with her lover and fellow writer Sophie Elkan, she undertook a trip to Italy, Greece, Egypt and Palestine in 1900. Immediately after arriving in Jerusalem, they visited the American Colony. Lagerlöf was well informed about the case of Swedish emigration from Nås in the province of Dalarna and set out to follow in the footsteps of these settlers. She wrote to her mother (Lagerlöf, 2016): "They are extraordinarily strange people, I must say, but it is pleasant to see how clean, well-kept and well-organized everything is with them. They say they are happy, and the men also look cheerful and lively, but the women less so." During her visit, Lagerlöf discovered that the Swedes among the colonists had all learned English and that the preacher Olof Henrik Larsson has been deposed and "now ekes out his existence in a shed on the farm". Although her companion Sophie Elkan had a letter for the Chief Rabbi of Jerusalem, she kept it to herself so as not to be recognized as Jewish. Otherwise, she would not have been allowed to enter the Holy Sepulchre or the Omar Mosque right next to it, she reported in a letter to Betty Warburg.

Lagerlöf did not treat her journey to Palestine as a travel diary, but develops a novel in two parts from the story of sectarians from the Swedish province of Dalarna: *Jerusalem*. While being a work of fiction, the novel portrays the colony and its Swedish inhabitants in a sympathetic manner, albeit under a thin disguise.

Lester I. Vogel, in *To See a Promised Land: Americans and the Holy Land in the Nineteenth Century* (1993) draws a sobering conclusion: "American efforts to colonize the Holy Land were, on the whole, aberrant, poignant, and illusory. Despite differences in the sizes of the ventures, and despite differences in the programs or relative successes, these efforts were based on an image of the Holy Land that was based in esoteric meaning. Each group expected to find conditions in the Holy Land at a low ebb, but their anticipations were keyed to an idealistic image of a potential biblical utopia, not to a realistic assessment of an Ottoman province."

The First Package Trip Tourists with Thomas Cook

"ARE YOU PILGRIMS HERE?" HE CONTINUED.
"Not precisely."
"Only tourists, perhaps?"
"Something that way," volunteered the Californian. "Just so, sort half and half—killing two birds with one stone—blending the performance of a spiritual obligation with the desire of seeing the country."

This is what Albert Rhodes (then US consul in Jerusalem) in *Jerusalem As It Is* (1865).

As early as in the 1850s, de Saulcy already complained about the loss of the poetic qualities that he had perceived on his previous visits to Jerusalem, now that the streets were home to cabarets with French or Italian names: *Café du Jourdain, À la Mer Morte, On donne à boire et à manger* (he admitted to having stayed at the comfortable Hotel Hauser, though, not without shame).

Mark Twain's lament for the Holy Land may have been a turn-off for some, but it couldn't by any means stop the continuing flow of travellers. By the end of the 1860s, right after Twain's visit, the travel entrepreneur Thomas Cook, who had been working in Great Britain until then, began to bring pilgrims and tourists to the Orient; travel conditions had already fundamentally improved and the road between Jaffa and Jerusalem was now passable for carriages. The Palestine tour led by Cook usually included 60 travellers, 80 servants, 21 sleeping tents and various horses. In addition to the Solomon's Pools, the Church of the Holy Sepulchre and the birthplace of Jesus in Bethlehem, the destinations included missions, mosques, ancient synagogues and Roman ruins, thus demonstrating already a somewhat more varied understanding of the country's history. Cook's typical itinerary led south from Jaffa via Gaza and Beersheba to Jerusalem, from there to the Dead Sea, Jericho, Samaria, Nazareth, Cana, the Sea of Galilee, Baalbek and on to Beirut.

As a former Baptist minister, Cook was very passionate about these activities; entrepreneurial profit was not his top priority. Nevertheless, he himself refrained from praying under the mosaics of the Church of the Holy Sepulchre and did not kneel where the empty tomb of Jesus is said to be. In doing so, he clearly set himself apart from both Roman Catholics and members of the Orthodox churches. As might be expected, he also had no interest in religious souvenirs. When his son John later joined the company, he is said to have frequently come to blows with his father because he was pushing harder for the company's profitability.

Through a wide network of Bedouins, Arabs and consuls from many countries Cook recruited trustworthy guides, porters and drivers who welcomed the travellers as soon as the steamships arrived in Jaffa and never left their side from then on. Hotels were contracted in Jerusalem, including the Mediterranean Hotel run by Moses Hornstein in the Old City of Jerusalem, where Mark Twain, Herman Melville and the American President Ulysses S. Grant, among others, stayed.

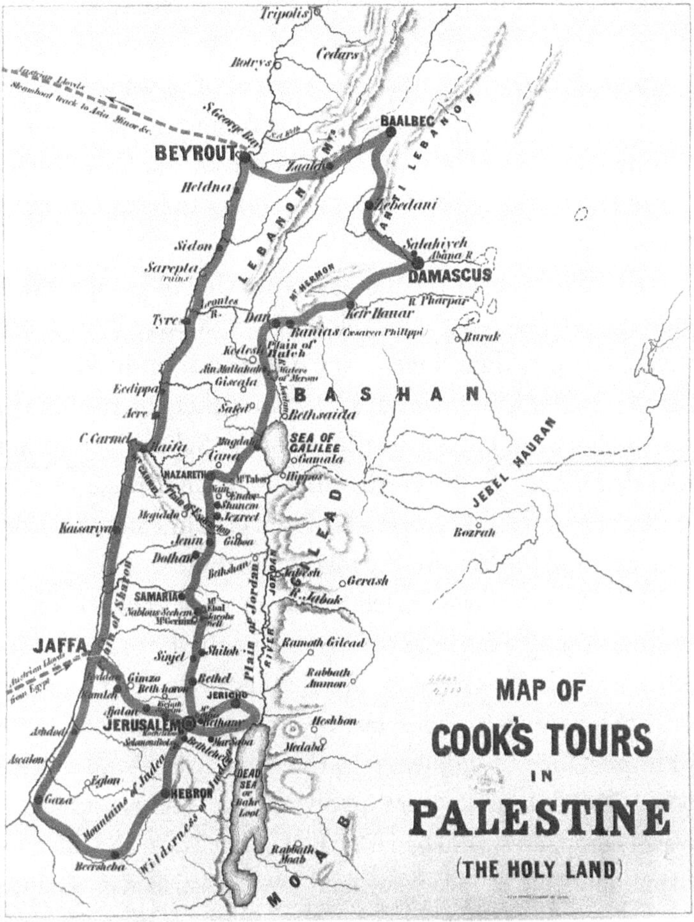

FIGURE 6. Map of Thomas Cook's Tours in Palestine (1873).

The majority of the tourist groups consisted of Americans, Brits and Germans, who carried bibles and hymn books as well as maps and travel guides. Cook's activities provoked mixed feelings among foreigners who had settled there permanently. "They come like locusts into a room, and it is hard for habitues to find board and lodging during their stay," Isabel Burton described the arrival of one of his groups in Jerusalem in 1871. Locals would speak of "Cookii" to refer to the travellers. Burton continued: "The caravans are menageries of curious human bipeds. Surely the enterprising Mr. Cook must advertise for his incongruous assemblage and the pick and choose the queerest." Burton ironically refers to her own journey to Jerusalem in her book as "our Haj to Jerusalem".

The advantage for the foreigners arriving in groups was, of course, that they were not exploited or treated as it often happened to individual travellers. Cook also supported philanthropic causes with his groups by visiting them on the itineraries, such as the Jaffa-Tabeetha Mission School, which was founded in 1863 by the Presbyterian Scot Jane Walker-Arnott. It was one of the first schools for Arab girls in Palestine. Cook had acquired the land for the mission in this case.

The influx of travellers led to the opening of various small stores, money exchange offices, souvenir shops, and cafés. Also, Thomas Cook & Co. was the first travel company not only to hire Jewish guides, but also to integrate historical sites of importance to Judaism into the itineraries—and not just when Jewish tourists were involved. Arab representatives of travel companies, who had long had control over the selection of suitable guides, rarely engaged Jews and also avoided businesses run by Jews. Cook was now consciously countering this trend.

Apart from this, the various Christian groups ran their own guesthouses. The "Casa Nova" of the Italian, Spanish and French Franciscans in the Christian quarter of the Old Town, the Assumptionists (Catholic order of men), the "Notre Dame de France Hostel" in the New Town, the "Prussian Hospice" of the German Lutherans in the Muslim quarter of the Old Town, the "St. Paulus Hospice" of the German Catholics outside the

Damascus Gate, and the "Austrian Hospice" in the Muslim quarter.

Repeatedly, Thomas Cook brought pilgrims from other countries to Palestine, such as groups of French Catholics. By 1882, a total of around five thousand tourists had come to the Holy Land with his company, accounting for around three quarters of all British and American visitors. The first railroad connection in the region, established between Jaffa and Jerusalem in 1892, gave his business a further boost. By the end of the century, the number had risen to around fourteen thousand persons.

In the meantime, the German publisher Baedeker started to print travel guides for the region, adding the curious understatement that the Holy Land was "the best guide to the Bible". The British rival publisher John Murray, on the other hand, declared the Bible itself to be "the best guide to the Holy Land." To be sure, there was plenty to tell. In the first edition of the Baedeker volume *Palestine and Syria. Handbook for Travellers* (1876), Albert Socin, a German professor of Oriental languages, wrote: "Palestine and Syria cannot be considered tourist destinations in the usual sense. The country offers little in the way of natural beauty, and the type of the Orient with its wealth of colour is far more pronounced in Egypt. The main attraction of the trip is the historical memories." Socin pointed out that strict Muslims would be "extremely reluctant" to see "unbelievers" visiting their holy places, but that it was no longer forbidden. And for communication, the Protestant recommended: "Talking about religion in Palestine is just as obvious as talking about politics in Europe; in order not to divide people, it will be a good idea to exclude any exchange of opinions about it from the conversation." Socin had no particular sympathy for neither Catholics nor the local Christians.

This was followed by further suggestions for dealing with the population:

> "The foreigner should never get involved in too much intimacy with people: genuine friendship is rare in the Orient, and unselfishness is the rarest quality among Orientals. Behind all the endless expressions of friendship with which people shower Europeans, lurks self-interest and the expectation of a higher tip (baksheesh), the more the foreigner allows himself to be deceived by fine phrases." And in the passage "Rules for dealing with Orientals" Socin stated: "In Muslim houses, you must wait until the women who are in the courtyard, for example, have withdrawn to the back house or the upper rooms . . . The stranger is advised never to ask a Muslim about his wives; these relationships are considered to be under the veil (sitr). Even just looking at women on the street or in the houses is considered indecent and can even have dangerous consequences under certain circumstances."

Among the traveling souvenir dealers of the time was Moses Wilhelm Shapira, who was born in western Ukraine and emigrated to Palestine in 1856, where he converted from Judaism to Protestantism. Shapira developed a lively trade in artefacts there. These included supposedly authentic clay pots ("pseudo-Moabitica") from the Moabite period, which initially attracted the interest of archaeologists after the discovery of the Mesha Stele with its inscription, but then turned out to be fakes. Another fiasco followed when Shapira tried to sell the British Museum 15 scrolls with pieces of text from Deuteronomy, which were also quickly exposed as imitations. Shapira committed suicide the following year.

French author Pierre Loti could sing a song about Jerusalem's tourists. Magically drawn to the Holy Land, he set off on his "unbelieving pilgrimage" in 1884. He saw Christianity as being on the wane and wanted "to describe the actual aspect of its desolation and its ruins; to tell what, in our transitory epoch, is the degree of effacement suffered by its great and holy shade, which a generation soon to come will no longer be able even to discern."

That very night, he heard

> "an exalted call to prayer, reminding men of their nothingness and their death. The muezzins are shepherds standing on their earthen roofs, and they sing all together in a kind of perpetual fugue; and always it is the name of Allah, the name of Mahomet, surprising and gloomy, here, in this land of the Bible and of Christ." To him, everything seemed to have degenerated into a big spectacle: "Two more wagonettes pass us, filled with the noisy tourists of the agencies: men in sun helmets, stout women in otter caps and green veils. We were not prepared for such an encounter; and our mental reverie, our religious dream, is more than ever disconcerted. Oh, their bearing, their noisy chatter, their laughter on this holy ground to which we have come, humbly pensive, by the old road of the prophets!"

And he obviously mislead many with his skilful play of garments and identities:

> "Finally there is the pretence of our Arab costumes, which we wear to-day for the last time—they mystify two parties of tourists making their way to Hebron: for while they are staring at us as if we were great sheiks, their Syrian guide explains that we are Moghrebis—that is to say, men from that vague Moghreb (Occident) which, for the Arabs of

FIGURE 7. The steps leading to the Holy Sepulchre (between 1898 and 1914).

Palestine, begins in Egypt and ends in Morocco. On this side of the desert, indeed, the long veils of white wool in which we are enveloped are not worn, and are an immediate indication of distinguished pilgrims from the west."

The darkness of the Church of the Holy Sepulchre then demanded his full attention. On the steps down into the Chapel of St. Helena, he encountered "begging cripples, half-witted creatures covered with ulcers" cowering at the sides. But then a ray of hope: "Amongst these poor scarecrows is a young man, blind, enveloped in his magnificent fair curls as in a mantle, beautiful as the Christ he strangely resembles." He observed some Abyssinian priests coming out of a subterranean room,

> "who might be taken for the ancient Wise Kings issuing from the bowels of the earth: black faces under large gilt tiaras shaped like turbans, long robes of cloth of gold ornamented with imaginary red and blue flowers. Hurriedly, with that sort of excited eagerness which is customary here, they cross the crypt of Saint Helena and ascend towards the other sanctuaries by the wide ruinous staircase—illuminated on the first steps by the light which falls from the loopholes of the vault, archaically splendid then in their golden robes amid the squatting gnomes at the foot of the walls—and then suddenly disappear above in the dark distance."

There is something masochistic in the way Loti, the disillusioned romantic, visited the places each time in the expectation of finding something that could breathe new life into his faith in this ancient land where "one can scarcely distinguish the real rocks from the debris of human buildings, the remains of churches and fortresses, of funerary mounds and tombs that are made one with the mountain."

As much as all this put him off, he still found it fascinating. There were the Russian pilgrims in the church of Bethlehem, "whose eyes, it's true, are filled with tears", the "chattering tourists with their Baedekers". And young women moving about, "very simply pretty all of them, under the whiteness of these veils which accentuate a strange resemblance, especially when they carry in their arms a little child: one might imagine, at each turning of the dark old streets, that he saw appearing the Virgin Mary, such as she is shown to us in the pictures of our Primitives."

Perhaps it is precisely his melancholy mood, so often bordering on despair, that allowed him to delve into the historical depths of the city, pondering the "transience of religions and empires". The blue pavilion near the blue mosque, for example, prompted him to think about "Jerusalem's terrible past":

> "This blue kiosk, near the blue Mosque, would alone suffice to tell of the tremendous past of Jerusalem. Its double row of marble columns is, as it were, a museum of relics of every epoch; there are capitals there of all kinds; Greek, Roman, Byzantine and Hebrew; and some of unknown age, of savage and unknown style. But now over all this has descended the tranquillity of death; the remains of so many hostile sanctuaries have been grouped together, in honour of the God of Islam, in an unlooked-for harmony—to remain so perhaps indefinitely, until the final return to dust."

The "Turkish friend on duty", as he was often derisively referred to because of his unclouded love of Turkey, summed up soberly: "But those times have gone by for ever and the eyes of men are directed now towards the countries of the west and north, where the new ages are beginning, fearful and chilling; and these ruins here will never be rebuilt; and no one will come any more to Palestine, save some last pilgrims, rare and solitary, and in addition perhaps a certain select few of curious idlers, worse profaners than Saracens or Bedouins."

Loti's "anxious pilgrimage" came to an end "like a drop of useless water into the immense gulf of things past and forgotten."

Walking the Fine Line Between Irritation and Fascination— Encounters with Bedouins in the Desert

AT THE TIME, Bedouins were often associated with the "Israelites", the study of their nomadic way of life promised certain insights into the distant past—at least that was the idea. In any case, they aroused more fascination than sedentary Muslims and were usually treated with more benevolence in the descriptions. For many French authors, they represented an ideal society that had not yet been corrupted by civilization. The scientist Jean-Marie Dubois-Aimé, who was a member of Bonaparte's expedition, was not at a loss to project the ideals of the French Revolution onto the Bedouins: Equality, liberty and fraternity.

Only in exceptional cases did Bedouins play a role at the level of local rule in Ottoman lands. From 1847, for example, the Bedouin leader Aqil Agha was the most important power in Lower Galilee: the commander of an "irregular" force of the Ottoman

FIGURE 8. Bedouins in front of their tent, photograph taken by Maison Bonfils.

Empire. Despite several attempts, authorities did not succeed in disempowering him until 1864.

Whether or not Bedouins eventually turned out to be a real threat to travellers depended on several factors. The Ottomans wanted them to settle down so that they could be subjected to control and become useful citizens, as they would then no longer be able to avoid taxation and military service. The Bedouins therefore contented themselves with making makeshift renovations to ruins or building very simple houses that were not difficult to leave. As the Ottoman Empire or its local representatives lost power and access, control over the Bedouins was increasingly lost and they now pushed into regions they had previously avoided, which in turn increased the likelihood of encounters with overland travellers. Conversely, over time, travellers increasingly moved away from the usual routes to explore regions that were in the hands of Bedouins.

Seetzen drew an interesting comparison: "The extraordinary care that the European police take for public safety, and the severe and unavoidable punishment that threatens robbers if they are caught, makes these people far more dangerous with us than here. Our robbers often feel compelled to resort to abuse, even murder, in order to protect themselves against the danger of being betrayed, even if the robbed person is unarmed and does not defend himself at all. The local robber, on the other hand, and these are all Bedouins almost without exception, never needs to resort to such cruel means, as he fears no punishment and expects no disgrace from his acquaintances, but rather honour for a robbery."

Seetzen's conclusion is likely to have met with some fierce opposition: "The Bedouin really is a humane robber; if you do not resist him, you can always be sure that he will leave you as much clothing as is sufficient to cover and warm you at all times. . . . The Arab, on the other hand, behaves quite differently towards his enemies, he often shows himself to be truly cruel, sometimes sparing neither child nor woman in such attacks." Seetzen speaks from experience, as he himself was the victim of an attack and was lucky to have only lost his watch and turban; his papers were left with him. The fact that he was otherwise not harmed is most likely due to the fact that he showed no resistance.

De Chateaubriand was among those unfortunate ones who actually experienced a violent confrontation with Bedouins first-hand when he was attacked by a troop of them on his way to Mar Saba, a Greek Orthodox monastery in the desert of Judah. He was only able to flee behind the walls of the monastery with great difficulty after a battle. De Chateaubriand assumed that the Bedouins' ways had begun to deteriorate as a result of their lively intercourse with the Turks and Europeans. He had the impression that they gave away their wives and daughters and murdered the traveller, whom they would have otherwise only plundered.

After Ida Pfeiffer had traversed "the most terrible rocky paths, gorges and bends" near the Dead Sea, she came across a Bedouin camp:

> "We rode up to their tents and asked them for a drink of water, instead of which, with true kindness of heart, they gave us several bowls of delicious buttermilk. In all my life I have probably never enjoyed anything with such delight and desire as this cooling drink after such a strenuous, arduous ride in the great heat. When Count Z. wanted to give them money, they didn't take it. The chief approached us and shook hands with some of them as a sign of friendship, because from the moment you enjoy something with the Bedouins or Arabs or ask them for their protection, you are not only completely safe among their horde, but you would even be defended by them against attacks from others to the death. Only in the open is it not advisable to encounter them. Their customs and traditions are so contradictory!"

Pfeiffer was undaunted:

> "I would almost like to believe that some travellers only describe robberies and dangerous incidents that they have not experienced in order to make their stories sound more interesting. I made a great journey, sometimes through very precarious regions, often quite alone with an Arab servant, and nowhere did I encounter any serious misadventure."

Charles van de Velde set off for Masada and the south-west coast of the Dead Sea, relying on Bedouins:

> "Their roving propensity nevertheless did not belie itself, for instead of going straight on as we did, they went off to the left and right like bloodhounds, without any conceivable reason for their doing so, except their own peculiar habits; for, as they themselves said, there was no reason to apprehend danger. But the Bedouin is always seeing something, though nobody else may see it,—a bird, some game, or whatever else it may happen to be. Thus, for example, one of these guides came to me unexpectedly with half-a-score of partridges' eggs, which he had discovered under some solitary bush"—which was a welcome reason for the guide to ask for a baksheesh.

Bedouins repeatedly turned to him for medical advice. He was irritated by the frequent gunshot wounds, which he wanted to treat with a cauterizing iron, which the victims always refused. Gradually, he managed to find peace in a tent with the Bedouins: "The poor Bedouins, although nominally attached to the Mohammedan faith, can hardly be said to have any religion at all. They seemed, nevertheless, to understand me when I besought them to leave me alone with my Bible."

Ignorant travellers were easy prey for the local guides. De Velde mentioned a Bedouin called Abû Dahûk:

> "Show him that you are anxious to recognize in every stone squared off by the hand of nature a piece of antiquity; excite his covetousness by presenting him continually with piastres, whenever he shews you something that he calls a ruin; and you may be certain that he will shew you ruins (khurbets) every quarter of an hour, with names and sur—names;

> if not near you, then, at all events, at a distance. This is the reason that, in those regions of the Bedouins, one hears of so many names mentioned by some travellers, which other travellers are never able to re-find."

Van de Velde recognized the inescapable dilemma in which the travellers found themselves when they wanted to explore the less explored southern and eastern parts of the country: They had to make "a sort of contract" with them. And while they were dependent on the Bedouins as guides, they were also at the mercy of their not always honourable behaviour.

Mary Eliza Rogers painted a rather conciliatory picture: "The real poetry of the country is unwritten. It is the every-day language of the people. They are all—more especially the Bedouins and the peasants—unconscious poets. Their natural artistic feeling, and their sense of beauty and fitness, are shown in their costumes, which are always harmonious in colour, and never embroidered except with pure and graceful designs. They show their skill and taste in the simple and appropriate forms of their home-made lamps, jars, dishes, stoves, and other articles of domestic use, which they model in clay and expose to the sun till they are thoroughly baked."

In the second half of the nineteenth century, the Tamira—Bedouins living between Jerusalem and the Dead Sea—realized that they were not only in demand as guides for groups on their excursions, but could also stage spectacles that would appeal to the visitors, in which a certain degree of thrill was deliberately factored in. A certain Hermann von Wedewer, a theology teacher from Wiesbaden, who undertook his journey with the unnamed Russian prince "O." and meant for his readers to "see and get to know many things that remain closed to most pilgrims, since the connections of a Russian prince in this country are extraordinarily powerful", noted in *A Voyage to the Orient* (1877):

> "Around a fire, which lit up the square in the darkness, we saw the wild, brown figures of about 20 sturdy Bedouins. Their women, dressed from head to toe in a large, linen shirt of blue colour, stood behind them in a row, leaning gracefully on each other. After we had taken our seats on field chairs, the men divided into two choirs, which moved against each other in slow, solemn steps to a monotonous melody sung by the women and swayed gracefully back and forth. . . . Then they drew their crooked swords from their sheaths and swung them above their heads. . . . Now the beat changed and quickly and ever faster they moved against each other, representing two enemy battle lines, and wildly and ever more wildly they swung their swords, until finally the passionate, rapid turning and leaping forward, the softening and bending down, swaying in the most fantastic and incredible way on their knees and the wild swinging of the steel looked extremely similar to a real battle."

To which extent such theatrical productions were based on the reality of Bedouin life didn't really matter to the visitors.

New Settlers in the Holy Land

UNTIL WELL into the 1830s, the only communities of Western Christians living in Palestine were the members of Catholic orders, namely Franciscans and Carmelites. As ambitiously as the Americans early on pursued their settlements in Palestine, their success did not match that of the Württemberg Templers from the second half of the nineteenth century on. The so-called Templer Society had its origins in a Pietist movement that emerged in Germany in the seventeenth century, which was inspired by the belief that it could breathe new life into the Protestant church. The central figure was the Bible scholar Johann Albrecht Bengel, who was convinced that Jesus would return in 1837 and begin his millennial reign.

The impetus for further development came from Leonberg-born theologian Christoph Hoffmann. The actual Templer Society developed in the 1850s after Hoffmann had returned from Frankfurt and met the merchant Georg David Hardegg.

The Templers' interest in Jerusalem was related to economic hardship experienced in Württemberg. But they also believed that the approaching 400th anniversary of the Turkish conquest of Constantinople signalled the end of the "deniers of God." The Crimean War, which the Ottoman Empire was only able to win with the help of European powers, reinforced the feeling among many that the Turks would sooner or later lose control of Palestine.

The Templers saw the Holy Land as a refuge from all evil. Could the gathering of the "people of God" in Jerusalem restore the world order, which had fallen apart at the seams, and overcome the famine in Württemberg? The Templers were firmly convinced. Christoph Hoffmann's brother Wilhelm, a confidant of the Prussian king, founded the "Jerusalem Association" in Berlin in 1852 together with Friedrich Adolph Strauss, which worked to represent the Protestant Church in the Holy Land and to proselytize the locals.

In the summer of 1854, the "Society for the Gathering of the People of God in Jerusalem" was announced in Ludwigsburg and candidates were appointed to set off for the Holy Land and found a settlement there. However, their arrival in Palestine in 1858 was ill-fated: in an attack by Arabs, some Germans and Americans, participants in a settlement project near Jaffa, had just been seriously injured or killed. After travelling through the country for three months and assessing the situation, the three Templers returned to Germany disillusioned. In view of the hostile attitude of the Muslim inhabitants and the Turkish government, they did not consider settlement to be promising. So, the decision was made to send only four missionaries at first. However, no one could have expected their fate: One converted to Islam, another joined a mission hostile to the Templers, another died of malaria and the fourth disappeared without a trace.

During this time, disturbing news reached Europe from Lebanon. In June 1860, Druze stormed the Catholic monastery of Deir El Mochalles, two women's monasteries and two Maronite monasteries, set them on fire, beat the monks to death and defiled the nuns. Around three hundred Christians were killed. Although the Muslim governor was ordered to put a stop to the riots between the two groups, he continued to incite the Druze and even supplied them with weapons. One reason for this was that the French, who were the protecting power of the Maronites, had ensured in the Treaty of Paris in 1856 that the Maronites would no longer be subject to special taxation in future. Around six thousand Christians fell victim to the massacre. In 1861, the Templers left the church and elected Hoffmann as their bishop. Things came to a head in 1866: many Templers feared that they would have to fight with France, which they hated, against Prussia. They were encouraged to emigrate by the news from Palestine that 156 Americans had just arrived there to set up a settlement. Rumours also spread that Jews were planning to emigrate to the Holy Land, which the Templers perceived as potential competition for their settlement project. After the philanthropist and founder of the Red Cross Henry Dunant called on the world powers to rebuild the Orient and Palestine in 1863, Hardegg travelled to Paris to ask Dunant for support and money for the Templers' settlement project. In the end, however, the agreement concluded was not worth much because Dunant invested his entire fortune in agriculture in Algeria and lost it in the process. His reputation was destroyed and any further ability to act was ruined.

At the end of October 1868, Hoffmann and Hardegg finally reached Haifa with the firm intention of starting the settlement, but without having received a *ferman*, a written decree and letter of protection, from the Sublime Porte. An Ottoman citizen arranged the first plots of land, as the Germans were not allowed to purchase land, and the first buildings were erected with the help of Arab workers. During the first seven years, hundreds of Templers arrived in the country. After agriculture and viticulture were not very successful—the soil quality was poor and the vines were infested with pests—the settlers switched to other tasks: Many became involved in transportation, others as plasterers. The Templers introduced wagons as a means of transportation and started a regular carriage service between Haifa and Acre. This was followed by another colony in Jaffa, from where the increasing numbers of new Jewish arrivals were brought to Jerusalem. The travel agent Thomas Cook concluded a contract with the settlers for the transportation of its tourists in the country. Craft products were offered in a store, among other places, where wealthy Arabs were among the most important customers.

Soon, another swampy area was acquired for a new colony that was given the name "Sarona"—an hour away from the Jaffa colony, where the north of Tel Aviv is located today. Several settlers fell victim to malaria until—following an Algerian example—eucalyptus trees were planted. At this time, it was still assumed that the essential oil of the tree had a disinfectant effect. It took some time until it was understood that the planting of the trees would dry out the area and thus deprive the mosquitoes of their breeding grounds.

Coexistence with the locals was overshadowed by considerable problems. The Muslim population perceived the Templers as unwanted intruders and the Germans' deep-seated prejudices towards them stood in the way of unbiased encounters. There was talk, for example, of the Arabs being "inherently impudent and conceited" or, as Christoph Paulus, one of Hoffmann's successors, wrote, they "should first be made into human beings before they can become Christians". Or even that the German settler "will hopefully never make friends with the natives in such a way that he finds pleasure and companionship in their midst". Yet the relationship between the settlers and the native or Arab Christians was apparently hardly any better than that between them and the Muslims. Unsurprisingly, the Templers were also not on good terms with the Carmelites, a religious community founded around 1150 on Mount Carmel, which was under the protectorate of the Greek Orthodox community. In 1898, the Arabic newspaper *al-Ahram* accused the German settlers of enriching themselves at the expense of the local population, "throwing themselves on the natives like leeches to suck them dry".

Even though the "Christian butchery" feared by the settlers did not occur, there were repeated serious attacks from both sides. The settlers feared being dispossessed and expelled. But there is also evidence of harmonious coexistence: when Jakob Schumacher, an architect from Tübingen and "Prussian", as he was often referred to, died in 1891 (he had first emigrated to America in 1848 before reaching Palestine in 1869 and had long served as the American consul in Haifa), many Muslims also came to bid him farewell.

Although there was no real threat to the continued existence of the settlements, the Templers had to repeatedly assert their interests against obstacles from the Ottoman authorities. The German government denied them the much-desired support. And when Germany and Turkey formed an alliance, it seemed completely hopeless that the Templers would ever be able to strengthen their position in Palestine, let alone "inherit" the country.

From the 1880s onwards, Jews came to the country in two waves (the so-called first "aliyah", literally "ascent"), for the most part fleeing the pogroms in Russia and Romania, and, supported by Baron Rothschild, founded agricultural schools and colonies. As Barbara Tuchman reminds in *Bible and Sword,* "nine tenths of the Jews were not Montefiores and Rothschilds, but submerged minorities living on the edge of subsistence. These enthusiasts failed to realize that the Jews who wanted to go to Palestine had neither money nor influence . . . and that the Jews who had money and influence did not want to go to Palestine. . . . Among the grand dukes only Rothschild (after the death of Montefiore) had faith in Palestine. . . . The family scoffed. They called his Palestine colonies "la fantaisie du Baron."

In 1882, twenty Russian families settled on the sand dunes of Jaffa, naming their moshav village Rishon LeZion ("First in Zion", today a large city south of Tel Aviv) and initially focused on viticulture. They too were actually prohibited from acquiring land by an edict issued by the Sultan in 1885, which expressly forbade the formation of Jewish colonies. But they knew how to make do through intermediaries. By 1889, they had over 76,000 acres spread over 22 settlements, in which around five thousand people lived.

The beginnings were marked by several setbacks. Many of the farmers, who came from what is now Ukraine, found that the maize and wheat varieties they were familiar with were not suitable for cultivation.

The Templers initially welcomed the Jewish immigrants because they gave the transportation system a boost. However, they were soon perceived as economic competitors rather than customers. There were even business boycotts by the Germans against the Jews. However, this did not last long because both groups realized that they also benefitted from each other.

When the activities of the Zionist movement were intensifying towards the end of the century, this unsettled the Germans already living there. They assumed that "Jewish gold" was being transferred to the Sultan to balance his finances so that he would allow the Jewish settlement of Palestine. The expert on colonial agriculture and later president of the Zionist Organization Otto Warburg emphasized, in the magazine *Altneuland* in 1904, the merits of the "Palestinian Germans" for the spread of Western culture in the Orient and their role as a "natural link between the Orient and the Occident": "With true Swabian tenacity, these people have understood how to adapt to Oriental living conditions without losing their German nationality—both internally and externally." And he added: "Nevertheless, there is little sign of the colonies making strong progress . . . so that some of the new generation prefer to seek their fortune elsewhere in the world." In any case, Warburg's intervention helped to calm things down for the time being. His comments can probably also be understood as a piece of wishful thinking with regard to the future of the next generation.

Time and again, obstacles were placed in the way of Jewish immigration. In 1892, a group of 200 Iranian Jews were sent back at the border—presumably because they could not count on the support of a European consulate. It is important to note, however, that the Ottoman Empire's resistance to Jewish immigration was not so much based on the fear that the balance of power could shift regarding the ratio of non-Muslim to Muslim population in the country, but rather that immigrants from Europe were under the legal protection of their respective countries and could thus at least partially evade the grip of the Turks.

Africa played a role in another context besides the one mentioned above. In the late 1890s, tens of thousands of Eastern European Jews found refuge in London's East End, a fact that drew the displeasure of the population. In 1903, the British colonial minister Joseph Chamberlain put forward the idea of a "New Jerusalem" on the plateau of Uasin Gishu, part of the protectorate of East Africa (today in Kenya), to Theodor Herzl.

The plan bears the official name "Uganda Plan" and the unofficial name "Jewganda". In a Jewish settlement colony on an area of around 13,000 square kilometres, the members would be able to "cultivate their national customs". The *Jewish Chronicle* expressed outrage: instead of returning to the "ancestral homeland of the race", the Jews were to establish a "settlement among semi-wild tribes, far from the climes of civilization". "Is Zion to be exchanged for Kikuyu and the cedars of the Lebanon for the Taru jungle?"

At the Zionist Congress in Basel, which took place in the same year, the plan was described as "night asylum", yet it divided the Zionists. Finally, an expedition was sent, whose verdict was negative. The matter also failed due to the resistance of British colonists who had already given options on the land. However, as Barbara Tuchman wrote: "England thus became the first country to negotiate officially with the Jews as a political entity and the first to make them an offer for territory."

Images of the Holy Land

HOW DID Europeans imagine Jerusalem and the Holy Land? Until the nineteenth century, depictions of Palestine were mostly limited to descriptions—with exceptions such as the illustrated book by Bernhard von Breidenbach mentioned earlier. Painters of the Baroque and Renaissance periods consistently transferred biblical scenes to their European settings and landscapes. Later woodcuts, engravings and drawings, inspired by reports from other sources, conveyed a certain idea of what the landscape looked like. This applies, for example, to William Turner, who contributed drawings for the engravings in the lavishly designed volume *Landscape Illustrations of the Bible* (1836),which were based on sketches travellers had made on location. The Catholic artist Gustave Doré created 241 wood engravings to illustrate the Bible (*La grande bible de Tours*, published in 1866); these scenes were set in oriental-looking landscapes. Doré is said to have trained his eye for dramatic natural phenomena and rugged cliffs during his hikes in the Vosges mountains.

One of the best-known artists who actually took the trouble to visit there was the Protestant Scotsman David Roberts (Sim, 1984). In 1838/39, he travelled through Egypt, Nubia, the Holy

FIGURE 9. The Scottish artist David Roberts travelled to the Holy Land in 1838/39. Here, a group of people who appear to be pilgrims prepare for the last stage to Jerusalem.

Land, Jordan and Lebanon. Together with Louis Haghe, he produced a large number of lithographs and paintings based on sketches and watercolours he had made on the way. Their journey was a difficult one, in the company of armed servants and a group of Bedouins with no fewer than twenty-one camels. Roberts is regarded as the first artist to be allowed to draw in mosques, although only under the condition that he put on oriental clothing, shaved his moustache and gave up his brushes made with pig bristles. Later on, critics accused Roberts of taking considerable liberties in the depiction of the panoramic landscapes. In general, there was a marked tendency among most artists traveling in the Holy Land to purge their depictions of ugly or even offensive elements.

Among the handful of American painters who travelled to Palestine the aforementioned Frederic Church, usually associated with the Hudson River School, has a special place. After spending years exploring and painting landscapes of South America, Maine, Jamaica, and the Arctic he went to the Old World in the autumn of 1867, accompanied by Isabel, his wife, his mother-in-law and their young son. They rushed trough England and France, taking a ship from Marseilles to Alexandria, relinquishing a planned trip to Cairo, moving on to Jaffa and then to Beirut—it was the Middle East that exerted particular attraction to Church. In Jerusalem he happened to meet Charles Warren, the head of the field operation of the British Palestine Exploration Fund, which was a scientific enterprise under the patronage of Queen Victoria that made a significant contribution to Palestinian archaeology and geography, but also provided the groundwork for a Western conquest of Ottoman territories. Church then became involved with the American Palestine Exploration Society (APES), being the only artist member among fifty ministers, missionaries, industrial magnates and explorers. Founded in New York in the early 1870s, the organization undertook various survey expeditions with the aim of mapping the Holy Land. As John Davis states in *The Landscape of Belief*, "It would be difficult to overestimate the significance of Church's involvement with this organization; it is perhaps the most concrete tie known to exist between the acquisitive, ideologically charged enterprise of Palestinian exploration and the painted depictions of its landscape. In the publications of the society, covert and overt appeals were repeatedly made to racist, imperialist, or nationalist sentiments".

Among the large Middle Eastern canvasses that Church executed, *Jerusalem from the Mount of Olives* occupies a unique spot. Extremely intricate in detail, with various important buildings of Jerusalem in the far distance, it wasn't easily accessible. In fact, Goupil's Gallery in New York where it was on display, provided the visitors with an engraved key to facilitate the understanding.

After their stay they went via Constantinople to Rome. Church kept fond memories of the Middle East: "In all Europe I have seen nothing to equal the Syrian landscape for the brightest qualities. . . . Syria, with its barren mountains and parched valleys possess the magic key which unlocks our innermost heart."

Since in Islam images of living beings were strongly discouraged, early photographic works had been created by Western or non-Muslim artists, some of whom had studios in Cairo and Constantinople. Photographers such as the Englishman James Robertson and the Italian Felice Beato came to the Holy Land in the 1850s to capture the settings of the Bible on camera—these images were compiled in the album *Jerusalem* and published in Constantinople in 1864. Since the 1860s, there had been several photo studios in Jerusalem, the best known of which was that of the French-Huguenot Bonfils family, which also had branches in Beirut, Baalbek, Alexandria and Cairo. It sold photos of the holy sites and had locals pose in their typical costumes. A few decades later, the Armenian priest Garabed Krikorian opened his own studio—after he had left his convent. He learned to photograph from the Armenian Patriarch of Jerusalem, Yesayi Garabedian, who operated a studio in St. James' Monastery as early as 1850 and is considered a pioneer of the profession in this region. Krikorian later also benefited from the travellers brought to the country by Thomas Cook & Co. Models were often used flexibly, only their respective costumes changed. For example, the same person could be both the Chief Rabbi of Jerusalem and a mattress maker. Occasionally, praying

FIGURE 10. Jerusalem from the Mount of Olives by Frederic Church (1870).

Muslims who could not be persuaded to model were imitated by Christians or beggars. (There is a parallel here to the orientalist paintings of baths and harems—prostitutes sometimes served as nude models, who were then sparingly adorned with oriental textiles).

Palestine always represented a special attraction at World Fairs. At the one in London in 1851, a "large, moving diorama of the Holy Land" illustrating the "Exodus of the Israelites" was on display in the Egyptian Hall. Musicians, Singers and actors from Syria and the Holy Land performed there. The Old City of Jerusalem was built in miniature for the 1904 World's Fair in St. Louis: The Dome of the Rock, the Wailing Wall, the Church of the Holy Sepulchre and the Tower of David were set up on an area stretching over four hectares. In order to make the representation appear as realistic as possible, locals were embarked and guided tours of the improvised "holy sites", camel and donkey rides and oriental bazaars were organized. Thomas Cook & Co. had the dragoman Khalil S. Gandour from Jaffa perform there. Members of the Cadbury family, who had travelled to Palestine with his help, enjoyed Turkish coffee and were accompanied by Gandour to the "sights" of the World's Fair.

"You cannot go to Jerusalem, so Jerusalem comes to you. To American energy all things are possible!" enthused the author Lydia Mamreoff from Finkelstein Mountford at the opening. Incidentally, she had been born in Jerusalem in 1848, the daughter of parents of noble Russian origin. Even after the turn of the century, such ethnological expositions had evidently lost none of their appeal (they were indeed staged well into the twentieth century). In the context of "Palestine in Brighton", supposedly authentic scenes were recreated: "Life in a Jerusalem house", "The Life of a Shepherd in the East", or "A Picnic in Palestine".

Since the 1860s, stereoscopes have played a certain role in the dissemination of images of the Holy Land. This device lends a second dimension to retouched landscape photos, thereby creating an impression of depth. Charles Foster Kent, an expert on the Old Testament and author of a long series of books on Hebrew history, teaching at Yale University in his later years, developed a stereoscopic journey through the Holy Land around 1900, which was very popular. He understood Palestine as the "fifth gospel", which contained hitherto inaccessible truths, and encouraged users to "go back in imagination from the ignoble present of this land into its mighty past".

A Painter Turned Emigrant—Gustav Bauernfeind

THE ARCHITECT and painter Gustav Bauernfeind, who trained at the Stuttgart Polytechnic, repeatedly visited the Orient. He was attracted by the exotic motifs and the prospect of being able to sell his works to collectors in Great Britain and America. According to his testimony, he had no religious motives; he is even said to have called himself a "heretic". Initially, Bauernfeind focused on Italian scenes, but later his self-image developed into that of an "Oriental painter".

He perfected his art in Munich. His older sister Emilie had been living in Beirut for almost a decade. Her husband Wilhelm wrote to Bauernfeind: "You won't find any Italy in Syria. You should not look for such an abundance of architectural art treasures here as there, but I should think that, despite this, an artist's eye will find a rewarding field for his studies here and will not regret a trip." He was proved right. Bauernfeind's first voyage to the Orient took place in 1880 and lasted about a year and a half. He first travelled via Athens to Alexandria, from there to Cairo and finally to Beirut and the Holy Land. Using a camera, he began to capture interesting motifs. In a letter, he characterises Jerusalem as a "stone desert", in Jaffa he is impressed by the lush vegetation and the splendour of the orange gardens. On his return to Munich, he worked on paintings and saved the money he had received from sales to an American and an Englishman living in Stuttgart for another trip. It is also recorded that he was trying to get a *firman* for a study trip through Syria and Palestine lasting several years.

His second stay in the Orient lasted three years; he moved between Damascus, Beirut and Jaffa. His activities repeatedly aroused the suspicion of the police. He reassured his relatives in Baden-Baden: "You shouldn't be worried about me, because people are far too afraid of the Europeans to dare do me any serious harm. Also, the police are too developed. After all, the worst thing that can happen to me is deportation. But even that can be denied with great certainty." After nine months, he sent his new painting to England, the *Pottery Seller*, and soon began working on *The Jews at the Gate of the Temple Square in Jerusalem,* which he later sent to the art dealer Arthur Sulley in London.

Bauernfeind spent a summer in Lebanon to escape the heat. When he returned to Jaffa, he finally managed to find a sheikh who was willing to pose for him, but unfortunately the sheikh broke his leg. Immediately, rumours spread that the sheikh had been punished by fate for sitting as a model—therefore Bauernfeind could no longer win over anyone for his project. What kept him there? "Life here is generally a chain of hardships and yet I have to say that the gang of people among whom I live here always exerts its peculiar charm on me as soon as I step out onto the street and see these original figures marching past."

At the same time, his relationship with Elise Bertsch, whom he met by chance in Jaffa while she was on her way to her sister in Jerusalem, from where she wanted to travel on to India for a long stay on behalf of the Basel Mission, began to develop. Both of them obviously quickly felt that they were meant to be together, but Bauernfeind still had to convince her that he was a devout Christian, which he affirmed in the letters he sent to her in Mangalore, India, where the Catholic bishop's see in southwest India was located. "Dear Mr. Bauernfeind! Even if I am not convinced of everything in it," Elise Bertsch replies, "I know that God will be your guide and that under His guidance you will go towards the light, towards God, and I will go with you." Bauernfeind is euphoric and believes that he was guided by God when he fell in love with her. After her stay in India was shortened and a dispute over the cost of the return journey was resolved, nothing stood in the way of their marriage. However, a few more years passed before then.

Apart from a meeting with Conrad Schick, Bauernfeind's encounters with his compatriots were of a rather unpleasant nature. During his third trip to the Orient from 1888 to 1889, at a hotel in Damascus, "no less than 8 counts, 4 Austrians and 4 Germans, the latter, with the exception of one, highly unsympathetic, haughty, monocle-twitching, faces chopped-up in duels . . . are unpleasantly noticeable all around the table".

His workload was heavy, and he had to deal with constant disruption and hostility, with his dragoman Franz supporting him. He was cursed as a "Muscovite" and "Frendschi" (European) by a sugar seller outside a mosque, and even spat at another time. His work in proximity of the mosques was regarded with particular suspicion. Among the people he sketched are a scissor grinder from Afghanistan, an African, two fellah women, a "ragged Kurd", an old sheikh, a kneading baker, a fakir, a 14-year-old boy and a blind man who plays the drums shortly before sunrise during the fasting month of Ramadan.

FIGURE 11. “The Wailing Wall” (1904) by Gustav Bauernfeind.

Bauernfeind’s plan to photograph praying Mohammedans in a mosque failed despite the help of an agent whom Bauernfeind had hired to recruit models. He demonstrated great courage when he photographed the entry of dervishes into Damascus from an elevated position, watched by thousands of spectators:

"Many dervishes on horseback behaved like raptures, or rather madmen. They fell into convulsions and fainted, the foam came out of their mouths . . . A group singing excitedly behind a flag literally shouted at me . . . The flag holder on my side fell into raptures and wanted to throw himself at me." The incident only went smoothly because other men managed to grab the flag holder in time. A week later, when Bauernfeind was again watching a pilgrimage, two men suddenly held snakes in front of his face. Thanks to the courageous intervention of his companion, worse was prevented. Bauernfeind's courage is all the more astonishing when one considers that he had hardly any knowledge of Arabic and could not easily assess a dangerous situation.

Bauernfeind's curiosity was aroused when some man told him about a mummy in a cave grave which, according to an alleged inscription on the gravestone, was supposedly several hundred years old and completely preserved, wearing a helmet and an armoured shirt. After walking the lonely path, leaving the lights of the city behind them and crawling into the grave, pursued by barking dogs, the "mummy" turned out to be a half-decomposed corpse without an armoured shirt, helmet and sword. With great difficulty, Bauernfeind managed to crawl out and leave the place.

After a few more years in Munich, he finally set off on his fourth journey with his wife and child in 1896. It lasted eight long years; little is known about its exact course. His initial destination was the colony of the German Templers in Jerusalem, but he preferred to visit the hermits in the southern Jordan Valley near Jericho, an otherwise little-visited region that looks like a lunar landscape. Among the last more detailed mentions is a visit to a Greek monastery in the area, near a Bedouin camp. Bauernfeind does not appear to have followed political developments—the war between Greece and Turkey over

Crete was officially declared during this period—and perhaps he did not have access to information about it. In a letter to his long-time confidant P. F. Krell, which he wrote in March 1898, he praised the "solemn seriousness of the late evening and early morning moods", but also mentioned his hostile view of the population: "On closer inspection, the people are repulsive. It is not only their spiritual kinship with the Jews that makes them unpleasant; in moral terms, too, they are no higher than described in some drastic chapters of the Old Testament." Despite these circumstances (or perhaps precisely because of them), Bauernfeind was enormously productive during his last years and created several large-format works of high quality. Shortly before his death, he completed his famous painting *The Wailing Wall.* In the meantime, he had become an emigrant.

Bauernfeind died in 1904 and was buried at the edge of the Templers' cemetery. His wife, suffering from tuberculosis, committed suicide two years later. "From the hospital, her coffin was placed on a small cart that was normally used to transport barrels of wine, and a half-blind Arab drove with her to the cemetery of our colony an hour away through the clouds of dust in Jerusalem. I was the only companion," her son later recalled the morbid scene.

More Americans Arrive in the Holy Land

DAVID F. DORR is one of the few documented African-American travellers to the Holy Land in the nineteenth century. He arrived before the Civil War, during the 1850s, not as a free man, but as a slave of the wealthy lawyer Cornelius Fellowes. The journey took them to Europe and the Orient. After Dorr managed to escape slavery, he published his report *A Colored Man Round the World* (1858; cited in Yothers, 2007), which also contains a few pages about the Holy Land. "I was not inclined to believe anything I heard from the people about here, because I knew as much as they did about it. I came to Jerusalem with a submissive heart, but when I heard all the absurdities of these ignorant people, I was more inclined to ridicule right over these sacred dead bodies, and spots, than pay homage", he wrote. Unlike most American travellers to the Holy Land he expressed an awareness of the economic inequalities among the people involved in the business of accommodation: "The best place to locate for a short time, is in the convent attached to the church; they make no charges against a pilgrim, but no pilgrim can come here unless rich, and no rich man will go away without giving something to so sacred a place as the tomb of the Savior."

And he recorded a surprising observation: "We took a bath in the Jordan, and tried some of its water with eau de vie, and found it in quality like Mississippi water." His conclusion about his stay in the Holy City was unequivocal: "Having stayed in the city of Jerusalem seventeen days, I leave it, never wishing to return again."

American Catholics rarely came to the Holy Land; they generally didn't have the financial means to do so. Some of them may have read de Chateaubriand's or de Géramb's books, or the books of evangelical Protestants, which they then found fault with. If they nevertheless managed to get to Jerusalem, their judgment of the local Christians was more benevolent.

Among them was Eugene Vetromile, who had previously been a missionary among the Etchemin Indians in the US state of Maine. In his book *Travels in Europe, Egypt, Arabia Petraea, Palestine and Syria* (1871), he attacked the Protestant tourists: "the less they say concerning the sacred places of the holy land, the greater service they will render to the cause of knowledge and religion", he remarks pointedly. And he tried to refute the "ridiculous stories" about the ceremonies of the Greeks, Armenians and Copts, praising their "gravity and decorum". Vetromile also listed the places charged with religious significance that are hardly observed by American Protestants.

In 1880, the Holy See founded the Franciscan Commissariat of the Holy Land for the United States in New York. In its magazine *The Crusader's Almanac,* a "new spiritual crusade" was proclaimed. The goal was not the Christian conquest of the land, as the name might suggest, but the raising of funds for Franciscan institutions, first the expansion of the "Casa Nova Hostel" in Jerusalem and the construction of a new pilgrim hostel in Nazareth: "Our Lady of America" and later the Franciscan Monastery of the Holy Land in Washington, D.C., praised for its "unmistakable Byzantine atmosphere", which included a replica of the Church of the Holy Sepulchre, the Grotto of the Annunciation in Nazareth and the Grotto of the Manger in Bethlehem. This monastery on familiar American soil may have been a welcome substitute for the costly trip to the authentic holy sites for many visitors. The first organized Catholic pilgrimage from the United States finally took place in 1889. The Greeks initially forbade the group from entering the Church of the Holy Sepulchre with its American flag bearing a cross, but the American consul managed to have the ban lifted. One of the highlights of the trip was a three-hour performance imitating the washing and burial of Jesus' body.

For the earlier-mentioned Catholic priest Andrew Edward Breen the stay in Palestine in 1904/05 was a sobering experience. Plagued by fierce doubts about the authenticity of the Church of the Holy Sepulchre and Calvary, he found some solace in the idea of being at the site of the crucifixion and resurrection: "I would die tonight with a wild joy for that everlasting truth". He found his studies at the École biblique et archéologique française de Jérusalem, the papally recognized research centre founded in 1890 in the Dominican convent of St. Étienne, a waste of time. Modern theories were put forward there, such as that Jesus had adopted the popular beliefs of the first century. Breen was indignant that the professors, "accept every extravagant opinion of the German rationalists and explorers, in their desire to be advanced". His disillusionment may have been partly due to the mumbling of the ageing professor and founder of the school, Marie-Joseph Lagrange. Nevertheless, Breen knew how to make good use of his time. His book *A Diary of My Life in the Holy*

FIGURE 12. A. E. Breen, author of *A Diary of My Life in the Holy Land* (1906) in Oriental garb.

Land (1906) is a comprehensive study of the country with many photographs.

And there were travellers who were drawn there for purely commercial reasons. George F. Train, an American travelling salesman who undertook a trip around the world, showed little restraint in his assessment of conditions in Palestine in his popular book *An American Merchant in Europe, Asia and Australia* (1857):

> "Donkeys with heavy loads of water and of dirt rubbing against you; camels with a cargo of planks or a cartload of

stone upon their backs brushing past; women with covered faces, who would do well to hide their ugliness from the gaze of man; men dirty, savage and obscene; children with sore eyes and unclean faces, and tattered rags send a chill through the frame; all men, women and children begging for backsheesh; dogs whose lean, lank form is enough to breed a famine; lizards of enormous size crawling through the fissures of holy tombs; fleas fastening upon you at every turn—verily, it is sufficient to make the heart sick to visit the Holy Land, the wreck of what it was; and those who have not visited it will best retain their respect for it by staying at home, for distance lends enchantment for the view."

It comes as no surprise that his assessment of Jerusalem was just along these lines: "I have been to Jerusalem, and have returned again, delighted and disgusted; delighted while traveling in the hallowed associations of bygone ages—disgusted at the utter desolation of nature. My ride was tedious, my lunch bad, my horse sore-footed and sore-backed. . . . Jerusalem has been so often visited and described, that I shall make myself most agreeable by saying little regarding it."

Train later thought he recognized himself in Phileas Fogg, the protagonist of Jules Verne's *Journey Around the World in 80 Days*.

Other travellers made the long journey from America, travelled in the wider area of Palestine, but then decided against a detour there. Charles W. Elliot, a Unitarian and President of Harvard University, ventured to the Middle East with his wife in the spring of 1895, but gave the Holy Land a wide berth: "I have always heard that Palestine was immeasurably less interesting than Egypt, and that traveling there was arduous."

Armenian and Russian Pilgrims

IN COMPARISON with the Palestinian Christians, the number of Armenians permanently residing in the Holy Land was smaller, but, along with Russians, they made up a significant proportion of the pilgrims. According to a report from 1820, there were one-hundred monks in the three Armenian monasteries in Jerusalem and a further two-hundred people of Armenian origin in the city. Many visitors mentioned the special orderliness of the Armenian quarter in the Old City of Jerusalem. Marie Joseph de Géramb remarked: "The best built quarter is that of the Armenians: some cleanliness is kept up there, and there is even a certain look of comfort, which only serves to make the other parts of the city appear the more hideous". Friedrich Adolph Strauss had already noticed the Armenians in Constantinople, where they had a much stronger presence. They proved, he wrote, to be "the most enlightened and pious" and had "always cultivated fellowship with the Protestants most zealously". Persecutions in their homeland have led to them being "scattered in all parts of the Orient". According to Strauss, this also had to do with the fact that patriotism was less pronounced among Armenians than among other peoples. "In the Turkish empire, they actually have trade in their hands, especially all money transactions, for which the Jews are too despised, and thus gain significant influence." Even if he considers them to be rigid in their outward forms and the way they practise their religion, he wrote: "They are characterized by refinement of manners and have preserved more profound Christian knowledge and a more vibrant life than the other Christians of the Orient." Many visitors to Jerusalem were impressed by the splendour of St. James Cathedral, the seat of the Armenian Patriarch. Others praised the Armenian monastery with its beautiful courtyards, terraces and staircases. The economic success of the Armenians, their higher level of education and the fact that they are Christians contributed to their special position in the Ottoman Empire and repeatedly gave rise to suspicions that they are trying to dismantle the empire by secretly supporting alleged Western Christian powers or Russia. Between 1894 and 1896, violence against Armenians escalated in Constantinople and in the north-east of the Ottoman Empire. This was triggered by the Anatolian Armenians' aspirations for autonomy, which were linked to the demand for equal rights. According to estimates, between one hundred thousand and several hundred thousand Armenians fell victim to the pogrom. In the period that followed, Turkish aggression was extended to Christians in the wider region.

Strangely enough, the Protestant theologian Paul Rohrbach, who travelled to Russia, Turkestan, Armenia and Palestine in 1898, made no mention of these events. Rohrbach wrote in 1903, expressing his sympathies more than almost any other prominent German Christian: "Armenians are and will remain the salt of the land in economic terms, both within and outside their immediate and closest homeland. Without them, economic prosperity is not possible under the present circumstances and for a long time to come. To have failed to recognise this is a serious mistake on the part of the Turks, which has taken severe revenge and will probably take revenge in the future." While Rohrbach emphasized that the Armenians are an "Oriental people", "he tried to prove", as Maibritt Gustrau writes, "that they did not have an Oriental nature, because in terms of their educational drive, their national feeling and their intelligence. He considered them to be compatible with Western European standards. The fact that they were Aryans was also intended to reinforce their difference from the neighbouring peoples."

The complexity of Rohrbach's attitude towards Christians in the Orient is demonstrated not least by his comments related to Jerusalem: "It is not easy to convey the impression that a visit to the interior of the Church of the Holy Sepulchre makes on the educated Protestant Christian. The first thing we felt was unmixed disgust." He observed how the Greek patriarch took a box of matches from his trouser pocket and lighted the sacred fire. And he felt confirmed in his view that "the spiritual and sensual ecstasy of the ancient Near Eastern, especially the Semitic natural religions" had continued in the Orient. Rohrbach soon extended his interests to other regions and advocated German cultural imperialism and the colonial policy pursued in Africa.

In contrast to Great Britain and—to a lesser extent—France, Russia had neither pronounced trade interests nor a strong consular presence in the Ottoman provinces (the Orthodox Constantine Bazili, who acted as consul in Beirut, is worth mentioning), but showed a stronger interest in the religious affairs of Palestine from the second half of the century onwards. Influence on Syria was to be strengthened via religious networks. High-ranking church representatives were sent to pave the way for sovereignty over the Greek Orthodox Church in the

Holy Land. In the 1840s, the Tsarist government established a Russian Orthodox mission in Jerusalem. Russia shared the Eastern Orthodox rite with the largest Christian community in Syria, where they made up around a third of Christians. The Tsar called on all believers to make donations for the pilgrims, as up to this time only a few hundred had set off for the Holy Land each year.

The Russian Orthodox Imperial Palestine Society created a network of facilities for pilgrims along the travel routes between Russia and the Holy Land through Ottoman territories that were far beyond the reach of the Tsarist authorities. Soon, ten to fifteen thousand pilgrims a year were coming from Odessa by steamship to Jaffa to attend Orthodox Easter, visit holy sites and bathe or be baptized in the Jordan River. Western visitors often lumped these pilgrim groups in with the Orthodox Greeks, especially as there was hardly ever any personal contact.

As the number of Russians continued to increase in the second half of the nineteenth century and they began to appear in their typical clothing—coming from the Tartary and dressed in sheepskins, for example—they were easier to recognize as such. They could also be recognized by their black bread and the samovars they carried with them for making tea. The women liked to use old umbrellas as walking sticks. Simple buildings were erected especially for the Russian pilgrims. Their presence could no longer be overlooked and was viewed with suspicion from various sides, not least by the Greeks. They were convinced that the Tsar was determined to completely separate the Muscovite Church from the Greek Church and break off the remaining links with the Greek Patriarch residing in Constantinople.

For many Western pilgrims, the sight of the Russians offered the opportunity to clearly distinguish themselves from them and reassure themselves of their own alleged superiority. The American lawyer and journalist Charles Dudley Warner did not mince his words in his book *In the Levant* (1876): "These people will need to make a good many more pilgrimages, and perhaps to quit their morose land altogether, before they can fairly rank among the civilized of the earth." Although Warner did not have much good to say about them, he was nevertheless interested in them and realized that many of them had travelled from distant regions of the Tsarist Empire: "I spoke with a group of men and women who had walked over two thousand miles before they reached Odessa and took ship for Jaffa. There were among them Cossacks, wild and untidy, light-haired barbarians from the Caucasus, dark-skinned men and women from Moscow, representatives from the remotest provinces of great Russia; for the most part simple, rude, clumsy, honest boors."

And Warner kept a close eye on the souvenirs they bought: rosemary laid out to dry, blessed bread with the image of the Saviour stamped on it, palm branches, crowns of thorns and stalks of reeds brought from the banks of the Jordan, even tin boxes of Jordan water. A special feature of the Russian pilgrims were "long strips of cotton cloth stamped in black with various insignia of death, to serve at home for coffin-covers; there were skull-caps in red, yellow, and white, also stamped with holy images, to be put on the heads of the dead". Warner continued: "I could not but in mind follow these people to their distant homes, and think of the pride with which they would show these trophies of their pilgrimage; how the rude neighbours would handle with awe a stick cut on the banks of the Jordan, or eat with faith a bit of the holy bread. How sacred, in those homes of frost and snow, will not these mementos of a land of sun, of a land so sacred, become!"

The presence of Russian pilgrims in Jerusalem could no longer be overlooked:

> "We met this morning, outside the walls of Jerusalem, the funeral procession of a Russian pilgrim—for many of them die, alas! in the course of their journeys to Palestine—an old woman, her face of yellow wax uncovered, borne along by other matushkas [wives of Orthodox priests]. And hundreds of pilgrims, men and women, follow; all the old faded petticoats are there; all the old fur caps; all the grey beards of the moujiks, the whole sordid and dark-coloured crowd. But faith triumphant radiates from their eyes, and they sing together a canticle of joy. They deem her happy, envy her, who has died in this holy land."

Over time, these believers became increasingly hostile in their own country. When the British, Russian-speaking writer Stephen Graham accompanied a group of Russian pilgrims embarking from Odessa for the Levant in 1913, he witnessed the contempt with which crew members punished the passengers. The mood in the country had been changing for several years and the revolution was just around the corner. The people who sympathized with the revolutionaries had wanted nothing to do with the pilgrims accused of religious "superstition".

An Imperial Caravan

IN THE SECOND half of the nineteenth century a trip to the Holy Land was part of the itinerary of many European aristocrats and dignitaries. Prince Edward, who later became King of England, came to the Holy Land in 1862 and had a cross tattooed on his arm as a memento. His son, the Duke of York, who later became King George V, came two decades later and also had one tattooed, albeit on his nose, which was later removed. He also placed himself in the hands of the Christian Razzouk family, whose business had a 700-year tradition. It was customary for the Copts of Egypt to have a cross engraved on the inside of their wrist—as an entrance sign for church attendance. The Razzouks had moved to the Old City of Jerusalem half a millennium before.

The Prussian Crown Prince Friedrich Wilhelm [who briefly ruled as Frederick III] visited the Holy Land in connection with the opening of the Suez Canal in 1869. His arrival in Jerusalem was preceded by a restless night in the tent camp, with biting scorpions and the howling of jackals, "some of our gentlemen even claimed to have felt such an animal in their own tent!", he records in his *Diary of my journey to the Orient.* After being received in the city by the European consuls, the highest representatives of the local churches and the cavasses, the Ottoman police officers, he went to the Church of the Holy Sepulchre, where the crown prince was familiarized with the complicated premises: "I felt bitterly disappointed by everything, but was also so confused by the conglomerate of chapels, altars, staircases and corridors that I finally became quite dizzy with courage."

In addition to visiting the mosques, there was a reception at the German consulate with the Pasha, a meeting with Germans living in Jerusalem and a Jewish deputation, as well as excursions into the city's surroundings. The highlight of his trip was taking possession of the "Muristan", the former home of the Knights Hospitaller—a gift from the Turkish government. The ceremony and handover of the document took place on the ruins on which the Protestant church would later be built. The Crown Prince's trip concluded with visits to the deaconess girls' school "Talitha Kumi" and the boys' orphanage for survivors of the victims of the persecution of Christians in Syria in 1860.

Almost three decades later, it was the second trip to the Orient for Emperor Wilhelm II and his wife Auguste Viktoria; they had already visited the Sultan in Constantinople once. In a way, their fifty-day journey resembled a traditional pilgrimage: the group chose Venice as their port of departure and Constantinople as their first destination, from there they travelled on to Jaffa and then continued in a three-kilometre-long caravan; the ride to Jerusalem took four days. In addition to politicians, a number of dignitaries from the Protestant church were also taking part, mainly from Germany, but also from Scandinavia, Great Britain, the Netherlands, Switzerland, Italy and Hungary. Even representatives of the German Protestant Synod of North America joined the convoy—as can be read in the book *The German Imperial Couple in the Holy Land* (Anon, 1899), richly filled with reports of documentary value and authorized by the

Emperor himself. They all saw themselves "as the Protestant crusaders of the nineteenth century". This allowed the Emperor to present himself as the patron of Protestantism in the Holy Land. It was to be a "journey to Palestine" "such as has never been carried out more gloriously in honour of the German people and the Christian religion". The goal was ambitiously formulated:

> "What the Occident has received from the Orient, the love that transcends the world, the German spirit should now gratefully return there and will thus try to bring light into the darkness of the Oriental peoples as the main purpose of its work . . . Into this promised land, on which the decline of two millennia weighs heavily, whose Mohammedan population lives along in dull, distrustful apathy and renunciation, joyless and peaceful, poor and frugal, and only here and there, pressed, irritated and incited, rises up to terrible, The Emperor of the mighty German Empire, united by Emperor Wilhelm the Great, moves into this country with the Empress, not as an enemy with sword and blood, not with selfish intentions, but as a friend reaching out his hand in sincere, Christian love."

In Jerusalem, a visit to the Church of the Holy Sepulchre was on the agenda, before which a walk through the Street of David had to be mastered, there was the fear that a crime may happen. As Conrad Schick commented, "a fearful secret" was kept about the day's events: "The anarchist activities were, however, a justified reason for caution; for as sharp as the Turkish police's attention was, who immediately put every suspect behind bars, some assassin could still approach the emperor with ease."

This was followed by visits to the Dome of the Rock, the Al-Aqsa Mosque and the Mount of Olives, where the Emperor plucked an olive tree branch in the Garden of Gethsemane, which was later displayed in his palace like a touching relic. The consecration of the Protestant German Church of the Redeemer in Jerusalem finally took place on October 31, 1898, not coincidentally on Reformation Day. And the Catholics did not go away empty-handed either. Sultan Abdülhamid II, in power at the time, gave the Emperor the "Dormition", a site on Mount Zion that was also considered holy by Muslims and was intended for a church, for 120,000 Reichsmark, which he in turn passed on to the "German Association of the Holy Land". (Construction of the Benedictine Dormition Abbey began in 1900).

In Bethlehem, the monarch expressed his regret that the members of the various Christian groups in the holy places are often so hostile towards each other and recalls the dispute over the "Star of Bethlehem"—not the cosmic phenomenon that (allegedly) showed the Magi the way to Bethlehem, but the silver star in a grotto in the basement of the Church of the Nativity, which marked the place where Jesus is said to have been born. When the star suddenly disappeared in 1847, Franciscans, Greeks and Armenians accused each other of stealing it, which brought France, Great Britain and Russia onto the scene. The disappearance prompted Tsar Nicholas I to demand patronage over all Christians in the Holy Land, which the Ottoman Sultan saw as an affront to his sovereignty, and France and England sided with the Turks. The star reappeared five years later, but as the tsar's demand had been rejected, he invaded the Danube principalities (Moldavia and Wallachia) under Ottoman sovereignty in 1853—this was the beginning of the Crimean War, which severely shook the balance of the five great powers and was to throw Russia back into a much weaker role.

There has been much speculation about the possible political background to the Emperor's journey. Was it a question of whether he or Germany wanted to secure a "place in the sun", strengthen relations with the Sultan, expand the military alliance with the Ottoman Empire, commission the construction of the Hejaz Railway, which was to connect Damascus with Mecca, and extend the contract for the railroad line from Berlin to Baghdad? Several factors may have been at play, but not the affirmation of a political claim by Germany to Palestine itself. However, it later became known that Turkey had already been divided into areas of interest between Berlin, Paris, London and St. Petersburg at that time. Berlin was given the zone along the Baghdad Railway, which would enable it to develop Anatolia as well as parts of present-day Syria and Iraq (historical Mesopotamia) economically—in competition with France and Great Britain.

At Saladin's grave, the Emperor left behind a laurel wreath with the inscription "from one great Emperor to another" written in Arabic. Wilhelm II was the first German Emperor to enter the Holy Land after Frederick II, a full 670 years later.

The Emperor also invited Theodor Herzl to meet him, first in Constantinople and then again in Palestine: the invitation was the reason for the founder of Zionism to travel there for the first and only time, accompanied by a delegation. The eagerly awaited meeting in Constantinople lived up to expectations; Wilhelm II and Herzl were impressed by each other. Herzl wanted to win over the Emperor as a protector of Zionism. At this time, anti-Semitism was less pronounced in Germany than in the Tsarist Empire, Austria-Hungary and France, where the Dreyfus Affair had just triggered a political earthquake.

Herzl's biographer Derek Penslar notes that Herzl was barely aware of the natural conditions of Palestine prior to his arrival. The circumstances of the journey are surrounded by a number of legends, which is why we will limit ourselves here to some of his diary entries. Regarding his first glimpse of the "Jewish coast", Herzl wrote of the "mixed feelings" they entertained when they approached "the land of our fathers". Regarding Jaffa, he noted: "poverty, misery heat in gay colours." He was impressed by the agricultural settlement of Rechowoth and the Jewish agricultural school Mikweh Israel.

In Jerusalem, he expressed some irritation at the "superstition and fanaticism" of the local Jews, the Wailing Wall was "pervaded by a hideous, wretched, speculative beggary". His travel companions refused to enter the Via Dolorosa and did not allow Herzl to go to the Church of the Holy Sepulchre or the Temple Mount. On 29 October 1898 he sketched out his plans for Jerusalem: "clear out everything that is not something sacred, set up workers' homes outside the city, empty the nests of filth and tear them down, move the bazars elsewhere. . . . I would build around the Holy Places a comfortable, airy new city with proper sanitation while retaining the old architectural style as much as possible."

Herzl further developed his ideas for Jerusalem in his book *The Old New Land* (1902), which he described as a "utopian novel", about a "New Society" going to be formed in Palestine in 1923.

But back to his journey. The long-planned audience with the Emperor, which took place at the tent camp of the entourage, was brief. Herzl could not know that Sultan Abdülhamid II had taken a stand against the Zionist endeavours, which did not go unnoticed by the Emperor, for whom a protectorate of Jerusalem was now out of the question. A month later, the Emperor wrote in a letter to his mother Victoria, in English: "Jerusalem is entirely spoiled by the many, very modern suburbs . . . full of Jewish settlers. There were 60,000 of these people—greasy, miserable, sluggish and degenerate—who have nothing better to do than to become equally hated by Christians and Muslims by trying to get every hard-earned penny from these neighbours. Nothing but shylocks, all of them."

Epilogue

AT THE BEGINNING of the twentieth century, the majority of Palestine's population of around 375,000 people lived in the district of Jerusalem, with a further 200,000 to 250,000 people in the subprovinces (sanjaks) of Nablus and Acre, which were still part of the province of Beirut, and another 100,000 inhabitants in the region of East Jordan. Jerusalem also ruled over Gaza, Jaffa, Hebron, Bethlehem and Be'er Sheva. Since 1887, the mutessarifat (Ottoman province with a governor) of Jerusalem had been under the direct authority of the Sublime Porte in accordance with its increased importance. The majority of the Muslim population in the region—a mixture of Arabs who had invaded from the seventh century on and those already living in Syria—encompassed around 600,000 people. The rural population was divided into settled farmers (fellahs) and bedouins or shepherds. Besides these groups, there were also Circassians, Kurds, and Druze in Upper Galilee. European Christians accounted for approximately 5,000 of the population, with the majority (3,000) being German, and of these, most were Templers from Württemberg. The number of Jews had meanwhile risen to around 100,000. Numerous Jewish colonization companies and organizations worked in and for Palestine.

Back in 1860, the Alliance Israélite Universelle had been founded to improve conditions for Jews living in the Holy Land. For a long time, emphasis was placed on French education and language at school, so that students graduating could emigrate to other countries. The Esra organization, which was founded in Berlin in 1884, in contrast, aimed to help steer "the flow of Jewish emigrants from the Christian West to the countries of the Mohammedan Orient, especially to Palestine and Syria". The settlement of Yemeni Jews who arrived from around 1882 onwards from South Arabia, posed a challenge. The first Yemeni families sailed northwards on dhows from Sana'a. The colonists of Rehovot, the city where immigrants were initially given employment by labour unions, quickly identified their hardworking qualities and the possibility of using this cheap work to be less dependent on Muslims. Besides this, the Yemenites proved to be a link in the chain between the colonists and the Arab population because they could speak both Arabic and Hebrew with ease.

The Aid Organization of German Jews, founded in Berlin in 1901, who concentrated their efforts on developing a Jewish education system in Palestine, wrote in its report in 1909: "If the Orient develops as predicted, and if our fellow Jews in Turkey take part in this development to an outstanding degree, it will thereupon be possible to bring Russian, Galician and Rumanian Jews, who have to endure such terrible conditions at the moment, to Asia and thereby divert some of those emigrating, possibly a very significant number, from current destinations, which are overcrowded developed countries and the United States to the Orient . . . Our fellow Jews in the Orient seemed predestined to become the mediators between Western culture on the one hand and the slowly developing culture of the Orient on the other."

Western travellers often saw the people living in the Holy Land as 'Orientals' connected by a common culture. They envisioned the Jews, Orthodox Christians, and Muslims who lived there as a kind of living museum. They were puzzled by the iconodulism, icons, and pronounced spiritualism of the Christians. But didn't they have more in common than the things that set them apart? Hadn't the journey to this region of Christianity, Judaism, and Islam resulted in more respect and humility? A problematic issue was that Jerusalem, which was sometimes the only destination, came to represent the entire Holy Land, even though the composition of its population did not match Palestine, which had had a Muslim majority for centuries.

Reports exist of both peaceful coexistence and tensions among the various religious and ethnic communities. A book by the American historian Michelle Campos investigates the relationships between Muslim, Christian, and Jewish families and neighbours in Jerusalem's Old City in the late nineteenth century: these groups shared a courtyard, paid each other visits, and maintained long-standing business relations.

> "Muslim girls learned Judeo-Spanish from their Sephardi Jewish neighbors; Christian and Jewish musicians performed at Muslim weddings and holidays; and all three shared beliefs and traditions about the evil eye, droughts, and visiting the tombs of local saints. At the same time, religious, economic, and political rivalry appeared from time to time, and the practical aspects of 'living together' could be a source of tension."

Christians and Jews in particular had fraught intergroup relationships, especially around religious holidays and holy sites, Campos writes in *Ottoman Brothers* (2010). It wasn't until the final stages of the Ottoman Empire that Muslims and Jews living in Palestine began to see each other as rival political communities, both laying claim to Filastin (a term for Palestine that had long since fallen out of use), or Eretz Israel.

Initially, they did so as citizens of the Ottoman Empire, even though Palestinian Muslims and Turks were somewhat estranged. Khalil as-Sakanini, a renowned Palestinian Christian and intellectual in Jerusalem, who had spent a few years living in America, conveyed in 1913 how weak nationalist feeling was at the time. "He pinned his hopes on the next generation and on émigrés who, he believed, would return to Palestine and spread nationalist ideas," according to the Israeli historian Shimon Shamir. As-Sakanini himself was allegedly not certain of his national identity. "Many Ottoman pashas believed that the Christians, unlike the Jews, did not sincerely wish to integrate into the Ottoman society, but desired to overthrow it with the help of Christian European powers," notes Shamir's colleague, Moshe Ma'oz in the same volume, *Studies on Palestine during the Ottoman Period* (1975).

Between 1915 and 1917, the British government signed three agreements regarding the division of the Ottoman Empire. Together with Hussein ibn Ali, Sharif of Mecca, which belonged to the Ottoman Empire, they supported the creation of an Arab kingdom. The negotiations over the exact drawing of the borders proved tough: in the Sharif's eyes, he wanted all of Syria and Mesopotamia to belong to his kingdom. In May 1916, the British and French signed the secret Sykes-Picot Agreement, which established their respective spheres of influence in Syria and Mesopotamia for the postwar period. Germany, the Ottoman Empire's ally and Great Britain's adversary in the war, played no role. On 2 November 1917, the British foreign minister Arthur Balfour promised in a letter to Lionel Walter

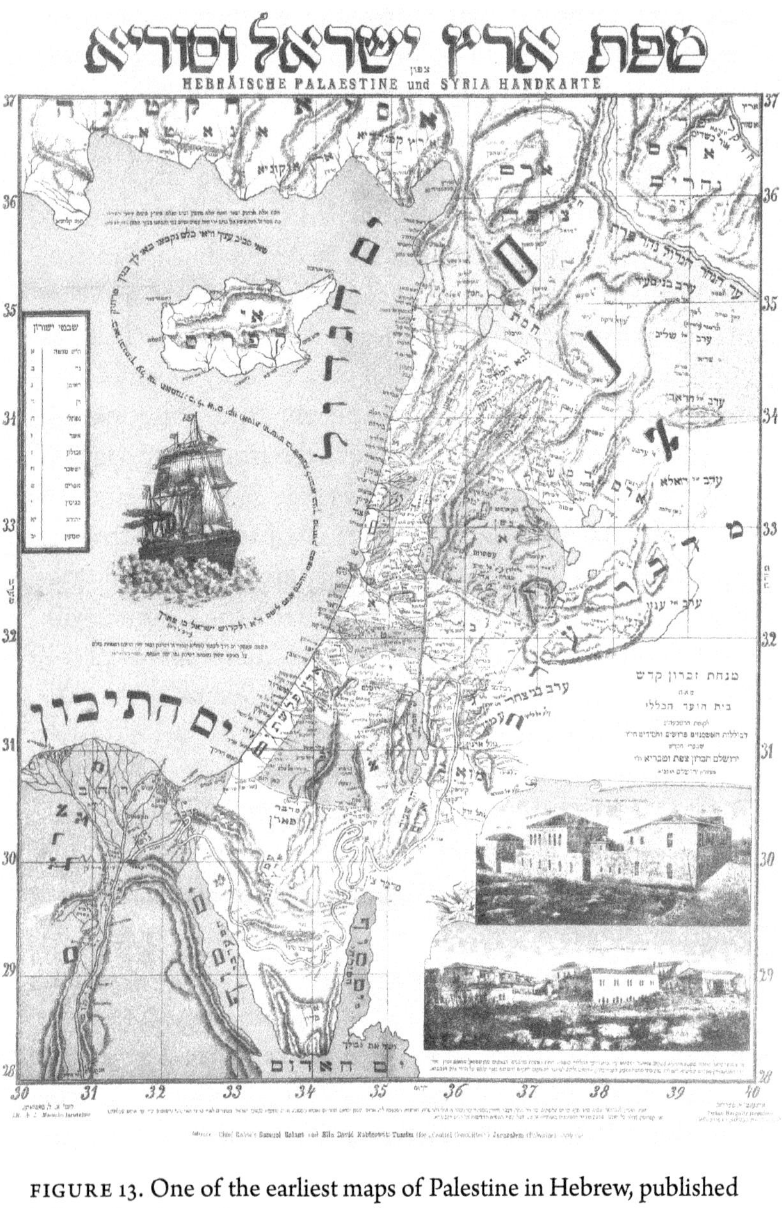

FIGURE 13. One of the earliest maps of Palestine in Hebrew, published in Jerusalem in 1908.

Rothschild, honorary chairman of the Zionist Federation of Great Britain and Ireland, a vaguely worded "national home for the Jewish people," provided that nothing shall be done which may prejudice the civil and religious rights of existing non-Jewish communities in Palestine, or the rights and political status enjoyed by Jews in any other country. The wording was chosen in agreement with the US President Woodrow Wilson. It entered history as the Balfour Declaration and brought about a radical development.

In December of that year, after a bloody battle, General Edmund Allenby marched his troops to victory through the hills leading to Jerusalem and through Jaffa Gate. After the end of the war, the League of Nations conferred Great Britain with a mandate to govern Palestine and Iraq, while France administered the territories of Syria and Lebanon. The political situation changed decisively and the end of the Ottoman Empire came as a surprise to many if not most living in Palestine. It was turned into a political entity. In July 1922, the League of Nations officially gave Great Britain a mandate over Palestine. Transjordan was established to the east as a semi-autonomous emirate. The influx of pilgrims soon began once more. Jewish travellers arrived on "Zionist tours" to strengthen their ties with Eretz Israel. They wished to have firsthand experience of the conditions and develop their own attitude towards them. Later many immigrated there or were forced to flee their own countries. In the meantime, conflicts and tensions between the Muslims and Jews who already lived there began to simmer.

ACKNOWLEDGEMENTS

MY INTEREST in Israel and Palestine dates back to the mid-1980s. Although this book is about the past, I most likely would not have written it without having visited most of the places mentioned.

During my first visits, I stayed and worked in two kibbutzim for most of the time: Urim in the Negev and Ami'ad, which is located just north of the Sea of Galilee. Having been born in Germany, these trips were part of my wish to better understand, and perhaps come to terms with, my country's monstrous past. The visit to Yad Vashem was particularly memorable. At that time, the Sinai was still occupied by Israel. I visited St. Catherine's Monastery and walked up Mount Sinai. I returned much later, after it had become part of Egypt.

Although I was raised in the Protestant tradition, I have always been fascinated by pilgrimages and their sites, whether in Jerusalem, Rome, Lourdes (France), Fátima (Portugal), or Santiago de Compostela (Spain). During my many years in Istanbul, I developed an interest in the history of the Ottoman Empire, which I then combined with my reading of pilgrims' and other travellers' reports of the Holy Land. A few years ago, this culminated in the idea for this book.

They Came to the Holy Land was first published in German in early 2024 as *Unterwegs ins Morgenland*, just a few months after Hamas's horrific attacks in Israel. First, I would like to thank my longtime editor, Wolfgang Hörner of Galiani Berlin, a literary imprint of Kiepenheuer & Witsch, for working with me on this book, my sixth with him. As always, the resources of the Berlin State Library were invaluable in locating books and articles. I would also like to warmly thank Suzanne Marchand, Kerstin Volker-Saad, and Tobias Becker for taking the time to read an early draft. Their comments were very helpful.

Eva Schoening pointed me to Muhammad Marmaduke Pickthall's book, and Richard Berrong drew my attention to Ernest Renan's work. My friend and colleague, David Chaffetz, read the manuscript and provided valuable feedback. My thanks also extend to the anonymous readers. Of course, I alone am responsible for any mistakes that may have been made.

Acclaimed translator Lucy Jones did a terrific job translating some of the chapters into English. The remaining chapters were translated through a collaboration between me and my friend Kaan Cahit Dewan, an American who is an English instructor at Bilkent University in Ankara, Turkey. This edition does not always correspond in every detail to the German edition. Here and there, we have made changes, added comments, expanded or shortened quotations. Also, I have written some new parts. The selection of texts spans more than 1500 years and must, by its very nature, be incomplete. I have selected them to highlight the diversity of the travellers and their various motivations. I consider myself fortunate that Ben Tate of Princeton University Press became interested in an English language edition of the book and I would like to thank Catja Pafort for their thoughtful copy editing and everyone who was involved in producing and marketing this book. Last but not least I would like to thank Aleksandra Erakovic at Kiepenheuer & Witsch for patiently handling the contractual matters.

BIBLIOGRAPHY

Pilgrimage

Adomnán (aka Saint Adamnán). *Pilgrimage of Arculfus in the Holy Land (about the year A.D. 670)*. Palestine Pilgrims' Text Society 1895

Bekemeier, Annemone. *Reisen nach Jerusalem. Das Heilige Land in Karten und Ansichten aus fünf Jahrhunderten. Sammlung Loewenhardt* (Catalogue of the exhibition of the Jewish Museum). Wiesbaden: Ludwig Reichert 1993

Ben-Naeh, Yaron. "Thousands great saints: Evliya Çelebi in Ottoman Palestine". In: *Quest—Issues in Contemporary Jewish History.* No. 6, December 2013

Chareyron, Nicole. *Pilgrims to Jerusalem in the Middle Ages.* New York: Columbia University Press 2005

Craig, Leigh Ann. *Wandering Women and Holy Matrons: Women as Pilgrims in the Later Middle Ages.* Leiden: Brill 2009

Davies, Paul, Deborah Howard and Wendy Pullan (eds). *Architecture and Pilgrimage, 1000–1500: Southern Europe and Beyond.* Farnham: Ashgate 2013

Doležal, Daniel, and Hartmut Kühne (eds). *Wallfahrten in der europäischen Kultur. Pilgrimage in European Culture.* Frankfurt am Main: Peter Lang 2005

Donner, Herbert. *Pilgerfahrt ins Heilige Land: Die ältesten Berichte christlicher Palästinapilger.* Stuttgart: Verlag Katholisches Bibelwerk 2002

Férotin, Dom Marius. "Le véritable auteur de la 'Peregrinatio Silviae'. La vierge espagnole Aetheria." In: *Revue des Questions historiques* 74, 1903, pp. 367–397

Haupt, Barbara and Wilhelm G. Busse. *Pilgerreisen in Mittelalter und Renaissance.* Düsseldorf: Droste Verlag 2006

Hochheimer, Albert. *Die Strassen der Völker. Entdeckung und Abenteuer.* Zurich: Benziger Verlag 1977

Hopper, Sarah. *Mothers, Mystics and Merrymakers: Medieval Women Pilgrims.* Stroud: Sutton Publishing 2006

Hunt, E. D. "The Itinerary of Egeria: Reliving the Bible in Fourth-Century Palestine". In: Swanson, R. N. (ed.). *The Holy Land, Holy Lands, and Christian History.*

Woodbridge: Published for the Ecclesiastical History Society by The Boydell Press 2000, pp. 34–54

Janes, Dominic and Gary Waller (eds). *Walsingham in Literature and Culture from the Middle Ages to Modernity.* Aldershot, Ashgate 2010

Ohler, Norbert. *Pilgerstab und Jakobsmuschel. Wallfahrten in Mittelalter und Neuzeit.* Munich: Artemis & Winkler Publishers 2000

Penth, Sabine. *Die Reise nach Jerusalem: Pilgerfahrten ins Heilige Land.* Darmstadt: Primus Verlag 2010

Reichert, Folker. *Erfahrung der Welt: Reisen und Kulturbegegnung im späten Mittelalter.* Stuttgart: W. Kohlhammer 2001

Reichert, Folker and Alexander Rosenstock (eds). *Die Welt des Frater Felix Fabri.* Weissenhorn: Anton H. Konrad Verlag 2018

Röhricht, Reinhold. *Deutsche Pilgerreisen nach dem Heiligen Lande.* Gotha: Perthes 1889

Rouxpetel, Camille. *L'Occident au Miroir de l'Orient Chrétien: Cilicie, Syrie, Palestine et Égypte.* Rome: École Française de Rome 2015

Schick, Robert. "Who Came on Pilgrimage to Jerusalem in the Mamluk and Ottoman Periods? An Interreligious Comparison". In: Ariantzi, Despoina and Ina Eichner (eds). *Für Seelenheil und Lebensglück: Das byzantinische Pilgerwesen und seine Wurzeln.* Mainz: Leibniz-Zentrum für Archäologie 2018, pp. 243–257

Schreiner, Stefan (ed. and trans.) *Jüdische Reisen im Mittelalter: Benjamin von Tudela; Petachja von Regensburg.* Leipzig: Dieterich 1991

Swanson, R. N. (ed.). *The Holy Land, Holy Lands, and Christian History.* London: The Boydell Press 2000

Van Eck, Marianne P. Ritsema. *The Holy Land in Observant Franciscan Texts (ca. 1480–1650): Theology, Travel, and Territoriality.* Leiden/Bosten: Brill 2019

Wilkinson, John. *Egeria's Travels. Newly translated with supporting documents and notes.* London: S.P.C.K 1971

Palestine

Anon. *Das Deutsche Kaiserpaar im Heiligen Lande.* Berlin: Mittler 1899

Bar-Yosef, Eitan. *The Holy Land in English Culture, 1799–1917: Palestine and the Question of Orientalism.* Oxford: Oxford University Press 2005

Ben-Arieh, Yehoshu'a. *The Rediscovery of the Holy Land in the Nineteenth Century.* Jerusalem: The Magnes Press, The Hebrew University, Israel Exploration Society 1979

———*Jerusalem in the Nineteenth Century: The Old City.* New York: St. Martin's Press 1985

———*Painting the Holy Land in the Nineteenth Century*. Jerusalem: Yad Izhak Ben-Zvi Publications 1997

Ben-Arieh, Yehoshu'a and Moshe Davis (eds). *Jerusalem in the Mind of the Western World, 1800–1948*. Westport: Praeger 1997

Campos, Michelle. *Ottoman Brothers: Muslims, Christians, and Jews in Early Twentieth-Century Palestine*. Stanford: Stanford University Press 2010

Carmel, Alex (or Carmel, Aleks). *Christen als Pioniere im Heiligen Land: ein Beitrag zur Geschichte der Pilgermission und des Wiederaufbaus Palästinas im 19. Jahrhundert*. Basel: Reinhardt 1981

Carmel, Alex and Ejal Jakob Eisler. *Der Kaiser reist ins Heilige Land: die Palästinareise Wilhelms II. 1898*. Stuttgart: Verlag W. Kohlhammer 1999

Davis, John. *The Landscape of Belief: Encountering the Holy Land in Nineteenth-Century American Art and Culture*. Princeton: Princeton University Press 1996

Doumani, Beshara. *Rediscovering Palestine: Merchants and Peasants in Jabal Nablus, 1700–1900*. Berkeley: University of California Press 1995

Fishman, Louis A. *Jews and Palestinians in the Late Ottoman Era, 1908–1914. Claiming the Homeland*. Edinburgh: Edinburgh University Press 2020

Galazka, Guy. *À la découverte de la Palestine: Voyageurs Français en Terre sainte au XIVe. siècle*. Paris: Presses de l'université Paris-Sorbonne 2011

Geniesse, Jane Fletcher. *American Priestess: The Extraordinary Story of Anna Spafford and the American Colony in Jerusalem*. New York: Nan A. Talese 2008

Gibson, Shimon, Yoni Shapira and Rupert L. Chapman III *Tourists, travellers and Hotels in Nineteenth-Century Jerusalem*. Leeds: Maney Publishing 2013

Grafton, David D. *An American biblical orientalism: the construction of Jews, Christians, and Muslims in nineteenth-century American evangelical piety*. Lanham: Lexington Books/Fortress Academic 2019

Gustrau, Maibritt. *Orientalen oder Christen? Orientalisches Christentum in Reiseberichten deutscher Theologen*. Göttingen: Vandenhoeck & Ruprecht unipress 2016

Halbwachs, Maurice. *La topographie légendaire des Évangiles en Terre sainte: étude de mémoire collective*. Paris: Presses universitaires de France 1941

Hallote, Rachel. *Bible, Map, and Spade: The American Palestine Exploration Society, Frederick Jones Bliss, and the Forgotten Story of Early American Biblical Archaeology*. Piscataway: Gorgias Press 2006

Hayden, Judy A. and Nabil I. Matar (eds). *Through the Eyes of the Beholder: The Holy Land, 1517–1713*. Leiden: Brill 2013

Jacobs, Martin. *Reorienting the East: Jewish travelers to the Medieval Muslim World*. Philadelphia: University of Pennsylvania Press 2014

Kane, Eileen. *Russian Hajj: Empire and the Pilgrimage to Mecca*. Ithaca: Cornell University Press 2015

Kawerau, Peter. *Amerika und die orientalischen Christen. Ursprung und Anfang der amerikanischen Mission unter den Nationalkirchen Westasiens*. Berlin: Walter de Gruyter 1958

Kernohan, R. D. *The Road to Zion: Travellers to Palestine and the Land of Israel*. Carberry: Handsel Press 1994

Klatzker, David. *American Christian travelers to the Holy Land, 1821–1939* (Doctoral dissertation, Temple University) Philadelphia 1987

Kollek, Teddy and Moshe Pearlman. *Pilgrims to the Holy Land: The Story of Pilgrimage through the Ages*. London: Weidenfeld and Nicolson 1970

Ma'oz, Moshe (ed.). *Studies on Palestine during the Ottoman Period*. Jerusalem: The Magnes Press 1975

Nawratzki, Curt. *Die jüdische Kolonisation Palästinas: Eine volkswirtschaftliche Untersuchung ihrer Grundlagen*. Munich: Verlag Ernst Reinhardt 1914

Obenzinger, Hilton. *American Palestine: Melville, Twain, and the Holy Land Mania*. Princeton: Princeton University Press 1999

Osband, Linda (ed.). *Famous Travellers to the Holy Land: Their Personal Impressions and Reflections*. London: Prion 1989

Prudential Committee of the American Board of Commissioners for Foreign Missions. *Religious Intelligence: Palestine. The Panoplist and Missionary Herald*. Boston: Samuel T. Armstrong 1819. pp. 545–6. https://babel.hathitrust.org/cgi/pt?id=hvd.ah6kz1&seq=561 [accessed March 19, 2026]

Rogers, Stephanie Stidham. *Inventing the Holy Land: American Protestant Pilgrimage to Palestine, 1865–1941*. Plymouth: Lexington Books 2011

Schölch, Alexander. *Palästina im Umbruch: Untersuchungen zur wirtschaftlichen und sozio-politischen Entwicklung*. Stuttgart: F. Steiner 1986

Shepherd, Naomi. *The Zealous Intruders: The Western Rediscovery of Palestine*. San Francisco: Harper & Row Publishers 1987

Silberman, Neil Asher. *Digging for God and Country: Exploration, archaeology, and the secret struggle for the Holy Land, 1799–1917*. New York: Knopf 1982

Socin, Albert. *Palestine and Syria. Handbook for Travellers*. Leipzig: Karl Baedeker 1876

Tuchman, Barbara W. *Bible and Sword: England and Palestine from the Bronze Age to Balfour*. New York: New York University Press 1956

Vogel, Lester I. *To See a Promised Land. Americans and the Holy Land in the Nineteenth Century*. University Park: The Pennsylvania State University Press 1993

Jerusalem

Budde, Hendrik and Andreas Nachama (eds). *Die Reise nach Jerusalem. Eine kulturhistorische Exkursion in die Stadt der Städte. 3000 Jahre Davidsstadt*. Berlin: Jüdische Gemeinde zu Berlin/Argon Verlag 1996

Croitoru, Joseph. *Al-Aqsa oder Tempelberg: Der ewige Kampf um Jerusalems heilige Stätten*. Munich: C. H. Beck 2021

Goldhill, Simon. *Jerusalem: City of Longing*. Cambridge: Belknap Press of Harvard University Press 2008

Kampmeyer, Margret and Cilly Kugelmann. *Welcome to Jerusalem*. Cologne: Wienand Verlag 2019

Lawler, Andrew. *Under Jerusalem: The Buried History of the World's Most Contested City*. New York: Doubleday 2021

Lemire, Vincent. *Jerusalem 1900: The Holy City in the Age of Possibilities*. Chicago: The University of Chicago Press 2017

Mack, Merav and Benjamin Balint. *Jerusalem: City of the Book*. New Haven: Yale University Press 2019

Montefiore, Simon Sebag. *Jerusalem: The Biography*. London: Weidenfeld & Nicolson 2011

Noonan, F. Thomas. *The Road to Jerusalem: Pilgrimage and Travel in the Age of Discovery*. Philadelphia: University of Pennsylvania Press 2007

Peters, Francis Edward. *Jerusalem: The Holy City in the Eyes of Chroniclers, Visitors, Pilgrims, and Prophets From the Days of Abraham to the Beginnings of Modern Times*. Princeton: Princeton University Press 1985

Poser, Rachel. "Common Ground: The Politics of Archaeology in Jerusalem". *Harper's*. September 2019. https://harpers.org/archive/2019/09/common-ground-archeology-israel-palestine/ [accessed March 13, 2026]

Robertson, James and Felice Beato. *Jerusalem Album Photographique de Robertson & Beato*. Constantinople: Köhler & Weiss Libraires Editeurs 1864

Other Works

Anguiano, Mateo de. *La nueva Jerusalén en que la perfidia hebraica reitero con nuevos ultrages*. Madrid: Imprenta de Manuel Ruiz de Murga 1709

Bayard, Pierre. *Comment parler des lieux où l'on n'a pas été*. Paris: Éditions de Minuit 2012

Burckhardt, Jacob. *Die Zeit Constantin's des Großen*. Basel: Schweighauser'sche Verlagsbuchhandlung 1853

Carboni, Stefan (ed.). *Venice and the Islamic World, 828–1797*. New Haven: Yale University Press 2007

Doré, Gustave. *La grande bible de Tours*. Tours: Alfred Mame et fils 1866

Esch, Arnold. *Zeitalter und Menschenalter: Der Historiker und die Erfahrung vergangener Gegenwart*. Munich: C.H. Beck 1994

Goer, Charis and Michael Hofmann (eds). *Der Deutschen Morgenland: Bilder des Orients in der deutschen Literatur und Kultur von 1770 bis 1850*. Munich: Wilhelm Fink 2008

Greenblatt, Stephen. *Marvelous Possessions: The Wonder of the New World*. Chicago: The University of Chicago Press 1991

Hammer-Purgstall, Joseph von. *Fundgruben des Orients bearbeitet durch eine Gesellschaft von Liebhabern*. Vienna: Schmid 1809

Hourani, Albert. *A History of The Arab Peoples*. London: Faber and Faber 1991

Howard, Douglas A. *A History of the Ottoman Empire*. Cambridge: Cambridge University Press 2017

Krämer, Gudrun. *A History of Palestine: From the Ottoman Conquest to the Founding of the State of Israel*. Princeton and Oxford: Princeton University Press 2006

Luchterhandt, Manfred, Lisa Marie Roemer and Verena Suchy (eds). *Das unschuldige Auge: Orientbilder in der frühen Fotografie*. Petersberg: Michael Imhof Verlag 2017

Mairs, Rachel and Maya Muratov. *Archaeologists, Tourists, Interpreters: Exploring Egypt and the Near East in the Late 19th-Early 20th Centuries*. London: Bloomsbury 2015

Melman, Billie. *Women's Orient: English Women and the Middle East, 1718–1918*. Ann Arbor: University of Michigan Press 1992

Oren, Michael B. *Power, Faith, and Fantasy: America in the Middle East 1776 to the Present*. New York: W. W. Norton 2007

Osterhammel, Jürgen. *Unfabling the East. The Enlightenment's Encounter with Asia*. Princeton and London: Princeton University Press 2018

Polaschegg, Andrea. *Der andere Orientalismus. Regeln deutsch-morgenländischer Imagination im 19. Jahrhundert*. Berlin: Walter de Gruyter 2005

Rogan, Eugene. *The Arabs: A History*. New York: Basic Books 2011

Said, Edward W. *Orientalism*. London: Routledge 1978

Yothers, Brian. *The Romance of the Holy Land in American Travel Writing, 1790–1876*. Aldershot: Ashgate 2007

Books on Specific Persons

Adomnán (aka Saint Adamnán). *Pilgrimage of Arculfus in the Holy Land (about the year A.D. 670)*. London: Palestine Pilgrims' Text Society 1895

Balcou, Jean with Sophie Guermès and Jean Glaser (ed.). *Renan en Orient*. Rennes: Presses Universitaires de Rennes 2022

Bell, Gertrude. *A Woman in Arabia: The Writings of the Queen of the Desert* (edited by Georgina Howell). New York: Penguin 2015

Berrong, Richard M. *Pierre Loti*. London: Reaktion Books 2018

Blake, William. *Between Fire and Fire: Poetical Works, bilingual edition*. Munich: dtv 2007

Carmel, Alex and Hugo Schmid. *Der Orientmaler Gustav Bauernfeind. 1848–1904. Leben und Werk*. Stuttgart: Hauswedell 1990

Chernik, Karen. "Mark Twain and the Adams Colony". In: *Shapell Manuscript Foundation*, 2019. https://www.shapell.org/historical-perspectives/between-the-lines/mark-twain-and-the-adams-colony/ [accessed April 17, 2026]

Delaney, Carol. "Columbus's Ultimate Goal: Jerusalem". In: *Comparative Studies in Society and History*, Vol. 48, No. 2 (Apr. 2006), pp. 260–92

Green, Abigail. *Moses Montefiore: Jewish Liberator, Imperial Hero*. Cambridge: Belknap Press of Harvard University Press 2010

Hecht, Louise (ed.). *Ludwig August Frankl (1810–1894): Eine jüdische Biographie zwischen Okzident und Orient*. Cologne: Böhlau Verlag 2016

Jaeghere, Michel de. *Le Menteur magnifique: Chateaubriand en Grèce*. Paris: Les Belles Lettres 2006

Kreiger, Barbara and Shalom Goldman. *Divine Expectations: An American Woman in nineteenth-Century Palestine*. Athens: Ohio University Press 1999

Lagerlöf, Selma (ed. Holger Wolandt). *Liebe Sophie—Liebe Valborg. Eine Dreiecksgeschichte in Briefen*. Stuttgart: Urachhaus 2016

Lohmeier, Dieter (ed.). *Mit Carsten Niebuhr im Orient. Zwanzig Briefe von der Arabischen Reise 1760–1767*. Heide: Boyens 2011

Mairs, Rachel. *From Khartoum to Jerusalem. The Dragoman Solomon Negima and his Clients (1885–1933)*. London: Bloomsbury 2016

Östlund, Joachim. "A Lutheran in the Holy Land: Michael Eneman's Journey, 1711–12". In: Hayden, Judy A. and Nabil I. Matar (eds). *Through the Eyes of the Beholder: The Holy Land, 1517–1713*. Leiden: Brill 2013, pp. 207–224

Penslar, Derek. *Theodor Herzl: The Charismatic Leader*. New Haven: Yale University Press 2020

Saint Augustine of Hippo (trans. Henry Chadwick). *Confessions*. Oxford: Oxford University Press 1998

Schaff, Phillip (ed.) and Freemantle, M. A. (trans.). NPNF2-06. *Jerome: The Principal Works of St. Jerome: The Letters of St. Jerome*. New York: Christian Literature 1892. https://www.documentacatholicaomnia.eu/03d/0347-0420,_Hieronymus,_Epistolae_[Schaff],_EN.pdf [accessed March 27, 2026]

Schreiner, Stefan (ed. and trans.) *Jüdische Reisen im Mittelalter: Benjamin von Tudela; Petachja von Regensburg*. Leipzig: Dieterich 1991

Schwabe, Fabian (ed.). *Von Island nach Jerusalem. Ein Reisebericht aus dem 12. Jahrhundert*. Universität Tübingen Digital Humanities website, 2025. https://digital-humanities.uni-tuebingen.de/nikulas-itinerar/# [accessed April 17, 2026]

Sim, Katharine. *Jean Louis Burckhardt: A Biography*. London: Quartet Books 1981

—*David Roberts, R. A., 1796–1864: A Biography*. London: Quartet Books 1984

Vermeulen, Han F. *Anthropology and the Orient. C. Niebuhr and the Danish-German Arabia Expedition*. In: Han F. Vermeulen: *Before Boas. The Genesis of Ethnography and Ethnology in the German Enlightenment*. Lincoln & London: University of Nebraska Press 2016

Volker-Saad, Kerstin. *Unterwegs im Gelobten Land: Hermann Fürst von Pückler-Muskaus Spurensuche biblischer Geschichte im Jahr 1838 in Palästina*. Bad Muskau: Foundation Fürst-Pückler-Park Bad Muskau 2022

Wilkinson, John. *Egeria's Travels. Newly translated with supporting documents and notes*. London: S.P.C.K 1971

Ya'ari, Avraham (1947) *Zikhronot Erez Yisrael [Memories of the Land of Israel]*, Vol. 2, Ch. 68: "A Doctor in the Land, Hillel Yaffe" (in Hebrew). Mossad 1947. Hillel Jaffe's papers are held at the Central Zionist Archives in Jerusalem (http://www.zionistarchives.org.il/en); a precise citation for the letter quoted in the text is not available.

Zielonka, Anthony. "Gustave Flaubert's Journey to the Holy Land: Anticipation, Disenchantment and Enduring Fascination." In: *Aller(s)-Retour(s): Nineteenth-Century France in Motion*, edited by Loïc Guyon and Andrew Watts, Newcastle upon Tyne: Cambridge Scholars Publishing, 2013, pp. 125–35

Quoted Travel Reports

Bartlett, William Henry. *Walks about the City and Environs of Jerusalem*. London: Hall, Virtue and Company ca. 1850

Bassi, Alessandro. *Pellegrinaggio storico e descritivo di Terrasanta*. Turin: 1857

Benjamin, Israel Joseph. *Acht Jahre in Asien und Afrika. Von 1846 bis 1855*. Hanover: 1858

Bonar, Andrew A. and Robert Murray McCheyne. *Narrative of a Mission of Inquiry to the Jews from the Church of Scotland in 1839*. Edinburgh: William Whyte 1839

Bowring, John. *Report on the Commercial Statistics of Syria*. London: William Clowes and Sons 1840

Brasca, Santo. *Itinerario alla santissima città di Gerusalemme*. Milan: Leonard Pachel and Ulrich Scinzenzeler 1481

Breen, Arnold Edward. *A Diary of My Life in the Holy Land*. Rochester: John P. Smith 1906

Breidenbach, Bernhard von. *Peregrinatio in terram sanctam*. Mainz: Reuwich 1486

Browne, John Ross. *Yusef; Or the Journey of the Frangi. A Crusade in the East*. New York: Harper & Brothers 1853

Buchenbach, Hans Jacob Breuning von. *Orientalische Reyß*. Strasbourg: Carolus 1612. https://www.digitale-sammlungen.de/de/view/bsb10625255?page=,1 [accessed April 17, 2026]

Bünting, Heinrich. *Itinerarium sacrae scripturae, das ist ein Reisebuch über die ganze Heilige Schrift.* Magdeburg: Kirchner 1587

Burton, Isabel. *The Inner Life of Syria, Palestine, and the Holy Land.* London: Henry S. King & Co. 1875

Busch, Moritz. *Eine Wallfahrt nach Jerusalem. Bilder ohne Heiligenschein.* Leipzig: Friedrich Wilhelm Grunow 1861

Casola, Canon Pietro (ed. and trans. M. Margaret Newett). *Canon Pietro Casola's Pilgrimage to Jerusalem.* Manchester: Manchester University Press 1907

Chartres, Fulcher of (ed. Harold S. Fink). *A History of the Expedition to Jerusalem, 1095–1127.* Knoxville: University of Tennessee Press 1969

Chateaubriand, François René de. *Travels in Greece, Palestine, Egypt, and Barbary, during the years 1806 and 1807.* London: Henry Colborn 1812

Clarke, Edward Daniel. *Travels in Various Countries of Europe, Asia, and Africa* (second volume: *Greece, Egypt, and the Holy Land*). New York: D. Huntington 1814

Conder, Claude Regnier. *Tent Work in Palestine: A Record of Discovery and Adventure.* London: Bentley & Son 1878

de Géramb, Marie Joseph. *Pilgrimage to Jerusalem and Mount Sinai.* Philadelphia: Carey and Hart 1840

de Saulcy, Louis Félicien. *Narrative of a journey round the Dead Sea, and in the Bible lands, in 1850 and 1851.* London: R. Bentley 1854

Dorr, David F. *A Colored Man Round the World.* Cleveland 1858

Ebers, Georg and Hermann Guthe. *Palästina in Bild und Wort.* Stuttgart and Leipzig: Deutsche Verlags-Anstalt 1882

Fabri, Felix (trans. Aubrey Stewart). *The Wanderings of Felix Fabri.* London: Committee of the Palestine Exploration Fund 1892

Fabri, Felix. *Galeere und Karawane: Pilgerreise ins Heilige Land, zum Sina und nach Ägypten 1483.* Stuttgart: Edition Erdmann 1996

Flaubert, Gustave (trans. and ed. Frances Steegmuller). *The Letters of Gustave Flaubert, 1857–1880.* Cambridge: Belknap Press 1980

———*Voyage en Orient.* Paris: Gallimard 2006

Frankl, Ludwig August. *Nach Jerusalem!* Leipzig: Baumgärtner 1858

Friedrich Wilhelm, Kronprinz von Preußen. *Tagebuch meiner Reise nach dem Morgenlande.* 1869

Furrer, Konrad. *Wanderungen durch Palästina.* Zurich: Orell, Füßli und Companie 1865

———*Die Bedeutung der biblischen Geographie für die biblische Exegese.* Zurich: Orell, Füßli und Companie 1870

Graham, Stephen. *With the Russian Pilgrims to Jerusalem.* London: Macmillan & Co. 1913

Hasselquist, Fredrik. *Iter Palestinum eller resa til Heliga Landet: förrättad ifrån år 1749 til 1752.* Stockholm: Lars Salvii 1757

Lamartine, Alphonse de. *A Pilgrimage to the Holy Land. Comprising Recollections, Sketches, And Reflections, Made During A Tour In The East, In 1832–1833*. London. Richard Bentley 1837 (three volumes)

Lortet, Louis. *La Syrie d'aujourd'hui: Voyages dans la Phénicie, le Liban et la Judée 1879–1880*. Paris: Hachette & Cie. 1884

Loti, Pierre. *Le désert—Jérusalem—La Galilée*. Paris: Calmann Lévy 1895

Lynch, William Francis. *Narrative of the United States' Expedition to the River Jordan and the Dead Sea*. Philadelphia: Lea and Blanchard 1849

MacGregor, John. *The Rob Roy on the Jordan, Nile, Red Sea and Gennesareth, a Canoe Cruise in Palestine and Egypt, and the Waters of Damascus*. London: John Murray 1886

Mandeville, John. *The travels of Sir John Mandeville*. London: Penguin 2005

Melville, Herman (ed. Howard C. Horsford). *Journal of a Visit to Europe and the Levant, October 11, 1856–May 6, 1857*. Princeton: Princeton University Press 1955

Miller, Ellen E. *Alone Through Syria*. London: Paul 1891

Maleo, Mariano Morone da. *Terra Santa nuovamente illustrata dal p.fr. Mariano Morone da Maleo*. Piacenza: Stamperia ducale di Giovanni Bazachi 1669

Neubauer, Adolf (trans.). "Zwei Briefe Obadjah's aus Bartenuro aus dem Jahre 5248 und 5249 und Ein anonymer Reisebrief vom Jahre 1495". In: *Jahrbuch für die Geschichte der Juden und des Judentums*, Band III, Leipzig 1863, pp. 193–302

Ohly, Carl. *Reiseerinnerungen aus dem Morgenlande*. Elberfeld: Buchhandlung der Evangelischen Gesellschaft 1898

Pappenheim, Alexander von (ed. Heimo Reinitzer): *Alexander von Pappenheim, Reichserbmarschall (1530–1612). Autobiographie*. Vol. II: Reisebericht nach Rom und Jerusalem (1563/64) nach der Handschrift der Universitätsbibliothek Gießen Nr. 164. Hamburg: Verlag Dr. Kovač 2020

Péchenard, Monseigneur Pierre-Louis. *De Reims à Jérusalem*. Paris: Dubois Poplimont 1893

Pfeiffer, Ida (ed. Gabriele Habinger). *Reisen in das Heilige Land: Konstantinopel, Palästina, Ägypten im Jahre 1842*. Vienna: Promedia-Verlags-Gesellschaft 1995

Pickthall, Marmaduke William. *Oriental Encounters: Palestine and Syria 1894-6*. New York: A. A. Knopf 1927

Pococke, Richard. *Description of the East and some other countries* (second volume). London: W. Bowyer 1743

Poggibonsi, Niccolò da. (ed. Alberto Bacchi della Lega) *Libro d'Oltramare*. Bologna: G. Romagnoli 1881

Porges, Mose ben Israel Naftali (aka Moses Präger). *Darkhe Tsiyon (Paths to Zion)*. Frankfurt am Main, Amsterdam or Prague 1650. Available from https://www.posenlibrary.com/author/moses-hirsh-porges [accessed April 17, 2026]

Renan, Ernest. *Mission de Phénicie.* Paris: Imprimerie impériale 1864

Rhodes, Albert. *Jerusalem As It Is.* London: John Maxwell and Company 1865

Robinson, Edward. *Biblical Researches in Palestine and Adjacent Countries.* London: J. Murray 1841

Robinson, George. *An Additional Account of George Robinson's: Shewing his Call to go to Jerusalem,* etc. In: *A Brief History of the Voyage of Katharine Evans and Sarah Cheevers to the Island of Malta.* London 1715, pp. 207–216

———*Later Biblical Researches in Palestine and the Adjacent Regions: A Journal of Travels in the Year 1852.* London: J. Murray 1856

Rogers, Mary Eliza. *Domestic Life in Palestine.* London: Bell and Daldy 1862

Rohrbach, Paul. *Vom Kaukasus zum Mittelmeer: Eine Hochzeits- und Studienreise durch Armenien.* Leipzig and Berlin: Teubner 1903

Romieu, Auguste. "Douzième lettre". In: Pigeory, Félix. *Les Pèlerins d'Orient: Lettres artistiques et historiques sur un voyage dans les Provinces danubiennes, la Turquie, la Syrie et la Palestine.* Paris: E. Dentu 1858

Scholz, Johann Martin Augustin. *Reise in die Gegend zwischen Alexandrien und Parätonium, die libysche Wüste, Siqa, Egypten, Palästina und Syrien in den Jahren 1820 und 1821.* Leipzig and Sorau: Friedrich Fleischer 1822

Schwarz, Joseph. *The Cycles of the Sun.* Jerusalem 1843

———*Tvu'ot Ha'aretz.* Jerusalem 1845

———*A Descriptive Biography and Brief Historical Sketch of Palestine.* Philadelphia: A. Hart 1850

Seetzen, Ulrich Jasper (ed. Friedrich Kruse). *Ulrich Jasper Seetzen's Reisen durch Syrien, Palästina, Phönicien, die Transjordan-Länder, Arabia Petraca und Unter-Aegypten.* Berlin: G. Reimer 1854

Smith, George Adam. *Historical Geography of the Holy Land.* London: Hodder and Stoughton 1894

Soden, Hermann von. *Reisebriefe aus Palästina.* Berlin: Julius Springer 1898

Stanley, Arthur Penrhyn. *Sinai and Palestine: in Connexion with their History.* London: John Murray 1856

Stephens, John Lloyd. *Incidents of Travel in Egypt, Arabia Petræa, and the Holy Land* (ed. Hagen, Victor Wolfgang). Norman: University of Oklahoma Press 1970

Strauss, Friedrich Adolph. *Sinai und Golgatha: Reise in das Morgenland.* Berlin: Jonas Verlagsbuchhandlung 1848

Suriano, Francesco (trans. B. Bellorini and E. Hoade, ed. B. Bagatti). Treatise on the Holy Land. Jerusalem: Franciscan Printing Press 1949

Tobler, Titus. *Lustreise ins Morgenland.* Zurich: Orell, Füßli und Compagnie 1839

Train, George F. *An American Merchant in Europe, Asia and Australia.* New York: G. P. Putnam & Co. 1857

Turner, William. *Journal of a tour in the Levant*. London: John Murray 1820

Twain, Mark. *The Innocents Abroad. Or: The New Pilgrim's Progress*. Hartford: American Publishing Company 1876

van de Velde, Charles (Carel) William M. *Narrative of a Journey through Syria and Palestine in 1851 and 1852*. Edinburgh and London: William Blackwood and Sons 1854

Van Dyke, Henry. *Out-of-Doors in the Holy Land: Impressions of Travel in Body and Spirit*. New York: Charles Scribner's Sons 1908

Vetromile, Eugene. *Travels in Europe, Egypt, Arabia Petraea, Palestine and Syria*. New York: D. & J. Sadlier & Co. 1871

Vitry, James (aka Jacques, Jakob) of. *Historia orientalis et occidentalis*. Douai (lat. Duacum): Baltazaris Belleri 1597. https://www.digitale-sammlungen.de/de/view/bsb10189102 [accessed April 17, 2026]

Volney, Constantin-François. *Travels through Syria and Egypt, in the years 1783, 1784, and 1785. Containing the present natural and political state of those countries*. Dublin 1793

Warner, Charles Dudley. *In the Levant*. Boston: Houghton, Mufflin and Company 1876

Wedewer, Hermann von. *Eine Reise nach dem Orient*. Regensburg: Manz 1877

Wegelin, Daniel. *Palästina. Bilder aus dem heiligen Land, aufgezeichnet durch Daniel Wegelin aus St. Gallen, während seines Aufenthaltes in Jerusalem* (ed. H. Leemann). Zürich: Schulthess 1845

Werlauff, Erich Christian (ed.). *Symbolae ad geographiam medii ævi, ex monumentis Islandicis*. Copenhagen 1821 (contains the report by Nikulás Bergþórsson aka Nikulás of Munkaþverá). https://archive.org/details/Symbolaeadgeogra000384414v0WerlReyk/page/n5/mode/2up [accessed April 17, 2026]

Willard, Frances E. *Journal of Frances E. Willard*. Evanston: National Women's Christian Temperance Union Headquarters 2005

Wood, A. L. (pseudonym of Clorinda S. Minor). *Meshullam! Or: Tidings From Jerusalem*. Philadelphia 1851

INDEX

Pages numbers in *italics* indicate figures.

Absalom's Tomb, 63
Abyssinians, 152, 215
accommodations, 39, 55, 118, 207, 208, 210–11, 245–46. *See also* travel
Acre, 12, 37–38, 69, 81, 156–57, 227
Adams, George J., 202–3
African-Americans, 178–79, 195, 245–46
Agha, Aqil, 217–18
Aid Organization of German Jews, 263
Al-Aqsa Mosque, 13, 37, 47, 172
Alexander, Michael Solomon, 128
Alexander II (emperor of Russia), 137
Alexius I Comneus (emperor of the East), 11
Ali, Mehemet, 144
Ali, Muhammad, 98
Alliance Israélite Universelle, 263
alms, 81. *See also* fees
Alone Through Syria (Miller), 177–78
al-Quds, xvii, 46. *See also* Jerusalem
American Board of Commissioners for Foreign Missions, 95
American Indians, 137
American Oriental Society, 102
American Palestine Exploration Society (APES), 234
Americans: African-Americans, 178–79, 195, 245–46; Catholics, 246–48; colonists, 202–7; missionaries, 95–106; pilgrims, 200; salesmen, 248–49; Zionists, 137–38
Anguiano, Matheo de, 35–36
animals, 27
anonymous Jewish traveller, 43–44
antiquities, 53, 169. *See also* relics
anti-Semitism, xiv, 103, 136–37, 147–48, 171–73. *See also* Judaism
Apocalypse, xiv. *See also* Second Coming
Arabic language, 17, 19, 64, 74, 97, 102, 164–65
Arabs: Arab Christians, 129; Arab women, 152–54; the Bedouin and, 219; impressions of, 25, 74–75, 79, 104–5; Jews and, 195; stories about, 60; use of term, xvii. *See also* Islam; Muslims
Aramaic language, 52, 64, 169
archaeology, 160–70
Archbishop of York, 131
architectural history, 165–66
Arculf (Bishop), 10
Armenian churches, 15, 56, 74, 97
Armenian language, 97
Armenians, xv, 16, 33, 101–2, 103, 250–52

Arraba, 152
artefacts, 212. *See also* antiquities
artists, 232–38, 239–44
Ashkenazi Jews (Ashkenazis, Ashkenazim), 140, 142, 146–47, 155. *See also* Jews; Judaism
as-Sakanini, Khalil, 265
attire, 16–17, 88–89, 117, 150–52, 157, 181, 182–83
Augustine of Hippo, 7
Austrians, 142
authenticity, 53, 78, 99, 112, 114–15, 163–64, 247
Ayyubid dynasty, 38

Badra, Yusef Simon (dragonman), 175–77
Baedeker (publisher, travel guide), 211, 215
Balfour, Arthur, 265–66
Balfour Declaration, 267
bandits, 12, 60, 175, 219
Barbary corsairs, 86
Bartlett, William Henry, 158
Bar-Yosef, Eitan, 186
Basilica of the Annunciation, 35
Bassi, Alessandro, 147–48
Bauernfeind, Gustav, 239–44
Baurenfeind, Georg Wilhelm, 58
Bayard, Pierre, 76
Bedouins, 43–44, 88, 217–23, *218*, 219
Bedouins in front of their tent (Bonfils), *218*
Bek, Mohammed, 152, 154
Bell, Gertrude, 195–96
bells, 17, 60–61, 125
Bengel, Johann Albrecht, 224
Benjamin, Israel Joseph, 144–45
Benjamin of Tudela, 41–42
ben Jonah, Benjamin, 41–42
Bergsson (or Bergþórsson), Nikulás, 30
Bertsch, Elise, 240–41, 244
Beta Israel, 147
Bethlehem, 8, 38, 39, 73–74, 91, *92*, 150, 215, 259
Bible: illustrated versions of, 232; Luther Bible, 84; as relic, 105; sale of, 97, 100, 101, 201; as travel guide, 4, 77, 177, 211
Bible and Sword (Tuchman), 228
biblical archaeology, 164–65
Biblical Researches in Palestine, Mount Sinai, and Arabia Petraea (Robinson and Smith), 164–65
Bishop Arculf, 9
Black Americans. *See* African-Americans
Blake, William, 86–88
Blessed Virgin, 73–74. *See also* Mary of Nazareth
"blood libel," 148
Board of Commissioners for Foreign Missions, 100
Bonar, Andrew A., 144
Bonfils, Felix, 92
Bonfils, Maison, *218*
Bossina, Stefano di, 36
Bowring, John, 187
Brasca, Santo, 26–28
Breen, Andrew Edward, 247–48, *248*
Breidenbach, Bernhard von, 26, 27
Britain. *See* Great Britain
British Palestine Exploration Fund, 234
Brother Elia, 38
Browne, Abraham, 86
Buchenbach, Hans Jacob Breuning von, 51

Bünting, Heinrich, 19–20, *20*
Burckhardt, Jacob, 9
Burton, Isabel, v, 180–81, 209–10
Busch, Moritz, 120–21
"Butcher," the, 65–66, 70
Byzantium, 10–12, 32

Calvin, John, 50
Campos, Michelle, 264
Cana, 52–53
captivity, 86
Carmel, Alex (Aleks), 189
Carmelites, 228
carriages, 208, 227
Casa Santa, 35
Casola, Pietro, 28–29
Catholics: American Catholics, 246–48; Catholic pilgrims, 122–26, 148; Muslims and, 60–61, 80; Protestants and, 51–52, 59, 246; Roman Catholics, 14–15, 38, 52, 55, 59, 91, 111; traditions and beliefs of, 52, 53, 97; violence against, 225–26. *See also* Christianity; Franciscans
Çelebi, Evliya, 48
Chamberlain, Joseph, 230–31
Chapel of St. Helena, 214–15
Chateaubriand, François-René de, 71–76, 192, 193–94, 219–20
Christ. *See* divine Christ; Jesus Christ
"Christian family from Madaba, Transjordan, in festive attire, visiting Jerusalem in 1904/05, A," *103*
Christianity: beliefs of, 7–8, 65, 80; conversion to, 49, 94–98, 110, 125, 128–29, 139; denominations in, xv, 16, 73, 111–12, 200; divisions in, xv–xvi, 54–55, 93; and missionaries, 94–98, 100, 101–2, 128–29, 144; as "open-air religion," 104–5; in Palestine, xv; recognition of, 127–28; and rule of Jerusalem, 12–13; Western and Eastern Christianity, 14–17. *See also* Catholics; Christians; Oriental Christians; Orthodox Christians; Protestant Christians; Western Christians
Christians: Armenian Christians, 101–2; and Christian quarter, 11, 210; conflicts between, 199, 259; Druze and, 225–26; Jews and, xv, 123, 147–48, 264–65; Maronite Christians, 16, 226; Muslims and, xv, 64–65, 93, 100–101, 130; Ottomans and, 110; Syrian Christians, 16, 24; taxation on, 12; Temple Mount and, 120–21; traditions of, 163–64; violence against, 110, 251; Western Christians, 14–17, 111, 124–25, 264. *See also* Catholics; Christianity; Oriental Christians; Orthodox Christians; Protestant Christians
Church, Frederic, 202, 234–35, *236*
church of Nazareth, 78, 80–81
Church of Scotland, 144
Church of the Annunciation, 78, 80–81
Church of the Holy Sepulchre: access to, 29; authenticity of, 112, 247; building of, 4–5, 9; ceremonies at, 117; Constantinian basilica at, 165–66; control of, 54–55, 199; descriptions of, 73, 114, 214–15, 257; Easter at, 109–10; fire and renovation of, 75–76; Georgian pilgrims and, 32; and the Holy

Church of the Holy Sepulchre (*continued*)
Sepulchre, 9, 50, 53, *214*; impressions of, 78, 99, 120, 252; knighthood at, 23, 31; location of, 164; replicas of, 247
Church of the Nativity in Bethlehem, 38, 39
Church of the Nativity, 9, 73–74, 259
citizenship, 70, 127
citrus fruits, 187, 190, 240
Clarel: A Poem and Pilgrimage in the Holy Land (Melville), 203
Clarke, Edward Daniel, 77–79, 81, 188
Clemens, Samuel Langhorne, 199–202, 207
Clement VI, Pope, 38
climate, 141, 172, 184–90
clothing, 16–17, 88–89, 117, 150–52, 157, 181, 182–83
Codex Arentinus, 3
coexistence, 64, 95–96, 264
colonists, 202–7, 227. *See also* settlers
Colored Man Round the World, A (Dorr), 245
Columbus, Christopher, 49
Constantine the Great, 9
Constantinople, 58, 72, 169, 224, 251
conversion, 49, 94–98, 110, 125, 128–29, 139
Cook, Thomas, 207–11, *209*, 227, 237
Coptic church, 16, 123–24
Copts, xv, 33, 103, 125, 246, 256
corsairs, 86
costumes, 182–83, 213–14. *See also* attire
cotton, 189
Council of Chalcedon, 14
Cozza, Lorenzo, 53–54
Cresson, Warder, 137–39
Crete, Emirate of, 11, 50, 244
Crimean War, 127, 151, 224–25, 259
crops, 184–90
crusades, 11–12, 15–16, 75
curiosity, 7, 51–52
Cycles of the Sun, The (Schwarz), 141
Cyprus, 28, 50, 130

Dahûk, Abû, 221–22
Damascus, 148, 186, 242–43
Damascus Affair, 148
Damiani, Bernard, 182–83
Darkhe Tsiyon (Porges), 44
Davis, John, 234
Dead Sea, v, 24, 184, 191–96, 220–22
Dead Souls (Gogol), 197
deism, 93. *See also* divine Christ
dervishes, 79, 81, 89, 242–43. *See also* Muslims; Sufism
Description of the East and some other countries, A (Pococke), 63
Descriptive Geography and Brief Historical Sketch of Palestine, A (Schwarz), 141
deserts, 105–6, 185–86
dhimma system, 12
Diary of my journey to the Orient (Friedrich Wilhelm, Prussian Crown Prince), 256
Diary of My Life in the Holy Land, A (Breen), 247–48
Dicksons settlement, 203
Didascalicon (Hugh of St. Victor), v
diseases, 91, 110, 117–18, 184
disguises, 72–73, 79, 181. *See also* attire
divine Christ, 14, 19, 93. *See also* Jesus Christ
Dodge, David Stuart, 202

Dome of the Rock, 13, 37, 46, 63, 99, 120
Domestic Life in Palestine (Rogers), 151–52
Donner, Herbert, 52
Doré, Gustave, 232
Dorr, David F., 245–46
Doumani, Beshara, 189
dragomans, 174–81, 208, 237
Druze people, 64, 161–62, 225–26, 262
Dubois-Aimé, Jean-Marie, 217
Dunant, Henry, 226

Easter, 33, 48, 108–10
Eastern Christianity, 14–17. *See also* Oriental Christians
Eberhard the Elder (duke of Württemberg), 22–23
Ebers, Georg, 107
École biblique et archéologique française de Jérusalem, 247
Edward VII (king of England), 256
Egeria (pilgrim), 3–6, 34
Egypt, 16, 38, 58, 88, 98–99, 118–19, 122–24, 198
Eight years in Africa from 1846–1855 (Benjamin), 144–45
Elia, da Cortona, frate, 38
Elkan, Sophie, 205–6
Elliot, Charles W., 249
Emilia Romagna, 42–43
Emirate of Crete, 11, 50, 244
Eneman, Michael Olofsson, 53–54
England, 86–88. *See also* Great Britain
Eretz Israel, 265, 267. *See also* Palestine
Esra organization, 263
Ethiopians, 16, 147
Eudocia (empress of Rome), 34–35
Europe, 35–36, 83–89, 127–28, 133, 136–37, 151, 256–61. *See also* Great Britain
"Evagatorium," 22
excavations, 9, 160–61, 165–66, 168–69. *See also* archaeology
exoticism, 85–86, 104, 157
export goods, 189–90. *See also* trade
extortion, 55, 108. *See also* fees
Ezekiel, book of, 186

Fabri, Felix, 21–26
Falasha Jews, 147
fatalism, 65, 93
Faverches, Richeldis de, 35
fees: alms, 81; extortion, 55, 108; levies, 72, 73, 134; taxation, 12, 32, 44, 61, 95, 98, 127, 226; tips, 212; tolls, 60
Ferdinand II of Aragon, 49
fertile land, 184–90
First Crusade, 11–12
Fisk, Pliny, 96–98, 100
Flaubert, Gustave, 198–99
food, 25–28, 113–14
Forsskål, Petrus, 58
France, 15, 70–71, 99, 127–28, 137, 265–67
Franciscan Commissariat of the Holy Land for the United States, 246–47
Franciscan Monastery of the Holy Land, 247
Franciscans: descriptions of, 78, 89, 180; donations to, 60; Greek Orthodox Church and, 54–55, 61; institutions of, 55, 56–57, 246–47; on Jews, 147–48; Protestants and, 51–52, 59; role of, 38–39, 53–55, 174. *See also* Catholics; Church of the Holy Sepulchre
Francis of Assisi, 38

Frandji. *See* Western Christians
Frankl, Ludwig August, 88–89, 141–42
Franks. *See* Western Christians
Frederick V. (king of Denmark), 57
French Ministry of Agriculture and Trade, 198
Frendschi. *See* Western Christians
Friedrich Wilhelm (prince of Germany), 256–57
From Reims to Jérusalem (Péchenard), 150–51
Fulcher of Chartres, 15
funerals, 91–92, 122, 132, 139, 244, 255
Furrer, Konrad, 105–6

Gähler, Sigismund Wilhelm von, 58
Galazka, Guy, 150
Galilee, Sea of, 39, 70, 181, 184, 208
Galland, Antoine, 83–84
Gamurrini, Gian Francesco, 3, 5
Gandour, Khalil S. (dragonman), 237
Garden of Gethsemane, 39, 104
Garden Tomb, 205
George V (king of England), 256
Georgians, 32
Géramb, Marie-Joseph de, 55, 109–10, 143–44, 250
German Association for the Exploration of Palestine, 131
German Imperial Couple in the Holy Land, The (Anon), 257
German Oriental Society (Deutsche Morgenländische Gesellschaft), 85, 102
German pilgrims, 28–29
German Protestant church, 131–32
German Protestant Synod of North America, 257–58
German settlers, 112, 224–28
Germany, 82, 84–85, 257–58
Gobat, Samuel, 128–29, 132
Goethe, Johann Wolfgang von, 84–85
Gogol, Nikolai, 197
Golgotha, 11, 13, 112
Goodell, William, 100
Gordon, Charles "Chinese," 205
"Gordon's Calvary," 205
Gospels, the, 8, 9, 38–39, 171
Graham, Stephen, 255
Great Britain, 86–88, 99, 127–28, 130–31, 136–37, 230, 265–67
Greece, 28
Greek Orthodox Church: American missionaries and, 101–2; Church of the Holy Sepulchre and, 75–76; Franciscans and, 54–55, 61; Jews and, 133–34; Kafr Kanna church, 52; Monastery of the Cross, 32, 113–14; Muslims and, 64–65; priests in, 89; rituals in, 124–25; Roman Churches vs., 91; Russian Orthodox Church and, 253; St. Catherine's Monastery, 25. *See also* Christianity; Oriental Christians
Grotto of the Annunciation, 81, 118, 247
Grotto of the Manger, 39, 247
guesthouses, 210–11. *See also* accommodations
Güglingen, Paul Walther von, 184
Gunther of Bamberg, Bishop, 11
Gustrau, Maibritt, 111–12, 252
gypsies. *See* Roma people

Hadrian (emperor of Rome), xvi
Halbwachs, Maurice, 17, 163
Hammer-Purgstall, Joseph von, 85
Hardegg, Georg David, 224, 226
harems, 152–54, 156–57

Hasidim Jews, 142
Hasselquist, Fredrik, 56–57
Haven, Frederik Christian von, 58–59
Hawes, Joel, 102
Hayden, Judy A., 48
Hebrew language, 144, 164–65, 263, *266*
Hebron, 47, 146–47. *See also* Palestine
Helena (Saint), 8–9, 78–79, 214–15
Helen of Adiabene, 169
Herz, Elise, 142
Herzl, Theodor, xvi, 230–31, 260–61
Historical and descriptive pilgrimage to the Holy Land (Bassi), 147–48
Historical Geography of the Holy Land (Smith), 185
Hoffmann, Christoph, 224, 226
Hoffmann, Wilhelm, 225
Holy Land: in America, 95; geographic location of, xiii; images of, 232–38; Jerusalem as, 264; nature in, 56–57, 104–6; romantic views of, 88–89; significance of, 9; use of term, xvi. *See also* holy sites; Palestine
Holy Land in English Culture 1799–1917, The (Bar-Yosef), 86
Holy Sepulchre, 9, 50, 53, 199, *214*. *See also* Church of the Holy Sepulchre
holy sites: authenticity of, 53, 78, 99, 112, 114–15, 163–64, 247; claims to, 13–14; condition of, 197; creation myths and, 9; desecration of, 23; Franciscans and, 38; impressions of, 171–72, 199; locations of, 52–53, 165–67; names for, 163–65; presence of God and, 7–8; related to Mary of Nazareth, 35, 123. *See also* Church of the Holy Sepulchre
Holy Tomb, 13. *See also* Church of the Holy Sepulchre; Holy Sepulchre
Horn, Elzear, 54
hospitals, 37–38, 131–32
hotels, 207, 208
house of the Holy Family of Nazareth, 35
Hugh of St. Victor, v
Humboldt, Alexander von, 145
Hussein ibn Ali (Sharif of Mecca), 265

Ibn Battuta, 47
Ibrahim Pasha, 98–99
Iceland, 30
idolatry, 50, 100, 158
"Imitatio Christi," 108
Importance of Biblical Geography for Biblical Exegesis, The (Furrer), 105
In a Canoe on Sacred Rivers (MacGregor), 169–70
Incidents of Travel in Egypt, Arabia Petraea, and the Holy Land (Stephens), 99–100
Inner Life of Syria, Palestine, and the Holy Land, The (Burton), v, 180–81
Innocents Abroad, or The New Pilgrim's Progress, The (Twain), 199
interpreters, 174–81
In the Levant (Warner), 254
Islam: Al-Aqsa Mosque and, 13, 37, 47, 142; beliefs and practice of, 65, 93, 213; Christian missionaries and, 95, 100–101; and direction of prayer, 46; and Dome of the Rock, 13, 37, 46, 63, 99, 120; photography and, 235, 237; Saracens and, 10, 18–19, 23, 24, 47; and Temple Mount, 9, 13, 42–43, 46, 120–21, 136, 166. *See also* Arabs; Muslims; Saracens

Israel, xiv
Italy, 28, 50–51, 257
itineraries, 22, 208, *209*, 210
Itinerarium sacrae scripturae. That is: a travel book about the whole of the Holy Scriptures (Bünting), 19
Itinerary to the Holy City of Jerusalem (Brasca), 26–28
Izmir (formerly Smyrna), 53, 72

Jacobites, 16, 42, 97, 111
Jacotin, Pierre, 70–71
Jaeghere, Michel de, 76
Jaffa, 69, 72, 107–8, 187, 190, 208, 211
Jaffe, Hillel, 149
James of Vitry, Cardinal, 16
Janissary guard, 61
Jazzar Pasha, Ahmad al-, 65–66, 70
Jerome, Saint, 8
Jerusalem: American consul in, 137–38; Armenian quarter of, 250; as center of the world, 20, *20*, 39, 185; Christian quarter of, 11, 210; Christian rule of, 12–13, 49; history of, 165–66, 216; as Holy Land, 264; impressions of, 157, 172, 198, 248–49; Jews in, 13, 41–44, 140; living conditions in, 80; maps of, 63; Mea Shearim neighbourhood in, 166; Mohammed and, 46; Muslim rule of, 12–13; Old City in, 264; Persian capture of, 9; road from Jaffa to, 108, 208, 211; tensions in, 264; use of term, xvii; walls around, 39
Jerusalem (Blake), 88
Jerusalem (Lagerlöf), 206
Jerusalem As It Is (Rhodes), 207
Jerusalem Association, 113, 225
"Jerusalem fever," 22
Jerusalem from the Mount of Olives (Church), 234–35, *236*
Jesuits, 39, 100, 101
Jesus Christ, 38–39, 148, 164, 165, 172–73, 205. *See also* Church of the Holy Sepulchre; divine Christ
"Jesus myth," 65
"Jewganda," 230–31
Jews: Arabs and, 195; archaeology and, 170; Ashkenazi Jews, 140, 142, 146–47, 155; Christians and, xv, 123, 147–48, 264–65; economic situation of, 210; Fashala Jews, 147; Greek Orthodox Church and, 133–34; Hasidim Jews, 142; in Hebron, 146–47; impressions of, 143–44, 158, 171–72; Jewish colonies, 228–31; Jewish immigrants, 140–41, 146–47; Jewish independence, 69–70; Jewish pilgrims, 41–45; Jewish quarter, 13; Jewish women, 155, 158; Karaite, 142; living conditions of, 54, 57, 145–46, 263; in Mea Shearim neighborhood, 166; Mizrahim Jews, 147; money collected for, 133; Muslims and, 264–65; Oriental Christians and, 154–55; in Palestine, 136–37; prejudice against, 148–49, 261; Samaritans and, 158–59; Sephardic Jews, 133, 140, 142, 146–47; as slaves, 165; taxation on, 12; Temple Mount and, 9, 42; and "Uganda Plan," 230–31. *See also* Judaism; Zionism
John 2, 52–53
Jordan River, 23, 30, 108, 169–70, 178, 192, 200, 246
Jordan Valley, 48, 195, 196, 243

Josephus, Flavius, 193
Journey to Syria and Egypt in 1783, 1784, 1785 (Volney), 63–66
Journey to the area between Alexandria and Parätenium, the Libyan desert, Siwa, Egypt, Palestine and Syria in 1820 and 1821 (Scholz), 32–33
Judaism: and anti-Semitism, 103, 136–37, 147–48, 171–73; and Christianity, conversion to, 94, 96, 110, 125, 128–29; ethnic groups in, 142, 146–47; recognition of, 127–28; secret practice of, 45; and tearing clothing, 43, 141–42; and Temple of Solomon, 13; views on, 173; and Wailing Wall, 9, 13, 54, 242, 261; and Yemeni Jews, 263. *See also* Jews; Zionism

Kafr Kanna, 52
Kalischer, Zvi Hirsch, 135
Kamil, Malik al- (sultan of Egypt), 38
Karaites, 142
Kebar river, 186
Kempe, Margery, 21–23
Kent, Charles Foster, 238
Khirbet Qana, 52–53
King, Jonas, 97–98, 100
knighthood, 23, 75
Knights Hospitaller (Order of St. John), 37–38, 257
Knights of the Holy Sepulchre, 23, 31, 75
Konstantinovsky, Matvey, 197
Koran, 150, 179
Kramer, Christian Carl, 58
Krikorian, Garabed, 235
Kural, Mosche, 142
Kurds, 241, 262

Lagerlöf, Selma, 205–6
La grande bible de Tours (illus. Doré), 232
Lamartine, Alphonse de, vi, 90–95, 162, 182–83
Landscape Illustrations of the Bible (illus. Turner), 232
Landscape of Belief, The (Davis), 234
languages: Arabic, 17, 19, 64, 74, 97, 102, 164–65; Aramaic, 52, 64, 169; Armenian, 97; and Bible translations, 97; in the Church of the Holy Sepulchre, 111; Hebrew, 144, 164–65, 263, *266*; liturgical languages, 17, 19, 113; and place names, 164–65; Turkish, 64; Yiddish, 44, 134, 144
"La Nueva Jerusalén," in Madrid, 35–36
Larsson, Olof Henrik, 206
Last Supper, location of, 38–39
latitude, 30
League of Nations, 267
Lebanon, 186, 225–26, 267
legendary topography of the Gospels in the Holy Land, The (Halbwachs), 163
Life of Jesus, The (Renan), 172–73
Linné, Carl von, 58
liturgical languages, 17, 19, 113
Loreto, Italy, 35
Lortet, Louis, 151
Loti, Pierre, 213–16
Luther, Martin, 50. *See also* Protestant Christians; Western Christians
"Luthero-Calvinists," 100–102. *See also* missionaries
Lynch, William Francis, 195

MacGregor, John, 169–70
Madrid, Spain, 35–36
Maleo, Mariano Morone, da, 52
Mamluk Sultanate, 32
Mamre oak grove, 166–67
Mamreoff, Lydia, 237
Mandeville, John, 18–19
Manzikert, Battle of, 11
Ma'oz, Moshe, 265
maps: of Cook's tours in Palestine, *209*; of the Holy Land, 234; of Jerusalem, *20*, 63; of Palestine, 63, 70–71, 131, 166, 170, *266*; of the world, *20*
Maronites, xv, 16, 33, 64, 111, 226
Mar Saba monastery, 31–32, 118, 219–20
Mary of Nazareth, 34–35, 73–74, 80–81, 123
Masada fortress, 194–95
masculinity, 157–58
Matar, Nabil I., 48
Matthew, Chapter 18, 7
Mattityahu (traveller), 45
McCheyne, Robert Murray, 144
Mecca, 46–48, 82, 85, 196
Mediterranean Hotel, 208
Mediterranean Sea, xiii, 10, 11, 12, 50, 146, 184
Melville, Herman, 139, 203
men, 117, 151, 153–54, 157–58. *See also* women
Meshullam! Or, Tidings From Jerusalem (Minor), 157
Mesopotamia, xiii, 3, 260, 265
Middle East, use of term, xvii
Milan, 28
Milk Grotto, 123–24
Miller, Ellen E., 177–78
Minor, Clorinda, 157
miracle of the wine, 52–53
miracles, 52–53, 81, 118, 173
Misk, Hanna, 180–81
missionaries, 94–98, 100, 101–2, 128–29, 144
Mizrahim Jews, 147
Mohammed, 13, 46, 93
Mohammedans. *See* Muslims
monasteries: Mar Saba monastery, 31–32, 118, 219–20; monastery of St. Salvator, 56–57; Monastery of the Cross, 32, 113–14; monastery of the holy Abbot Saba, 25; monastery of the Holy Redeemer, 55; St. Catherine's Monastery, 25, 59
Monastery of the Cross, 32, 113–14
monastery of the holy Abbot Saba, 25
monastery of the Holy Redeemer, 55
Monte Cassino, 3
Montefiore, Judith, 133–34
Montefiore, Moses, 133–36, 148, 158
Montefiore, Simon Sebag, 54
"Morgenland," 84. *See also* Orient, the
Moroccan corsairs, 86
Moses, 48
mosques, 13, 37, 47, 181. *See also* Islam; Muslims
Mount of Olives, 9, 23, 38, 61, 73–74, 141, 259
Mount of the Transfiguration of Jesus (Mount Tabor), 39
Mount Sinai, 4, 59
Mount Zion, 38, 43, 132, 259
"Muristan," 131–32, 257
Murray, John, 211
Muscovites, 33, 241, 253

music, 60–61, 81, 91–92, 117
Muslims: Christians and, xv, 12–13, 31, 60–61, 64–65, 80, 93, 100–101, 130; clothing of, 88–89; holy places of, 211; impressions of, 24–26, 74, 112–13, 119–20; Jews and, 264–65; pilgrims, 46–48; women, 150–54, 212; Ottoman rule and, 130; rules for conduct around, 39–40; Samaritans and, 159; taxation on, 12, 98; Templers and, 227–28. *See also* Islam; Saracens

Nabi Musa, 48, 81
Nablus, 189
Napoleon Bonaparte, 69–71
Narrative of a Mission of Inquiry to the Jews from the Church of Scotland in 1839 (Bonar and McCheyne), 144
Narrative of the United States' Expedition to the River Jordan and the Dead Sea (Lynch), 195
natural resources, 184–90
nature, 104–5, 115, 166–67, 184–90
"Náuar" people, 155
Navarre, Spain, 41
Nazareth, 35, 39, 78, 80–81, 118, 151
Near East, use of term, xvii
Negima, Solomon (dragoman), 177–79
Nestorians, 16, 97, 103, 111
Newett, M. Margaret, 28
"Next year in Jerusalem!," 41
Nicholas I (emperor of Russia), 259
Nicosia, Cyprus, 28
Niebuhr, Carsten, 58–63
Nile river, 6, 169, 186
Noah, Mordecai Manuel, 137–38
Nubians, 16

Obadiah of Bertinoro, Rabbi, 42–43
Ohly, Karl, xv
Old New Land, The (Herzl), 261
Old Testament, the, xiii–xiv, 164. *See also* Bible
Oliphant, Laurence, 136
olive oil, 188
On to Jerusalem! (Frankl), 88–89
"open-air religion," 104–5
oranges, 187, 190
Orient, the, xv, xvii, 14, 83–89
Oriental Christians: Americans and, 100, 103; clothing and traditions of, 16–17, *103*; Greek Church and, 111–12; Jews and, 154–55; rituals of, 101–2, 103; Western Christians and, 14–17, 18–19, 24–25, 96, 111, 264. *See also* Christianity; Christians
Oriental Encounters (Pickthall), 179–80
Orientals or Christians? (Gustrau), 111
Orthodox Christians, 31–32, 71, 264. *See also* Christianity; Greek Orthodox Church; Oriental Christians; Russians
Ottoman Brothers (Campos), 264
Ottoman Empire: division of, 260, 265; end of, 267; Europe and, 151, 265–67; Napoleon and, 69–71; nationalism under, 265; pirates and, 86; rule of, 39, 79, 95, 127–30, 228, 230; and Turks, 54, 55, 64, 79, 124
Out-of-Doors in the Holy Land (Van Dyke), 104
"Overcomers, the," 204–6
Oxford, 53

Palestine: Acre, 12, 37–38, 69, 81, 156–57, 227; animals and nature of, 130–31; Christian community in, xv;

Palestine (*continued*)
climate of, 184–90; Hebron, 47, 146–47; Jews in, 136–37; maps of, 63, 70–71, 131, 166, 170, *209*, *266*; occupation of, by Egypt, 98–99, 144; the Old Testament and, xiii–xiv; Ottoman rule of, 39, 127–30, 230; place names in, 164–65; population of, 262; use of term, xvi–xviii; Western powers and, 98–99, 267. *See also* Holy Land
Palestine and Syria: Handbook for Travellers (Socin), 211–12
Palestine Exploration Fund, 130–31, 166, 170
Palestinian Autonomous Territories, xiv
Palmerston, Henry John Temple, Lord, 137
Pappenheim, Alexander von, 31
Paris, 72
Paris peace treaty, 151
Parsons, Levi, 96–98
Passover, 39, 41
Paulus, Christoph, 227–28
Péchenard, Pierre-Louis, 150–51
Penny Magazine, The, *87*
Penslar, Derek, 260
per capita tax, 12
performances, 223, 247
Perushim, 142
Pesach, 39, 41
Petermann, Julius Heinrich, 14
Pfeiffer, Ida, 116–19, 156–57, 182, 187–88, 220
Phoenicia Mission (Renan), 171
photography, 235–37, 242, 247–48
Pickthall, Muhammad Marmaduke, 179–80
pilgrimages: advice for, 25–28; Church leaders on, 7–8, 50; costs of, 44; images of, *233*; mass pilgrimages, 11–12; popularity of, *87*; protection during, 37–40; by sea, 12, 107; statistics of, 31–33; women and, 3–6, 8–9, 21–22. See also *individual pilgrims*
Pilgrimage to Palestine, Egypt, Syria, A (de Géramb), 55
Pilgrimage to the Holy Land (von Breidenbach), 26, 27
piracy, 86
plague, 91, 110, 117–18
pleasure trip to the Orient, A (Tobler), v
Pococke, Richard, 63
Poggibonsi, Niccolò da, 47
Poland, 44, 146
Poles (Polish people), 142
polygamy, 152–54
Porges, Mose ben Israel Naftali, 44–45
Portugal, 146
Poser, Rachel, 170
postmillennialism, 95
"poulains," 15
Präger, Moses, 44–45
premillennialism, 95
primary relics, 34
Prophet Mohammed. *See* Mohammed
Protestant Christians: Catholics and, 51–52, 59, 246, 252; and Protestant diocese, 128; Protestant pilgrims, 50, 53–54, 57–63, 94–106, 110–13, 257–58. *See also* Christianity; missionaries
Prudential Committee of the American Board, 96, 102
Prussia, 127–28, 130, 256–57
Pückler-Muskau, Hermann, Fürst von, 119–20, 192–93

Quakers, 32, 137
Quaresmio, Francesco, 52

Rachel's tomb, 43, 134
racism, 148, 156, 195, 227–28
railroads, 108, 211
Ramadan, 241
Ramblings across Palestine (Furrer), 105
Ratti-Menton, Benoît Ulisse de, 148
Recollections of Travels to the Holy Land (Ohly), xv
Reichert, Folker, 31
relics, 23, 34–37, 114, 123, 164, 166–67, 201–2, 258–59. *See also* antiquities
religious conversion, 49, 94–98, 110, 125, 128–29, 139
Renan, Ernest, 170–73
Report on the Commercial Statistics of Syria (Bowring), 187
Resurrection flower, 194
Rhodes, Albert, 207
robbery, 12, 43–44, 60, 175, 219
Roberts, David, 232–33, 233
Robinson, Edward, 103, 164, 174
Robinson, George, 32
Rogers, Mary Eliza, 151–56, 158–59, 222
Rohrbach, Paul, 251–52
Roman Catholicism, 14–15, 38, 52, 55, 59, 91. *See also* Catholics; Franciscans
romanticism, 85–86, 104–5
Roma people, 79, 155–56
Rome, 50, 71, 146
Romieu, Auguste, 182
Rosen, Georg Friedrich Wilhelm, 168
Rose of Jericho, 194
Rothschild, Baron, 228–29
Russia, xiv, 71, 127–28, 137, 146
Russian Orthodox Imperial Palestine Society, 253
Russian Orthodox Palestinian Society, 165
Russians, 113, 125, 149, 152, 229, 252–55

Saint Augustine of Hippo, 7
St. Catherine's Monastery, 25
Saint Francis of Assisi, 38
Saint Helena, 8–9, 78–79, 214–15
Saint James Cathedral, 251
Saint Jerome, 8
Saint Salvator monastery, 56–57
Salisbury, Edward E., 102
Samaritans, 158–59
Saracens, 10, 18–19, 23–25, 47. *See also* Arabs; Muslims
sarcophagi, 168–69
Sardinia, 127–28
Sarona colony, 227
Saulcy, Louis Félicien, de, 167–69, 207
Schick, Conrad, 45, 165–66, 241, 258
Schölch, Alexander, 189
Scholz, Johann Martin Augustin, 32–33
schools, 156, 210, 257
Schuber, Maria, 122–26
Schumacher, Jakob, 228
Schwarz, Joseph (Yehoseph), 140–41
scientists, 56–62
Scutari (now Üsküdar, Istanbul), 116
Sea of Galilee, 39, 70, 181, 184, 208
sea travel, 107
secondary relics, 34
Second Coming, 49, 95, 204
Second Great Awakening, 94
Seetzen, Ulrich Jasper, 79–82, 155, 181, 191–93, 219
Sephardi, Zechariah, Rabbi, 43

Sephardic Jews (Sephardim), 133, 136, 140, 142, 146–47
settlers, 157, 189, 224–28, 229, 261. *See also* colonists
Shamir, Shimon, 265
Shapira, Moses Wilhelm, 212
Sinai, 4, 22, 39, 59, 95, 105, 164–65
Sinai and Golgotha: Journey to the Orient (Strauss), 110–11
Sinai and Palestine: In Connexion with their History (Stanley), 186
singing, 113, 117, 124. *See also* music
skepticism, 53, 81, 99, 114, 118
slaves, 88–89, 152, 156, 195, 201, 245–46
Smith, Eli, 100–101
Smith, George Adam, 185, 194–95
Smyrna (Izmir), 53, 72
"Society for the Gathering of the People of God in Jerusalem," 225
Socin, Albert, 211–12
Soden, Hermann von, 107, 113–15
Sodom apples, 193–94
souvenirs, 114, 123, 178–79, 201–2, 208, 212, 254
Spafford, Anna, 204–5
Spafford, Horatio, 204–6
Spain, 35–36, 133, 146
Stanhope, Hester Lucy, 160–63
Stanley, Arthur P., 186
"Star of Bethlehem," 259
St. Catherine's Monastery, 25
Stephens, John Lloyd, 99–100, 146
stereoscopes, 238
Strauss, Friedrich Adolph, 110–13, 145–46, 250
Studies on Palestine during the Ottoman Period (Ma'oz), 265
Sufism, 47–48, 79, 81, 89, 242–43. *See also* Islam
Suleymân (dragoman), 179–80
superstition, 53, 78, 100, 102, 111, 261
Suriano, Francesco, 184–85
Sykes-Picot Agreement, 265
synagogues, 143
Syria, 70–71, 130, 235, 267
Syrians, 16, 24. *See also* Oriental Christians
Syria of Today (Lortet), 151

Tales of the Thousand and One Nights, 83–84
Tanzimat ("New Order"), 127, 130
tattoos, 256
taxation, 12, 32, 44, 61, 95, 98, 127, 226. *See also* fees
tearing clothing, 43, 141–42
Templars, 37–38
Temple Mount, 9, 13, 42–43, 46, 120–21, 136, 166
Temple of Herod, the second, 13
Temple of Solomon, 13
Templers of Württemberg, 224–31
Temptation of St. Anthony, The (Flaubert), 198
Tent Life in Palestine (Conder), 186
That is: a travel book about the whole of the Holy Scriptures (Bünting), 19
Thomas Cook & Co, 237
Thomson, William McClure, 100
tips, 212. *See also* fees
Tobler, Titus, v, 129, 165
tolls, 60. *See also* fees
tomb of Jesus. *See* Church of the Holy Sepulchre; Jesus Christ
tombs: Absalom's Tomb, 63; Garden Tomb, 205; Holy Sepulchre, 9, 50, 53, 199, 214; of Moses, 48; of the

prophets, 61; of Rachel, 43, 134; Tomb of the Kings, 168–69
Topography of Jerusalem and its Environs (Tobler), 165
To See a Promised Land: Americans and the Holy Land in the Nineteenth Century (Vogel), 206
tour guides, 174–81
tourism, 174–81, 207–16, 227, 246
Tower of David, 42
trade, 10–11, 36, 63, 96–97, 187–89, 250–51
Train, George F., 248–49
travel, 25–28, 49–51, 81–82, 174–81, 207–16, 218–23
travel guides, 4, 44–45, 174–75, 184, 208, 211, 221–23
Travel Letters from Palestine (von Soden), 107
"travel philosophy in the Orient," 81–82
Travels in Europe, Egypt, Arabia Petraea, Palestine and Syria (Vetromile), 246
Travels in the East including a Journey in the Holy Land (de Lamartine), vi, 90–93
Treasure troves of the Orient edited by a society of enthusiasts (ed. Hammer-Purgstall), 85
Treaty of Paris, 127–28, 226
Tuchman, Barbara, 228–29, 231
Turkey, 146, 216, 228, 260. *See also* Ottoman Empire
Turks, 54, 55, 64, 79, 124. *See also* Ottoman Empire
Turner, William, 186–87, 232
Tvu'ot Ha'aretz (Schwarz), 141
Twain, Mark, 199–202, 207
"Uganda Plan," 230–31
Ultramontanes (German pilgrims), 28–29
United States. *See* Americans
Urban II, Pope, 11

Valerius of Bierzo, 5
Valley of Jehoshaphat, 23
van de Velde, Charles, 146–47, 166–67, 188, 194, 221–22
Van Dyke, Henry, 104–5
Venice, Italy, 50–51
Vetromile, Eugene, 246
Via Dolorosa, 39, 114–15
violence, 60, 72, 110, 148, 175–76, 219–20, 225–26
Vogel, Lester I., 206
Volney, Constantin-François, 63–66, 108
Voyage to the Orient, A (von Wedewer), 223

Wailing Wall, 9, 13, 54, 261
"Wailing Wall, The" (Bauernfeind), 242
Walker, Charles T., 178–79
Walsingham, Norfolk, England, 35
Warburg, Otto, 230
Warner, Charles Dudley, 254
Warren, Charles, 234
Wedewer, Hermann von, 222–23
Wegelin, David, 120
Western Christians, 12, 14–17, 111, 124–25, 144, 152, 264. *See also* Christianity; Christians; Oriental Christians
Western intervention, 85–86, 98–99, 157, 188
Wilde, Oscar, 173

Wilhelm II (emperor of Germany), 257–61
Willard, Frances, 157
Wilson, Woodrow, 267
wine, 188
women: appearances of, 117, 156, 157; Arab women, 152–54; Jewish women, 155, 158; men and, 117, 151; Muslim women, 150–54, 212; women pilgrims, 3–6, 8–9, 21–22, 116–19
wooden boards, 17, 117, 125
World Fairs, 237
Württemberg Templers, 202, 224–28, 262

Yemen, 57–58
Yemeni Jews, 263
Yerushalayim. *See* Jerusalem
Yiddish language, 44, 134, 144
"Young [Christian] Girls of Bethlehem" (Bonfils), 92

Zielonka, Anthony, 198
Zionism, xiv, 135–38, 145–46, 195, 203, 229–31, 260–61, 267. *See also* Judaism
Zionist Congress in Basel, 231
Zionist Federation of Great Britain and Ireland, 267
Zionist Organization, 230

A NOTE ON THE TYPE

This book has been composed in Arno, an Old-style serif typeface in the classic Venetian tradition, designed by Robert Slimbach at Adobe.